It was a long time ago in a faraway place called Nairobi in Kenya, when I was an 'angel with broken wings', I had to learn to fly again. I needed to recover my confidence.

With every thought we create our own reality, sometimes unconsciously attracting negative situations and having to experience the very worst of humanity [Reiner] to discover the very best [Amin] therefore, forgiveness healed my heart and eased my mind to whom I truly desired to be, at peace with myself and the Creator.

After several years as a Dr of Theology and Divinity, a successful spiritual, metaphysical, esoteric tutor and healer, I retired at sixty-six. I thought my life would slow down; however, in 2016 the universe had set out another plan for me. I had been working online with a professor friend from North Carolina University USA, assisting with his non-profit organisation. Also, Gabriel from Texas who I worked online with for a couple of years. I travelled to USA for three weeks work effort, to support my friend with his charity ideas. When staying in North Carolina, Gabriel flew down from Texas to meet me in person. After a week together we fell in love, we married in Denver in 2018. Another man younger than me, but a genius not a fool, like my previous experience. We are both authors, mentors of esoteric and metaphysical subjects.

I learned to turn the terrible Nairobi experience around, from being a victim of abuse, to taking control of my life and travelling the road of bliss, not chaos. Now after all these years have passed by, at seventy-four life's lessons continue, but differently. For the past twenty-three years, I have nourished my soul with compassion, goodness and forgiveness. By becoming a Reiki Master and energy healing teacher and using my laptop aura photography, I met hundreds of broken souls struggling to find their way in the world. Many dealing with pain and suffering that I could resonate with and therefore understand their plight. I discovered by helping others, it aided me to heal and give hope for them to find inner peace too. Once, long ago, I was wealthy and careless, now I am rich with love and contentment… and happier than most. I was a casualty of circumstances beyond my control, the madness of falling in love and reckless. Now I love being this me.

---

written by J L McKinney

KENYA

MY STORY

To Steph,

Hope you enjoy my story

Best Wishes,

Jan

J. L. McKinney

First published in paperback by
Michael Terence Publishing in 2024
www.mtp.agency

ISBN 9781800947986

Cover image
www.123rf.com (AI)

Cover design

Michael Terence
Publishing

Dedicated to…

Amin J Walji, MP for Westlands Nairobi Kenya, my true and loyal friend who saved my life, but sadly passed away 1996.

Tim Kenning aka TFK, a brilliant mind, NLP Master, Artist, Creative Writer, Author of THE HOUDINI PRINCIPLE, Eskrima and Wing Chung Martial Arts Expert, Escapologist and Salsa Dancer, who inspired and assisted me piecing the full story together. Twenty-two years of friendship, he sadly passed away aged 57 on June 1st, 2022.

Based on a true story.

Names have been changed but places and events remain the same.

From my journals, notes, photos and memories.

PART 1

THE FANTASY

ROMANY GYPSY LOVE STORY

I ran a Safari Lodge in Kenya at the border of Tanzania, on route to Amboseli National Park and Mount Kilimanjaro. The views were immeasurable, everything appearing in greatness with unsurpassed significance.

Namanga Safari Lodge was a rundown unfussy and low-priced accommodation. It was just a tourist stopping off place, mostly for back packers, and lorry drivers heading over the border, but it had great potential. I was setting up a partnership with my dear friend Amin Walji an MP in Nairobi; to take over the lodge from its owner Nazir, he and his wife Najma were creating an ostrich farm on some rough land nearby. They wanted to sell up and move on. Sadly, the partnership didn't progress further than hours of talk and empty promises from Nazir and his crazy wife Najma, nor turn out the way Amin and I had expected it to.

But nothing ever did in Kenya. Not for me, that is.

It was a warm still night; I was sitting outside on the old wooden veranda contemplating, remembering how it all began, and how things had changed since I first came to Kenya. If ever I get out of here alive, I am writing this story, I thought. As I sipped red wine, mesmerised by the iridescent flame coming from candles in the storm lamps, the peculiar sound of cicada, crickets and frogs began echoing through the grounds of the lodge. Rustling scratching noises as the animals were bedding down for the night. Indeed, without doubt Africa no more magical place could I be. I could hear the sounds so clearly that evening because the generator had broken down again. The generator was our only source of electricity for the lodge, we had to give out candles to guests when they came in. There was no breeze but the aroma of spices from the open-air cooking in Tanzania were drifting over.

A ghostly eerie luminous haze hovered in the skyline from the gleaming lamps in the small township. It gave an ethereal contrast, to the vivid silvery full moon casting her radiant glow over the vast African plains. The indistinct yet unmistakable Masai silhouettes displayed in the remoteness. A tall nomadic majestic tribe, adorned in fiery red robes, bejewelled with colourful beads. Such a spectacle as this, I would never behold nor experience again.

I gazed upward into the humbling dark night in awe of its immensity, captivated by the stars sparkling like diamonds against the deep blue sky. The stars appeared so near I could almost pluck them from the heavens, like fruit upon a tree. A vision so magnificent, and glorious it almost took my breath away. So splendid and inspiring, more stirring to my soul, than any imagining could ever have been.

It all at once reminded me.

For the very first time in many months, I sensed an inner peace, quietness, and composure a feeling that seemed quite alien to me. I reflected on how it was that I ended up here, running this broken-down safari lodge, with its bizarre menagerie of animals, akin to Noah's Ark. Now, this night, this moment, I felt reasonably safe. Although, my life continued to always be in some danger. I cast my thoughts on a time that had passed, a time that led me here, to this wonderful moment, and away from the madness of Nairobi. Now this night, I was so far removed from the apprehension and uneasiness. There would be no more fear, nor stress on such a night as this.

Remembering how everything beautiful and fine, became terribly wicked, and most evil. I thought of the man responsible, and to why so much suffering was placed upon me by him. His face haunted me, I so wanted to forget it all. I tried to erase the memories, but would I ever forget or forgive him, Reinhold (Reiner) Moser. I thought this man, this evil man whoever he really was, whatever he pretended to be would never harm me again. I breathed a deep sigh and poured more wine, over seen by the magnificence of the night sky. But this night was so glorious and resplendent, I became detached, separated from the painful time shared with him. I imagined I was watching a drama or movie unfold, and I, just in the audience rather than the victim in it.

Then, I was reminded how it all began.

PORTSMOUTH ENGLAND 1993

It was a cold dark and very stormy night in Portsmouth. Our house was a large Victorian four storey building that sat at the edge of the harbour overlooking the Royal Navy Fleet. The living room was up on the second floor, and the harbour view was amazing. Yachts, fishing boats and other sea going vessels clanged and bounced around on the ebb and flow of the spring tide. It was not unknown to have the complete street flooded during this time and a mad rush for the sandbags would always be the highlight of the day's entertainment.

My husband was out with his regular gathering of friends drinking at the local bar. It was a weekly ritual and habit for them to get together, exchange jokes and the latest events, they had experienced with or without their wives. I knew he would be out until the early hours of the morning; it was customary and expected to have a private party after closing hours. Now and then if provoked or goaded into going, I would accompany my husband but leave early. It had become too tedious and boring for me to continue meeting up with the same group of people gossiping and telling silly jokes. The entire area would be awakened by the disorderly rowdiness, shouting, and laughing as they left the bar.

My marriage was falling apart he was fifty-one and I was forty-three, we both knew it was pretty much an everyday chore and routine going to work, earning plenty of money and too weary to enjoy it. Sex became a sense of duty and a task I did not relish indulging in. Being mauled and bullied into sex games that only excited my husband. I yearned for a different life from the one I had, it was empty and devoid of love. I hungered for romance, passionate love and being caressed. I spent time alone yearning for a new experience or adventure and to meet interesting people. But mostly I desired to be swept off my feet.

Our businesses consumed every waking hour, my entire existence seemed to be nothing but hard physical work or waiting for Paddy to return drunk from the bars. I felt discarded, unwanted, and unloved. I had been systematically converted into his slave; I began to feel very resentful. If I dare to question him about anything he would punish me one way or the other. It was mental torture most of the time, however being brutally cruel was not the exclusion by any means. If I resisted any of his demands it would be to my detriment, and I would suffer the consequences for days after the incident.

An Irish Catholic with a very quick temper, a victim of abuse by the Christian Brothers in Ireland. He was emotionally damaged, with a deep bitterness and anger which would raise its ugly head when he drank whisky.

I could hear the wind howling and whistling through the cracks in the old house. The pouring rain crashing on the window pain, as I saw the intermittent flashes of lightening shimmering and reflecting on the open white Venetian blinds. It was an exceptionally stormy night and the strange clanging sounds from the boats as they tossed about on the sea made the atmosphere very eerie.

I snuggled up with my soft pink comfort blanket, alone, on the red leather Chesterfield sofa and watching a romantic film called Officer and a Gentleman. I was used to drinking alone and poured a large glass of chilled Chardonnay. The moment the film began it seemed as though I was transported into the movie and playing a part in it myself. I don't know if it was the stormy weather having a hypnotic effect on me. As I glared at the screen it was as if I became that young girl in the film, working in the factory and being swept off her feet by the handsome navy officer. It was a strange notion that flashed into my mind, that I would give up everything to have such a circumstance happen to me.

So often I had daydreamed on the topic of meeting a handsome young man and falling in love. I had heard rumours and read stories of older women, like me; falling in love with younger men that were labelled *toy boys.* If only I could have an experience just like that. I would trade all the money, jewellery, cars, and my possessions.

As I watched the film this overpowering feeling of excitement flowed through my body. I had in no way felt anything like it before. My hair stood on end, I shook, I couldn't breathe, and I became hot and clammy. I want to experience this with a man; I want to fall in love, the head over heels love. I want to be swept off my feet and kissed, caressed, and feel sexy.

What would it be like to share that experience with a man who could love me passionately? Who would share such ecstasy? I imagined a tall dark handsome young man who would love me and be loved in return.

I wished for a moment like this.

The caveat of desire:

Be careful what you wish for.

ROMANY GYPSY ENCOUNTER

THE MADNESS OF FALLING IN LOVE

It was a warm September evening when I met a beautiful young mysterious gypsy man, with dark wavy waist length hair and big sparkling brown eyes. An amazing physique, he was twenty-four. He said he couldn't read or write, penniless and uneducated. At first glance from behind, I thought he was a woman with such amazing long hair. He was sitting at the bar chatting to his brother, I discovered later. He turned around and smiled at me and leisurely trancelike walked over to where I was standing. I could vaguely hear noises going on around me, but it was as if I had been strangely transported into another dimension. Time stood still, and there was no one else around but this delightful man. I felt as if I was swirling around in space, weightless, helpless, and falling. Was this love at first sight that other people talked about, and I had longed to experience too?

"Hello are you okay?" he asked.

A moment passed then I was able to function in the real world for a split second to reply.

"Hello, yes I'm fine who are you?"

As I looked at him attentively, he grinned and touched my arm, shivers of electricity ran throughout my whole body. I had goosebumps and my hair were standing on end. I took a deep breath.

"I'm Janette."

As he pulled my arm he whispered softly with a sexy voice.

"My name is Dylan, twenty-four and single."

"I am forty-three and married."

He took my hand and told me I was beautiful, very sexy and forty-three was just a number. I couldn't believe what was unfolding, he put his arms around me.

"Dance with me?"

As he held me in his arms the sweet aroma from the heat of his body became intoxicating, I longed for a moment like this and here it was happening to me right now!

Falling, falling in love at first sight.

"I'm going to marry you one day," he whispered.

I laughed.

"One day, you will marry me, Janette."

We danced in a strange captivated hypnotic state for some time, and even when the music stopped, we were oblivious to it, and to the rest of the world. I was falling in love moment by moment with this young gypsy man that a few months earlier I longed for. It was real, and it was happening to me. I had no control over it, nor did I want to have, it was unerringly my desire, a moment like this.

"I haven't been out with anyone for over a year, you are the first lady I have really wanted to get to know, yes I fancy you like crazy but please believe me it's more than a sexual attraction," he remarked.

"You don't have to explain anything to me; I'm enjoying myself with you, I like you very much too, let's just have a nice time while we can."

I was swept off my feet by a delightful young gypsy man.

The chemistry was incredible, he was so enchanting, and mysterious. We fell madly in love; it was beyond understanding and completely out of our control.

THE HOTEL AND MY ROMANY GYPSY LOVER

A week later we looked for a small family run hotel in the city and stumbled across the perfect hide-away.

The room was pleasant and inviting with a large bay window draped in pink floral curtains. In one corner stood a small ornate cabinet next to a table with a television on it and a tray with tea, coffee, and biscuits. A double bed neatly covered with a plain pink quilt and a burgundy button back velvet chair with cabriole legs placed beside it. Opposite the bed an etched glass sliding door that led to a shower and toilet in pristine white, large soft white fluffy towels and an enormous mirror. I felt anxious about being in the hotel and concerned about revealing myself to this young man. He was going to see me naked. Very nervously I headed for the shower whilst he ordered a light snack and drinks.

"I'm back honey," he shouted.

After dropping the soap several times and slipping around in the shower tray I heard him say.

"Everything alright?"

"Yes," I replied.

By now the bathroom was thick with steam. I cautiously returned to the bedroom with a bath towel wrapped tightly around my wet naked body. Dylan's eyes were fixed on me, at the same time pouring a glass of white wine; it spilled over onto the table and floor.

"Wow, you are so lovely," he grinned.

I walked across the room and glanced at my reflection in the mirror, hoping the rest of my body would excite him too. Mostly covered with the towel, yet he appreciated what he saw. I was eagerly indulging in a love affair with this tall dark stranger who stole my heart in the nightclub. I didn't think about the consequences of my actions. My eyes feasted on him, and my heart leapt into my mouth, he simply took my breath away. Suddenly he leapt up from the chair and hastily stripped off his clothes without hesitation or embarrassment and strutted towards the bathroom. Singing as he showered, it seemed such a long and anxious wait for his return. Now he was emerging through the steamy mist, like an illusion. He grinned in a cheeky manner and casually sauntered over towards me. I drank two glasses of wine in his absence, to help my nervous tension. I reached out to touch his hand and feel his warm wet body. He glowed, radiantly smiling and eager for love. Without a second thought he dropped the towel to the floor revealing his astonishing physique.

Quite the most beautiful man I'd ever seen.

I could readily view his amazing body from every possible angle with his long dark hair dripping water down his muscular back. My eyes scanned every inch of his sun kissed flesh, as he stepped eagerly towards me. He was looking down at his penis growing and becoming erect and glanced at me with such tenderness. I knew he was hungry for sex. So was I.

He turned around exhibiting his amazing body, exposing a beautiful firm rounded bottom. Suddenly he bent over flicking the mass of long dark dripping wet hair and spraying the room with water. As he moved and stretched, my eyes were fixed on his body, observing his superb stature. I was transfixed, mesmerised, totally smitten and fascinated with my gypsy. He was a hot-blooded young man, and I a frustrated middle-aged woman eager for sexual fantasies. We indulged in an erotic harmony of excitement and pleasure with an insatiable appetite for sex, which lasted for hours.

I was experiencing this extraordinary passion. I wanted more of my gypsy lover and less of my Irish husband.

LEAVING MY OLD LIFE

One day I simply left from my old life of comfort and security, taking only a few clothes, books, and personal items. I found an apartment by the river Wensum in Norwich and moved in with Dylan.

The lawyer and court fees absorbed most of the money owed to me. My husband returned to our beautiful house in Ireland to start a new life.

After the stress of it all eased off, Dylan and I planned a romantic three-week holiday to Kenya, to discover another way of being together in love and free.

Far, far away from the chaos.

The madness of falling in love.

Running on adrenaline and sexual fantasies.

What are these crazy things we do when we are in love and not thinking rationally, normality turns to recklessness, random and impulsive behaviour.

PART 2

MOMBASA

DIANI BEACH STORY

It was April 1994.

The rainy season in Kenya.

Arriving in Kenya at Mombasa airport the humidity was quite a shock from England. But as we travelled to the hotel our minds were fixed on enjoying our time alone, away from friends and family influences.

Expecting a hot sunny African holiday, but it was April and the rainy season. We had arrived at the hotel in Diani Beach near Mombasa exhausted after the long journey from London England. The hotel was very grand painted white and so welcoming, typically a tourist attraction with a large swimming pool and bar. Inside a big reception area with red seating and huge plants in clay pots. We were greeted by staff smartly dressed in black and white, and offering a free drink of wine.

"Karibu sana, very welcome."

A nicely decorated restaurant with several tables neatly setup for dinner and smartly dressed staff greeted us.

Franticly running around outside and swinging from tree-to-tree large monkeys squealing and pulling things from the litter bins and tossing it into the pool.

A heavy downpour began just as we unpacked our luggage, we snuggled up on our cosy bed to rest listening to the rain falling on the open balcony. In the distance unfamiliar sounds echoed along the beach, only a few metres away. Drifting into a sleepy state I was suddenly disturbed by a bang; it was a large monkey climbing into our room.

"Shoo, shoo get out!!" I yelled.

Dylan jumped up quickly and shut the balcony door. We laughed at this strange encounter and intrigued what else to expect.

The rain fell for a further three days and nights as we sat watching the entertainment from the resident monkeys. The staff constantly trying to move them on to the next hotel. It was a spectacle to say the least. The people were so friendly and helpful; we had such fun with the staff. Finally, the weather changed, and the sun made an appearance, lighting up the hotel grounds and everything began to look incredibly beautiful. The gardens were lush and green, with hundreds of pretty flowerbeds bordering the stony paths leading to the beach. Steam rising from the patios that were ankle deep in water the previous day, the atmosphere changed to the paradise we had dreamed of.

We decided to explore the local vicinity the atmosphere felt very exciting, as people waved calling out.

"Jambo, habari sana."

Over the next week we spent many hours just lazing by the pool, and getting acclimatised, it was becoming extremely hot, but with intermittent showers. We walked along the endless white sandy beach and met other Europeans, most of them warning us about the young beach boys selling oranges. They offer you segments of an orange to quench your thirst.

"Mzuri." Lovely.

However, once you eat it, they expect you to purchase the rest of the orange. If you don't pay them, they hound you up and down the beach and tell others to annoy you. We didn't get caught or conned by the beach sellers, or the small kiosks offering tourist goods along the roadside. Further along the beach we discovered a nice shopping parade with several upmarket shops selling very interesting tourist goods. A very strange two-story open-air bar/café created from random timber. Several tourists sitting around drinking cold Tusker beer whilst enjoying the heat of the day.

THE TOURIST SHOP

We strolled into a delightful quaint shop selling beautiful gifts and chatted with the helpful attractive tall African man serving customers. After a general enquiry about the goods for sale, I asked him how difficult it would be to open a shop in Diani Beach.

"Hakuna matata." No problem.

It was an impromptu question that led to an interesting conversation about living in Kenya.

I wasn't really thinking about the official documentation that we would need to go through; it simply never crossed my mind at that point, it was curiosity and nothing more. His name was Joseph, he invited us to a hotel across the road for a drink and introduced us to his wife Rose. They informed us, there was an opportunity to rent a shop in the parade, it was a long row of small individual shops, mostly run by local whites and Asians. Nicely fitted out with an African theme, timber beams and typical local features. Rose explained how easy it was for her to get us a shop if we wanted it. There was only one shopping parade around for miles, and always full of tourists, potentially earning a lot of money. Dylan and I were very keen to find out more. We thought we could start a new life together away from our families. I was daydreaming and not thinking it through. When we considered what we had back home it then became a great prospect, a genuine reason to leave the UK, for a new beginning.

After a few days contemplation we decided to view a lovely empty shop in a prime position. It was perfect for us. We wanted to open a boutique and souvenir shop.

Back at the hotel over a few drinks we talked seriously about the chance of having a business and became extremely excited at the prospect.

VILLAGE EXPERIENCE

A friendly young Christian man called John working at the hotel invited us to his village. We didn't hesitate in seizing the opportunity to have an adventure away from the hotel. A long trek through rough bush ground to where the young man lived, was quite daunting and tiring. Before we set out for the day, we bought sweets for the children at his suggestion. Water and fruit for ourselves. On arrival we handed out the sweets to some children, when an old man offered us some local hooch, it was awful like drinking diesel. We ate some candy to end the appalling taste. However, we thoroughly enjoyed the outing and discovered a little of African life in Ukunda village. The following days were mostly filled with swimming in the beautiful ocean and lazing around the pool, eating, and drinking.

We decided to open an account with Barclays Bank nearby the hotel, in preparation of our possible return to Diani Beach. It was a surprisingly quick and effortless process to accomplish the bank account.

A few more visits to the shopping parade and a charming local open-air bar called Walter's Inn, not too far from the hotel. Enjoy a few beers and chat with some European tourists, local white people, and became friendly with the German owners Walter and Sylvia.

Walter and Sylvia owned a beautiful house with a small pig farm nearby and an excellent modern butcher shop in the parade.

DAY OUT TOUR

One day the hotel arranged for a trip out to visit a wood carving factory about an hour away and experience how the local crafts were created for the tourist. We enjoyed it so much because our ideas for the shop were becoming a potential reality. The dream of living here and having a shop was now becoming possible. It was recommended to seek accommodation for our return.

Before leaving Diani Beach, we met a charming young Italian lady called Barbara the manageress at Simba Village, an apartment complex opposite the hotel we stayed in. Barbara a very petite bubbly character with mousy shoulder length hair and big brown eyes. Appearing much younger than her years, with a sweet disposition and enthusiastic personality. We explained we wanted to rent an apartment from her and would return to Diani Beach in June. We paid a deposit to secure an apartment, with the idea of becoming permanent residents.

I had no idea how complex the immigration process would be, I naively believed we could return and stay in paradise without issue. Suddenly the three-week holiday in paradise ended, we felt very unhappy having to leave, and back to the cold air in England. After two months back in UK, I sold everything and bid farewell to family and friends. My family thought I was crazy, but I refused to listen and returned to Kenya with my Romany gypsy love.

When you are in love nothing makes sense, you behave illogically, foolishly, and senselessly. You act on the desire to please, on a whim and normality no longer exists in your in-love space.

Impulsive and reckless behaviour.

BACK TO KENYA DIANI BEACH

SELLING UP AND RETURNING

It was June 17th, 1994, when we left England. We could not get a suitable flight to Mombasa, but a cheap fare to Nairobi was available. We arrived at Nairobi airport and hired a silver saloon car. It was a nightmare trying to get out of Nairobi, the streets blocked with traffic and people, extremely hot and dusty. Finally, after weaving our way through the chaos, we found the road that would take us to our new home in Simba Village, Diani Beach. Driving along the Nairobi to Mombasa Road we passed different tribes by the roadside waving, and groups of women walking chatting with filled baskets on their heads. Zebras slowly strolling along the road. Dylan got out the car trying to encourage them to move along, however, they had their own pace, it was Africa.

Countless big old lorries creating huge clouds of dust and matatus, (local taxi minibuses) packed full of people sounding their horns as they thundered past us on route to Mombasa. Now and then we would stop and stretch our legs, eat fruit, and drink water. It was extremely hot and tiring. Finally, we arrived at Mombasa with the two enormous elephant tusks at the entrance, as crowds of people rushing about their business, shouting, and yelling, cars beeping their horns and total pandemonium. The contrast after hours of vastness, zebra, giraffe, wild animals, and small villages was obvious.

After weaving our way through the crowds, we headed for the ferry crossing where more chaos waited for us, and then took the Diani Beach Road. At last, we arrived very tired but so happy to be at Simba Village, however Barbara the Italian manageress was not there. We strolled across the road to the Italian Crismani family, the owners of the apartment complex where a short friendly African man dressed in shabby clothing greeted us.

> *"Karibu sana, very welcome,"* he uttered, and went with us to our apartment.

The apartment was bright, airy, an open plan living space, with a dark wooden fitted kitchen and bed sitting room. A short corridor to a white tiled shower and toilet. In the centre of the room an enormous bed covered with a green patterned throw, dark ornate wooden side cabinets and small green lamps. A huge dark framed mirror on the wall. Above the bed an exceptionally large white fan slowly turned causing a gentle breeze and a strange buzzing noise. Outside through the French windows the patio veranda, a seating area with colourful printed cushioned cane sofa and two small side tables.

Not long after arriving Barbara made her entrance carrying a big basket of fruit having mango, bananas, and oranges. A large glass jug filled to the brim with iced fruit juice and a box of mixed canned drinks. It was such a treat after the long hot tiring journey. After a quick chat she departed.

> *"Tionne hives karibuni, see you soon,"* she smiled and hurried back to her office.

Dylan and I unpacked our things, showered, and changed our clothes, then rested on the enormous, sumptuous bed for a few hours.

Within no time at all we were settled into our delightful ground floor apartment overlooking a large deep inviting swimming pool. Beautifully well-kept neat and tidy grounds, filled with an abundance of sweet, scented flowers and small colourful birds perched on every tree and shrub. The grounds were bordered by an eight-foot white wall; two heavy black iron gates constantly guarded by two askari, the local security guards. Smartly dressed in dark blue uniforms and peaked caps, parading around holding large heavy sticks. Both men were very friendly and helpful, expecting a tip known as *pesa kidogo* (small money) because this was the custom in Kenya.

On the 20th of June, I received a phone call I had become a grandmother, both mother and daughter were well. Later that day I called from the office at Simba Village to congratulate my daughter Sophie and her baby daughter Jols.

INSEPARABLE

As the days past Dylan and I became inseparable and extremely protective of each other. The constant sound of the crickets, cicada and frogs would not be the only noise disrupting our sleep, in the still of the warm humid night. The continuous buzz of mosquitoes was so infuriating as they hovered above the big net protecting us from their bloodthirsty bite. A large electric fan spinning round and round day and night with a faint but annoying hum. There was the odd moment of feeling a little homesick for things to be normal once more.

Dylan was intrigued and curious about everything and had no feelings about what and whom he had left behind in chilly UK. Everything seemed like a dream or fantasy that we both shared and nothing more than an illusion of the mind. Was it truly a reality that we were living in paradise and if so when would it all end? Would we awaken from the dream and discover we must return to the life we left behind.

Our nights of passion on the enormous king-size bed became an art. Constantly aware of the biting menace that lingered outside the safe zone of the net. Romping around in the tropical African nights on a jumbo bed with the only sound of nocturnal creatures somehow had a strange, yet romantic feel to it.

We kept the hired silver car for a week and then the Crismani family sold us a cheap old blue Volks Wagon Beetle to get around. We discovered a lovely local Pizza restaurant one night, enjoyed a few drinks and a huge, delicious pizza. Several local girls were flirting with Dylan which I found annoying, but he loved the attention, they called him Rambo. Chatting to local whites and ex-pats gave us a sense of normality.

GOING TO THE MARKET

One morning walking to the small open market we were introduced to a member of the local Christian church and invited to attend a service. It would be a wonderful opportunity for us to meet the preacher and the people from the Ukunda township.

It was Sunday, extremely hot and quite a trek across a rough terrain. We were warned not to go without a guard or someone from the church; it could be dangerous. However, we set off on our own. We walked for an hour or more in the sweltering heat and arrived at the gigantic open-air church with an amazingly high makuti (dry leaves) roof. An enormous open space with wooden seats and benches. We noticed many families gathered there, but we were the only white people at the service. Everyone well-dressed wearing colourful clothes, singing, and clapping their hands. It seemed very natural singing gospel songs with the local community. Later we were introduced to one of the preachers, his name was Francis a tall very thin and unassuming and seemingly soft-spoken man. We were given cakes, danced, and chatted with the children and their mothers. It was a very uplifting experience.

MEETING ROSE THE SHOP LADY

We arranged to meet up with Rose, the lady who told me about a shop in the parade, she took us to the property office. I noticed the awful mouldy and damp aroma, like an old church. The office was exceedingly small, barely enough room for a small battered wooden bench, a couple of broken chairs and a tall rusty metal filing cabinet. Piles of papers everywhere and cardboard boxes stacked up in one corner. The walls painted light green and a big black and white photograph of President Daniel arap Moi hanging from a large nail. A small thin peculiar looking old lady behind the desk stood up.

"U hali gani, how are you?"

Rose discussed the shop that I wanted, and I would have to pay a deposit of 15,000 Kenyan shillings to secure it. They chatted in Swahili, nothing seemed suspicious or underhand, I was satisfied with the introduction and the shop idea became ever closer.

We needed to buy goods for the apartment, although it was furnished there was no kitchen utensils or bedding. The mosquito net was too small, I wanted to create a huge square shape to hang over the entire bed. Rose came with us to Mombasa, where we found an interesting hardware store, then we stopped for a cold drink at the Blue Moon Café, on the way home.

OPEN AIR CAFÉ MEETING

A couple of days later we met up with Rose again at the odd timber open-air café, she explained that the property renting office required money for legal documents, security, and the full lease.

> *"This is the way it works here you must pay three months' rent in advance, a large deposit, we take it and give you a receipt,"* mumbled Rose.

Although my first reaction was to be cautious, she had the lease and all the necessary documents to hand. I had a strange intuitive feeling that I recognised as a warning however, I chose to ignore it. A basic lease with no complications, and I really wanted the shop; I could see such a fantastic opportunity, so I agreed to pay the fees. We headed to the bank, and I withdrew 90,000 KS, as asked. I signed the lease documents and Rose gave me a scruffy receipt for the money. Everything appeared legal and proper.

ASKING FOR SHOP KEYS

I was very keen to get started with the business. I had some great ideas to get working on, so the next day I went back to the property office. I asked the lady for the keys to the shop, but she looked puzzled and then explained there was no shop for me. I clarified the payment to Rose, the lease money she requested and offered her the receipt. The woman laughed and said Rose was only a local lady getting a small commission for introducing clients to the property office and nothing else.

"What are you doing giving it to her, she's only finding clients for us, we give her a small commission. She told me she was going into business with the mzungu lady," she laughed.

My heart sank, I felt sick.

Suddenly a strange sensation that my energy was pouring out of my body, I become anxious, shaking, and weak. I was melting away like a bar of chocolate left out in the noonday sun.

I thought to myself, that's what falling in love does to you. You can't see things as they really are or think clearly. Reality gets mixed up with fantasy and confusion sets in. I knew in my heart something was wrong. I simply wanted to experience the shop; I wanted to please my lover. It was too close to let go of, I didn't listen to my instincts. Perhaps I did, but chose to ignore them, what a mistake that was. Oh, how stupid can I get. Why did I ignore my gut feelings?

I'll find out if anyone knows where her husband resides and not mention Rose, I started to enquire and was directed to a place called Muthaiga Mini Market in the Diani Shopping Centre, run by Asians. They knew where he lived, finally I was getting somewhere.

FINDING ROSE

The following day Saturday, we decided to start looking for Rose in the village. Ukunda was a huge town packed with hundreds of small village houses. It was a dirty smelly place with dogs and chickens roaming around. Piles of rubbish just dumped everywhere. Children running up and down the narrow alleyways, and older people urinating in doorways. Heaps of wood stacked in broken down sheds and string washing lines with colourful clothing hanging. There was no running water, but noisy generators provided them with electricity and typical African music blasted out of parked cars on the roadside. A strong smell of food cooking outside the shabby houses on hot coal grills, clinging to the smoky heavy atmosphere. Small shops selling soap, cigarettes, sweets and washing powder. It was not a safe place for any stranger, never mind a mzungu.

After looking around for a bit in this strange unfamiliar place, I stopped someone and asked the way to Josephs house. It was right in the centre of the village; I made sure I could find my way back because when I returned it would be at night. They would not be expecting me, and mzungu people do not go in there.

VISITING ROSE

The only light in Ukunda village at night were tiny little oil lights placed around everywhere. Rose and Joseph were very shocked to see me. The dirty little house was sweltering hot and humid. A tiny room about ten feet square piled up with belongings, and a small generator creating a strange clicking noise. Crammed full of clothes and goods piled up high next to a small black portable TV, perched on wooden boxes. A dirty red couch with plastic bags of rubbish on it. No open windows, stale air reeking of body odour, urine and ugali, a sort of maze porridge. A small fan whirring in the corner churning up the stinking air, and no oxygen. Another room behind a yellow rag curtain nailed to the wall, was the bedroom.

"I want to know what you have done with my money Rose?"

"I was going to give it to the lady at the office, but she wasn't there. So, my friend and I thought it was better to put it into my bank account until Monday," she ranted.

Rose also had a Barclays Bank account.

"You need to give the money back to me Rose."

"What are you going to do mzungu, you're in Kenya 90,000 KS can buy a lot of stuff. I could have you killed for a bottle of whisky, you may not get out alive mzungu," she declared.

"You're messing with the wrong person I might be a mzungu, but I will not be conned by you Rose."

I told her that if she returned the money, I would forget all about it. She could have a job in the shop, and everything would be alright.

"Just meet me at the bank first thing Monday morning," I insisted.

She agreed, and I left Ukunda hastily.

SUNDAY CHURCH

There was nothing I could do until Monday so the next day we went to the church. It was a good two or three miles inland through the rough bush. Arriving at the church an ensemble of musicians and singers. The atmosphere electric with an authentic halleluiah experience. It reminded me of a time when I was a born-again Christian back home.

We met Francis chatting to his friends and I shared the story about Rose, and the money problem.

"We must get your money back Janette, a typical con move, they just take your money, and you never see them again. How much did she take?" He enquired.

"90,000 shillings."

"That's big money for Kenya, we need to see the bank manager, we must get your money back. I'll meet you there tomorrow morning when it opens," insisted Francis.

PETER THE PASTOR

Peter the pastor of the church was talking about the older people come to Christ and the church in Mombasa. He mentioned that I should be careful of the traditional thinking people, because they still believe in juju, the old ways and magic. I laughed and told him I was not afraid of any magic; I do magic myself. He shared a story of what happened to him five years back, a ghost kept attacking him in the night, an invisible force that terrified him.

One morning whilst having breakfast everything flew off the table crashing to the floor, it petrified the pastor. Francis and another preacher performed an exorcism. The pastor was never the same after the horrific experience said Francis.

Monday morning at 9am, we arrived at the bank to see Francis with a small bible tucked under his arm pacing up and down anxiously. I wasn't at all surprised Rose did not show up as promised. Francis and the bank manager spoke in Swahili for ten minutes. Then the manager looked at his computer.

"Yes, I can see that 90,000 KS has come out of your account, and 90,000 KS deposited into this Rose account, on the same day. Rather a lot of money for her to get overnight," he grinned.

"This is not good for tourism, I think we need to put it back where it belongs, hakuna matata sawa kabisa, no problem okay," said the smiling manager.

The bank manager leaned over putting his hand on my shoulder, and simply transferred the money from Rose's account back into mine.

"Sometimes I go up to Nairobi alone and have a long weekend up there, you are most welcomed to join me mummy," he grinned.

"Well, thank you for the invitation."

Of course, now I am in debt to the bank manager and totally entrusted to Francis.

BACK TO THE PROPERTY OFFICE

He took us back to the property office.

"We can't give it to you unless you have residency papers."

I hadn't thought of that, in our rush to get out here it never occurred to me would need residency papers to start a business. However, Francis offered to take responsibility of the shop, until the residency documentation was approved. Francis said we must meet with his advocate in Mombasa to create a company very soon. Then later he would travel to Nairobi immigration for the residency papers. All the legal papers would be sorted shortly, but I had to settle the bank situation with Rose.

VISIT ROSE AGAIN

Rose was unaware the money was safely back in my account and would not expect another visit from me. She gasped in disbelief as she opened the door and made excuses about the bank meeting.

"Get out of my village!" she screamed.

"Tomorrow we can go to the bank and property office together, or we can meet at the police station. All you need to do is give my money back."

She was laughing hysterically and shouting in Swahili, then English.

"Your money is gone mzungu and there is nothing you can do about it!"

I revealed to her that the manager had closed her account and informed the police. She was cursing me with Swahili magic! Finally, I needed to leave, I sensed an eeriness about the area. I hurried back to the car where Dylan was waiting for me.

The following night at 2am in the morning a loud thump woke Dylan up.

"Jan, what's going on?" he screamed.

It was dark no lights on outside, I thought that was odd. I slid across the bed and leaned over the side and peered underneath. Crouching under the bed staring back at me, a massive black cat with enormous eyes, I got back up. How did it get in I thought? I suggested to Dylan he ought to look under the bed.

"Fucking hell Jan is this for real, is this magic? I don't like it."

"Shut up! now talk nicely to the cat."

Magic in Africa.

There was no sign of the black cat in the morning, yet the gate remained closed. We were so relieved the Rose episode was behind us, but now more aware of mysterious cats appearing and magic in Africa.

Peter the pastor mentioned juju men and witches using cats and reminding me of old English witchy stories. The animals were called familiars by the witches and wizards. I had studied the mysteries and magic for many years and quite aware of these tales.

AFRICAN OASIS

Friday 1st July 1994

We travelled to Mombasa with Francis to his advocate; they chatted in Swahili then a little English. The advocate asked who the three directors are forming the company?

"There is only Dylan and me," I replied.

Francis said he would be a director on paper in our company, he had helped another foreign company formation before.

We all agreed.

"What are you going to call your company?"

"What about African Oasis?" I suggested.

"African Oasis is available, and after you receive the company documents you must immediately file for permanent residency."

Preliminary paperwork completed and copies to follow within the week. Whilst waiting for company papers I decided not to lease the shop until we had all the paperwork sorted out. Rose might try to cause trouble for us, and we needed to be more vigilant now.

TRIP TO MOMBASA

ASIAN WHOLESALERS AND ADVOCATE

The papers arrived and we paid the deposit for the shop. Francis needed to sign the documents with us. We headed to Mombasa to the advocate, and to buy stock for the shop. Francis directed us to an Asian dealer in one of the back streets, he was a friendly middle-aged man from Delhi, India. After a few hours of gathering clothes and tourist items we paid him and left Mombasa for Diani Beach. The ferry crossing was packed with people and vehicles, as we manoeuvred our way through the chaos. Great commotion with big trucks hooting and people yelling, as we slowly left Mombasa to the other side of the river.

FRANCIS WENT TO IMMIGRATION NAIROBI

Now that we had the company papers the next step was the residency papers. Francis mentioned he had a relative working in the immigration office in Nairobi and he would sort it out for a *peso kidogo,* a small fee. He left Diani Beach on a crowded bus heading to Nairobi.

After three days he returned with some paperwork.

"Where is the rest of the papers?"

He said there is an issue because we weren't married, we had to have individual papers and separate bank accounts. Or we needed to get a statement from the bank to show we had the 150,000 KS each, that they needed to apply for residency.

We revisited the friendly bank manager.

"Hello, we need your help again."

"What can I do for you mummy?"

After a brief explanation and a *pesa kidogo* bribe, he compiled an excellent official letter stating there were sufficient funds in the account, to cover the application requirement. I thanked him for his kindness. He winked.

We met up with Francis at church on Sunday, he was baffled that we managed to achieve the letter at such a small fee. The following day we visited the shop to explore ideas.

JOSEPH OBETTO

A tall thin unattractive African man wearing a scruffy blue baseball hat, red T-shirt with torn black jogging trousers, was approaching the steps of the shopping parade. He began chatting to Dylan as I was sitting on some steps watching the two men interact. Something felt wrong about this shop, it was too far back from the main parade. I called Dylan over and the stranger who introduced himself as Joseph Obetto a Luo tribesman.

Joseph was from up country, a carpenter helping someone in another shop. He mentioned he had several jobs lined up but nowhere to store timber and only a few tools. He asked if we needed any work done in the new shop and we could find him any day around Ukunda village. We asked him to meet up the next day to help us, because the shop was completely empty, we needed a counter and chairs. Joseph knew all the timber yards in Mombasa, he tried to describe where to go for wood, but we didn't understand how to get there. He said it would be easier to take us.

"Hakuna matata mummy, no problem."

TRIP TO MOMBASA

We met up with Joseph the following morning and headed to a Mombasa timber yard. We were introduced to a couple of friendly guys, who agreed to sell us some timber in bulk. At the time, I didn't need it, I only wanted a few things made for the shop. We moved on to the next timber merchant. There was an assortment of beautiful and inexpensive furniture in one corner of the yard. Joseph said he could make it cheaper, and we could make a huge profit selling it in Diani Beach.

"That sounds like a great idea. Let's go and have a bite to eat and discuss it more."

We stopped at the Blue Moon Café for a snack and some cold drinks and discussed Josephs plight, unable to store timber, but getting plenty of work making furniture, doors and much more in Diani Beach.

"What do you need Joseph?" I asked.

He said he could create a little carpentry business with his close friends and make a lot of money. They would require shelter, and several tools to get started.

"What if we helped you with the tools, and a place to work from?"

"That would be wonderful mummy."

"Or Dylan and I open a carpentry business, and employ you and your friends?"

Joseph jumped up clapping his hands and grinning.

"That's my dream come true! I can't believe it!"

"Well let's start planning it," Dylan remarked.

Drinking cold coke and drawing on serviettes some ideas of furniture that we could make, and the contracts that were already in place.

Off to another timber yard, and I began to get excited about this as a *bona fide* business. I didn't have to part with a lot of money, we could find the factory ourselves. I wouldn't hand over any money until I had legal papers from Francis. We returned to Diani Beach and Joseph came to the apartment for a meal of spicy chicken and cold beer. We chatted for hours about what would be ideal for a factory in Ukunda. Joseph said we needed to be near the roadside on the main Mombasa Nairobi route. Not too far inland, a good driveway because of heavy lorries delivering. Good shelter for the workers and the timber. Simply make a few things and put them outside along the driveway, and people will come.

DISCOVER ANOTHER SHOP

Returning to the empty shop, feeling apprehensive about getting it off the ground, especially with the modern furniture business idea with Joseph. A young African lady appeared from behind the building.

> *"Are you the mzungu African Oasis shop around the corner?"* she asked.
>
> *"Yes, as soon as my paperwork comes through."*
>
> *"I heard someone is going to burn you out lady, be careful."* she mumbled.

More problems, and it doesn't feel good, I'm not going forward with the shop idea. Rose was in the back of my mind, was it her? Even though I had bought some goods to sell in the shop, I decided to cut my losses and get out of the lease before it was too late.

ARGUMENT WITH DYLAN

Dylan and I sat in the car park quietly not speaking until I said to him.

> *"I am not going to open the shop it just doesn't feel right to me."*

Dylan wanted me to continue with the shop, and the furniture business, but my final answer was a definite no, something felt wrong. Why did I have these strange feelings about this shop, I was trying to think, but he wouldn't stop talking and began yelling at me.

> *"Be quiet for a moment I need to get some focus. I just need to think."*

> *"No, no Jan we have to do this it's why we came here,"* he was yelling!

Rose might create more problems for me.

> *"Oh God, you and your fucking magic and strange gut feelings!"* he screamed in my face.

I resolved to move forward with Joseph and the furniture factory concept and absorb the monetary loss of the stock. I didn't want to upset the Italian and German shopkeepers; they were the local Mafia.

Nor crazy Rose and her magic.

TWO DAYS ON THE BEACH

For two days I walked along the beach contemplating everything and hoping to achieve some insight to what was unfolding. I needed quiet time alone to empty my mind of all the clutter and to create some clear images, of what I needed to do next. Dylan detested being alone and came searching for me. I was sitting under a tree; it was a lovely sacred place to meditate.

Falling in love with a Romany gypsy toy boy, had many difficulties that I needed to solve. I began to miss my old secure life, I still had feelings for my ex-Paddy, but not in the way I loved Dylan. Now responsible for this young man, and I had no one to turn to. Dylan a naive boy at heart, and I needed to make sure that no harm came to either of us. Kenya was a dangerous place, and we were just novices playing at being something we were not.

I asked him not to follow me to the beach and interrupt my quiet time, but I caught sight of him lingering nearby. I slowly strolled up to the Forty Thieves bar along the beach and continued walking. I looked back but Dylan had vanished. I began sauntering back to the bar sat down with a large ice-cold Tusker beer and realised, nothing is what it appears to be in Kenya.

Not even myself.

FRANCIS AND RESIDENCY PAPERS

Francis demanded to take our passports and money to bribe his relation in the immigration office. I told him I would not part with the passports, and we would all go together to Nairobi.

> *"Oh mummy, it's not my fault I will come back with all your correct documents but remember you must get your passport stamped and a card to prove you are a resident. I'm afraid they won't do it unless you pay another chunk of money. This is Kenya, bribes are expected."*
>
> *"Dylan and I can go up with them later."*

"They won't see you; I am the agent."

I told Francis he couldn't have the passports because we had business to deal with in the UK first. He returned to Nairobi with more bribe money required, to move forward with the residency papers.

We were preparing to return to England on business.

CAFÉ PROPERTY

Joseph came to the apartment with news of an interesting property available for rent, on the main Ukunda to Mombasa Road. It was an old African café with a large frontage and long driveway from the busy road. We were invited to view the café and perhaps come to an arrangement to rent it. I was excited about the property. It was painted cream and black with a veranda. On the opposite side of the road a small church, a few small shops and a unit offering supplies for the building trade. This would suit us perfectly and be a new beginning.

After a long discussion with the friendly owner, we came to an agreement at a very fair rent and a visit to the advocate shortly followed for a lease. We stayed a couple of hours with the owner discussing the factory, rent and my situation. I explained to him I would want the factory in a few weeks, on my return from the UK. It was perfect because he wasn't ready to hand it over for another month. I also shared the Rose story and how she conned me, therefore rather cautious this time. He didn't ask for a deposit, and we were all very happy with the arrangement.

We were extremely excited about the factory becoming a reality so soon, however nothing would happen until my return from the UK. I needed to organise funds for the new business, visit my family and sort out my legal affairs. I would give him the money on my return and when the keys where in my hand.

> *"Hakuna matata mummy, no problem mummy,"* he smiled, and we shook hands.

We would be a niche in the market and making furniture between the jua kali boys and Keystones.

All the commercial and big contracts were given to Keystones. Local traders didn't trust the jua kali boys because they might just up and go.

Jua kali boys work outside, under the trees along the roadside.

LEAVING KENYA FOR ENGLAND

A few days before leaving Kenya we were invited to a Christian crusade on the beach and expected to see Francis there, he was going to baptise us in the sea. However, he didn't show up. Later we went to a big Christian wedding and provided several photos for the couple, and their families. It was a wonderful celebration.

Departing Kenya.

It was imperative to organise my divorce settlement, bank accounts and other business in England and visit family and friends. I didn't expect a big welcome home because they thought it a crazy idea to go. But my parents and daughter were very pleased to see me. I also met my beautiful baby granddaughter Jols, with golden hair and big blue eyes. Although very happy to see my friends and family, I couldn't wait to return to my home in Simba Village.

Constantly thinking about African Oasis and what we needed to get it up and running. I understood electrical equipment could be quite expensive in Mombasa, so I purchased several professional electric and hand tools at a discount price and forwarded via DHL to Kenya.

I booked a flight to Nairobi.

It was such a relief boarding the plane back to Kenya we chatted about our new life that was waiting for us on the other side of the world. Arriving in Nairobi to the glorious sunshine, we decided to take the train down to Mombasa and get picked up at the station. We stayed the night in a quaint hotel.

BACK AT DIANI BEACH

Back at the apartment and news came that there had been a terrible storm which destroyed the makuti roof of the church. Everyone trying to help in clearing the heaps of strewn poles and leaves. Francis left a message he would meet us at the bus stop the next day but did not turn up. The following day we caught him rushing by the post office grasping his battered old brown leather briefcase.

"I will come tonight don't worry," he muttered.

We were expecting to see Francis as promised and have the long-awaited residency papers, he made a few trips to Nairobi with fees and bribes, so I was expecting this whole business to be sorted out during our two weeks in England. However, there is still no sign of him and the residency papers. We told Joseph the whole story about Rose and Francis, he went looking for him in the early hours of the morning.

The next day we waited for Francis to show up, he didn't, and I was concerned for his absence. Joseph and I went to his house, he wasn't there. After an hour searching for the elusive Francis, we eventually found him at the church. He didn't have the documents because he was extremely busy with the church but would visit us at home later.

> *"You'll have to pay me more money to fix the problem,"* growled Francis.

I agreed with his demands and to meet the next day at the bank. It was so frustrating, I knew it would get sorted out eventually, but more money required as bribes, aside of the government fees.

KIDNAP FRANCIS

In the morning, we met Francis at the bank. He was very defensive, I sensed animosity between us. I mentioned constantly handing over cash was becoming an annoying habit of his. I chatted with the bank manager about the passport and bribe scenario. He said very clearly not to hand over the passports, but to go with him to immigration. I withdrew the cash for Francis and waved goodbye to the friendly manager. Francis was sitting in the back seat of the car talking to Dylan. I mentioned what the bank manager advised me to do.

> *"Right, that's it, off we go to Nairobi!"* insisted Dylan.

> *"Oh no. I can't go to Nairobi today. You're making a big mistake. Don't forget my name is on African Oasis, I am a director in the company."*

Francis panicked and tried to exit the car, yelling out that he was a director in another company, and he took them to court and won. Dylan ignored him and speedily drove off with Francis sitting in the back screaming in Swahili. We drove the four hundred miles to Nairobi; the atmosphere was very unpleasant. It was hot and stuffy like a sauna in the car, with a deathly silence.

THE IMMIGRATION BUILDING NAIROBI

25th October 1994

Arriving at the immigration building I became quite anxious; we were the only white people in there. You could almost smell the years of corruption in the heavy stuffy atmosphere and dark corridors. I imagined entering a room and disappearing. People shouting in different languages and the overwhelming stale body odour, lingering in the air. I asked Francis why are there guards on the doors?

"People get angry when they don't receive their papers."

After waiting an hour, a short scruffy guard escorted us to an office where a very stern man, peering over his thick glasses sat behind a desk piled up with papers and books.

"Passports and papers," he grunted.

Although they were chatting in Swahili, it was obvious they knew each other. I got the impression Francis was explaining he couldn't get any more money out of us.

"Now look here mzungu, I have been very good pushing your papers through quickly."

"Sir, I am just paying for residency documentation to be stamped today."

"If I choose, nothing is legal, and passports can disappear easily. I might not give them back to you mzungu. I think there is pesa kidogo owing to me," he grumbled.

In other words, no money - no passports. I had previously paid the government fees and several bribes to get it done quickly. I needed the proper stamp in the passport and residency card. I placed the passports and papers on his desk and suggested he should stamp them. He laughed, snatched the passports, and put them in his desk drawer. Demanding more money from me, reluctantly I agreed to pay him.

Removing them from the drawer he positioned one on top of the other, he pushed the top one across to me, but kept the other. Grinning, grunting, and playing mind games with me.

I looked straight into his soulless eyes.

"God is not happy with you today, my friend."

I handed over the *pesa kidogo* as he tossed the other passport across the desk.

"This is Kenya, mzungu, be careful," he snarled.

Finally, passports and residency cards with the proper stamp, we are now officially residents in Kenya. The whole procedure expense was twice as much as expected because Francis kept half of the bribe money. We drove back to Diani Beach stopping once to stretch our legs and drink cold orange juice from a roadside café. It was a long uncomfortable journey crunched up in a small car, with Francis in a silent mood. Finally arriving in Ukunda, we dropped him off at his house.

"Yes, Janette I kept some of the bribe money. This is how we help people in Kenya. If you think what I have done is bad, it is nothing to what is coming to you with that Joseph Obetto, he will destroy you," he retorted.

After dropping Francis off we made haste to Walter's Inn for a few much-needed cold beers. We shared with the guys at Walter's all the trouble we had obtaining our legal documents to stay in Kenya.

> *"Janette, you should have come to us first. We could have sorted it out for you."*

It never occurred to me to ask for help, we were so wrapped up with Francis, Rose and setting up the factory.

HIRING THE BOYS

The large trunk filled with electrical and carpentry tools arrived from England. Joseph Obetto knew some excellent carpenters and went looking for them. Later he returned with two genuinely nice young men, they were all good friends and co-workers. Ngala the eldest in his early thirties married with children, the other young man called Msambuku a brilliant carver and a shy gay person. I liked them both very much.

> *"Let's go for lunch and discuss what we can do to make African Oasis exclusive,"* I suggested.

There would be no competition, we found a niche in the market. Keystone factory only dealt with the big contracts and too expensive for the locals. People didn't trust the jua kali (jewa kali) boys, working along the roadside. The old café was divided in three areas, one exceptionally large open space and two more rooms behind it. To the left a smaller room suitable for my office and the larger space for storage. After a thorough clean we painted the walls black and cream. It was a bright and airy space with several barred windows, no glass.

THE OUTSIDE

A narrow pathway leading to a makeshift toilet, constructed of corrugated tin and timber, with an ill-fitting door and a slanting roof. Small and cramped with a long drop hole to crouch over the opening. An old black plastic bucket of filthy water to wash your hands in. Dirty old newspapers piled up on a box, not there for reading. The stench was unbearable.

> *"This is Africa mummy, you will get used to it, but we will clean it up a bit for you."*

I suggested putting sawdust in and around it, and then burn it.

> *"Great idea mummy."*

After a week of hard labour, the old café had vanished, it was now a furniture factory. I blessed the factory with prayers and burning incense. I sent the boys out to search for any old pieces of unwanted timber, boxes and anything that might be useful. They were to collect their own few tools and return later that day.

ORGANISING THE WORKSHOP

The boys arrived with their little bag of tools, mostly hand made things, a few hammers, chisels and one saw. I realised that I needed to rig them out with some proper clothes. They had old worn-out faded t-shirts, shorts and shoes made from rubber tyres or flip flops. All the shop stock in my apartment would be perfect for them. I knew they would feel good in new clothing, it would be an incentive to work hard, and be part of a team. I invited them to my home for a meal and let them choose their clothes. It gave me a warm feeling to know I could do this for these nice young men. Later I took

Ngala with me to Mombasa to purchase some much-needed things for his wife, children, and their small house. We filled boxes up with goods for his kitchen, bedding and some food.

BUYING THE NEW PICK-UP TRUCK

We needed a pick-up truck, and part exchanged the old beetle car for a sensible work vehicle, and a small generator for the tools. Joseph suggested we invite two very skilled young friends, Patrick, and Tyson. The two men arrived at the factory grinning from ear to ear, so excited to meet us.

> *"Mummy I have heard you wish for us to work with you at the wonderful new factory, and we are so pleased to say yes to you,"* smiled Tyson.
>
> *"I would like you all to come to my home tonight for a meal. I have some things for you both. Welcome to African Oasis Patrick and Tyson."*

Tyson was a thick set strong man in his mid to late twenties with boxing skills, aside of being a carpenter. Tyson was his nickname and Patrick tall slim and handsome with Rasta hair, wearing a big smile and donning a black beret with odd badges. I took to them at once.

Joseph, Dylan and I travelled to Mombasa to get the truck and generator, then on to the Blue Moon Café where the idea of the factory was first aired. It felt wonderful driving back to Diani Beach to begin a new phase in our life. The following day Joseph stencilled in black paint African Oasis with our business details on both sides of the truck. Now we were official.

MAKING MY DESK

The boys wanted to make me a desk for the office and Msambuku would carve African Oasis on the front panel. It was such a pleasure to watch these young men at work, singing and laughing under the shade of the trees in the heat of the midday sun. It was far too hot for me in the small stuffy office, no air, no breeze, and no electricity for a fan. When we leased the factory, the electricity had been cut off due to non-payment. I would have to wait for the electricity company to arrive within the next six months to reconnect it. I was expected to settle the bill, which wasn't part of the contract, hence the delay with negotiations and a stubborn landlord. It was checkmate and I wasn't about to pay his outstanding debts.

We made three worktables and two benches to sit on. I needed to hire more boys, James, Mohamed and two friends, all carpenters, and wonderful young men.

I created a brochure of new innovative designs with the boys help and we made samples of the furniture. I had several obstacles to overcome with limited shades of wood varnishes available, so I made my own after trial and error. I made a suitable selection of dyes and mixed them with varnish or just wax. Outside the factory a wonderful display of coffee tables, stools, dining tables and chairs, bookcases, bedside cabinets with unusual carvings and others plain. Msambuku carved mirrors and picture frames and trinket boxes and big storage trunks. The samples were displayed along the driveway and on the veranda.

THE POLICE CALL TO AFRICAN OASIS

The local police arrived to check that we had the proper documentation and business papers. After a couple of days, we are visited by immigration officers. They were informed I didn't have the correct papers and would give me a warning to sort it out. Obviously sent by an angry Francis and unaware of the full story.

> *"If you are coming for a payment up front pesa kidogo, you are too late I have my documents here and they are officially stamped."*

They asked for my papers, I held on to them tightly and refused to pass them over. They noted the official stamp and dated signature; they countersigned and stamped them also. Immigration warned me they would return for *pesa kidogo* (small money bribe). It's the way things work in Kenya, nothing comes to you legally, there's always a payment up front. They made it quite clear if our business was doing well, it will be good for them too. Sometimes things can be confiscated, or a business closed. You need to be liked in this country and you must make things comfortable for us and we make it easy for you. If you are difficult, we can be too.

I arranged for a delivery of timber from Mombasa, when the lorry arrived heavily laden, it got firmly stuck in the soft ground on the driveway. I realised this would be a problem for us in the rainy season. It was full of holes and bumps, I decided to have it repaired and re-laid with gravel.

This was finished 10th November.

BILL OMAMO CONTRACT

Soon after opening the factory a man called Bill Omamo called to my office, which felt like a sauna. Only one small window, no fan as the sun beat fiercely down on the corrugated tin roof, and I slowly baked like a potato.

"Jambo sana habari, layo jotto mingy sana mummy, I am Bill Omamo."

He was tall, grossly overweight with a huge personality.

This would be our first big break with Bill the son of Dr Omamo MP. A contract to refit and furnish his new bar and restaurant in Diani Beach called Bootleggers.

Joseph, Dylan, and I drove down to Bootleggers to chat with Bill and see exactly what he wanted us to do. He gave us ideas of the furniture and the theme as a type of *speak easy*. He put forward an idea for crates that were opened at the back of a lorry. He had already designed a bar I thought it looked ghastly. I quickly sketched a few ideas and presented them to Bill.

"This isn't going to work; I could come up with something much better than this," I suggested.

An attractive well-spoken female architect commented on the sketch and thought it was impressive. I put forward a few more designs but ignored by the lady competing for attention from Bill.

Eventually agreeing on wooden crates as tables and seats, a green cloth covered wagon as the bar. We established a fair price after much negotiating and received a cash deposit. Hired a few more men and set to work. We didn't foresee the problems we would have to overcome, without electricity at the workshop. The small generator was insufficient for the workload. Now in a predicament for power tools we would prepare the timber on site, at Bootleggers. This was frustrating, the pick-up truck was obviously too small for the job. It was extremely tiresome going back and forth from the site all day, also very time consuming.

BILL ARRIVED WITH THE FIRST PAYMENT

The sound of Bill puffing and panting as he made his way up the dusty driveway and his greeting call.

"Jambo Janette."

Was exactly what I needed to hear, on this sweltering hot day.

"Karibu Bill, habari gani, welcome how are you."

Bill stumbled through the doorway trying to catch his breath and slumped down on the seat in front of my desk. Beads of sweat rolling down his chubby black face, he reached over to offer me a cigarette.

"Asanti, thank you, hey you look exhausted Bill."

"I am, I need to lose some weight," he groaned.

With an enormous grin exposing his big white teeth he began to fumble with his briefcase. Exposing a stack of money inside, Bill put the first of three payments in cash on the desk.

"As promised Janette mummy," he huffed.

Bill grinned, sipped his warm coke, and made a grand exit waving and calling to the boys in Swahili.

OUR FRIENDSHIP

A few days passed when an invitation to Bill's home for a meal arrived, we were to meet his lovely wife, Jackie.

It was a beautiful house filled with unusual ornaments metal sculptures and nice heavy furniture.

Bill's wife Jackie, a beautiful slim lady like a model, but rather timid, a nervous disposition, I immediately liked her. We enjoyed a local Kenyan dish with plenty of wine and Tusker beer. Our friendship with Bill and Jackie grew rapidly and everything was going to plan with Bootleggers contract. Eventually the second payment for our work was due, we had agreed cash only, but Bill persuaded me that his cheques were good.

Bill arrived at the factory one hot afternoon.

> *"Here is a cheque for the second payment."*
>
> *"But we agreed cash only, that's why you had a good discount, Bill,"* said Dylan.
>
> *"My father is a very respected MP in government I can't imagine anyone refusing his cheques,"* he retorted.

Bill snarled at me gnashing his big white teeth with his eyes bulging out of their sockets and gasping for breath. I took the cheque.

The cheque bounced.

Bill and Jackie arrived at the workshop to discuss the bounced cheque. They apologised and handed over another one, it also bounced. We made another meeting at Bootleggers. I stayed firm about cash on the table as the first two cheques bounced, and we were well over the halfway stage. All the decor and fittings inside were completed, with the tables and chairs progressing reasonably well. It was only a few weeks away from the grand opening, when Bill called in the office, unfortunately this time there was no briefcase in his hand. No money just promises to pay on delivery, however, we agreed to the new terms.

We had several other small jobs to complete for private work and a restaurant, mostly handmade due to the absence of electricity.

WALTER'S INN

Walter and Sylvia originally from Germany had lived in Kenya over seventeen years and knew the local customs and laws. Walter's Inn was the local watering hole for the whites to meet up and exchange stories and get drunk. We had become friends with several other white settlers. There was so much to talk about, especially after revealing I previously owned butcher shops and an hotel in Ireland. I was trained in the butcher trade myself, by my master butcher ex-husband, he was an apprentice at Harrods in London. We had two shops, I made the sausages, pies, and burgers. We also owned an antique collectables business and properties that we rented out in England and Ireland.

One afternoon Walter randomly invited us to his house and small holding, where he was breeding pigs for the butcher shop.

"Here Janette, hold this baby piglet for me."

The piglet was so cute and pink, squealing and wriggling in my arms. I thought how sad he's going to be someone's pork chops one day. After a quick tour of the pigs and the small holding, we headed back to the bar for a drink. The local mzungu eccentrics John Bland and Bill Roberts were chatting to Sylvia at the bar. They were relics from the past, the old colonial days. John Bland appearing at all hour's day and night to sip wine under the shelter of the makuti roofed meeting place. It was always enjoyable listening to John, such great conversations. Or random fascinating stories about the Mau Mau uprising. John entertained his private audience with gusto.

Never far from his side the beautiful Narima an Asian Kenyan, the wife of wealthy businessman Joe Brunlehner (Joe the German) the landlord of Walter's Inn, and part of the shopping parade. They owned several holiday homes and a famous restaurant in Mombasa. I met Joe twice, but had the displeasure of meeting Mrs Bland many times, a very unsociable German lady with a chip on her shoulder. She had an instant dislike for most women, including myself? Yet, John always cheerful, an ex-policeman originally from Norfolk, like us.

He was in his mid-sixties but appeared much older with his bronzed weather-beaten face from hours out on his fishing boat. I liked John very much. Often in Walter's with his old buddy Bill, they would entertain me for hours with very interesting tales. One day Bill took me to his small, neat house for lunch and enjoy some classical music. We enjoyed Walter's delicious pork chops with a potato salad and drank lots of white wine. It was a comforting feeling having Bill and John as my British friends, we had so much to talk about.

I did feel sad for the piglet at Walter's farm; however, this pork chop was huge and most likely an old sow.

MEETING REINHOLD MOSER

One evening Walter put two large vodkas with sliced lemon on the bar and waved to me.

> *"Janette come have a drink at the bar. I'd like to introduce you to my old drinking buddy of many years, Mr. Reinhold Moser. Meet Janette and Dylan, African Oasis."*
>
> *"Hello, nice to meet you, call me Reiner,"* he smiled.

Tall a little overweight, nice looking with grey thinned hair. A rather rugged appearance with nice sparkling blue eyes. Very charismatic, yet somewhat arrogant with an air of importance, quite a noticeable man. I was immediately attracted to Reiner's self-importance.

He reminded me of Gene Hackman the American actor.

> *"I live in Nairobi, but I need to be in Diani Beach too, I have contracts all over the country,"* he boasted.

Reiner handed me his business card ITA, Nairobi.

> *"I need an office in Diani Beach and thinking about getting an apartment here. I have contracts coming up in Msambweni and Malindi."*

> *"We're a new small factory between jua kali and Keystone Furniture along the Mombasa Road,"* I replied.

> *"I'll come down and see you, we can do something together. I need a base. You need work, in fact, I've got something you could be getting on with now, Whispering Palms Hotel, are you interested?"*

> *"Yes, of course we are."*

I explained to Reiner we had several small contracts around Diani Beach, hotels, restaurants, and others private. African Oasis was quite busy.

Dylan walked over to a group of local people. In no time at all there were several drinks lined up on the bar. Every time Reiner spoke to me, he patted my hand with complimentary whispers.

> *"Who would expect to find a beautiful white woman in such a place as Kenya, perhaps you should be with me in Nairobi. Not with this boy, I have many connections in high places. Maybe you could come to Nairobi with me,"* he giggled.

Reiner flirted and entertained me for a couple of hours with stories about places he had lived and the women he met.

When in Germany he met and fell in love with a woman who was fifteen years older than him. She was the love of his life and taught him many things about sex. They separated a few times, but he was always drawn back to her. Forever attracted to those sexual and sensual experiences. He mentioned he was seeing a similar scenario with Dylan and me.

"You can see he is a boy pretending to be a man. I am a very big man in every department hahaha, it is good for the women don't you think?" Reiner laughed.

My mind went blank– as if the random comment didn't register, I decided to ignore it.

"You never know one day you may be laying in my arms. I'll show what a real lover can do. You will have experienced a real man. Not a boy."

Then he chuckled and smirked, I could see that he was always full of devilment. He was also a little drunk.

I told him about the problems I had with the Kenyans.

"This is normal, it's not just you, but you're an easy target because you're a white woman with an idiot boy. trying to live in black Africa," he remarked.

He winked and grinned, I was flattered by his comments but aware he had consumed several vodkas. However, I agreed to meet up sometime for business.

Walter came over and joined us.

"I'm so glad you have met Reiner we have been friends for over fifteen years. This is a great opportunity, perhaps you can make money together."

Reiner had secured a big property contract he wanted to discuss and would call at African Oasis workshop in a few days. At home Dylan and I talked about Reiner for hours and the possibility of doing business with him. I thought it was an interesting experience meeting him, he really made an impact on me.

NEXT TIME WITH WALTER

Walter remarked.

> *"So glad you met Reiner he has interesting connections in government and owns a hotel/nightclub. It's a pity you didn't know him before you met that preacher Francis and all that hassle for your papers. Reiner would have got them for you; in fact, I could have done it myself."*

We were simply the local gullible mzungus.

A few days passed and we met Reiner at Walter's Inn, he mentioned the possibility of big contracts coming in the new year. Although uncertain when, but this would be the Malindi contract. A few days later Reiner called to the factory, he was impressed at the quality of our work. After a quick chat about our handiwork he left Diani Beach, heading back to Nairobi. We must wait to hear from him. In the meantime, life simply continued as each day a new experience presented itself.

AUSSIE MIKE STORY

It was an exceptionally hot, dry day when the fierce roar of a Harley Davidson motorbike came to an abrupt halt causing a dust storm outside my office.

> *"Howdy you guys."*

That was the unexpected greeting from a very bronzed and extremely good-looking man, wearing cut off denim shorts and nothing else but a smile.

> *"Hi, I'm Janette and this is Dylan my partner, where are you from?"*

He wiped the sweat and dirt from his face with a bright red bandana and declared.

> *"Me name is Aussie Mike and I bed down along the beach at Tiwi in me little shack, I've been here in Kenya for years."*

Mike was so handsome with his dazzling white teeth, long sun-bleached blonde hair, and amazing tanned firm body, like a movie star.

> *"I wanna get some timba, not any old shit that is, the real stuff, good gear ya know. Yeah, like that over there."*

He was pointing to some rather expensive timber.

> *"I only use the very best for me furniture, they will sell mzungus any old crap, if they could, but not to me Aussie Mike,"* he laughed.

Mike was explaining how he started a little furniture business a few years back, making something he called Funzi beds and chairs, named after a small island. He made them with tree branches for the frames and used weaving for seating. We reviewed an album of photographs, and in exchange for information how to make them, we handed over some good timber. Other cut wood he purchased from us; we would deliver the following evening. We chatted for a while and sipped on a cold drink, laughing about some of his experiences and we shared some too. Suddenly he jumped back on the bike and with a big smile and a thunderous roar from the engine he shouted to us.

> *"You guys are invited to me shack for dinner tomorrow, be there at 7.30pm, just ask for Aussie Mike at Tiwi beach a couple of miles down coast alright. So, see you then folks, oh and be careful of the fucking bandits down by the river."*

As he sped off a huge cloud of dust covered all the freshly varnished tables, that were drying outside. The boys were not impressed with Aussie Mike.

But I was.

The next evening after a long sweltering day with traders coming and going, we showered and headed down the coast to Tiwi Beach. Dodging the local bandits as suggested was easier said than done. However, we made it in one piece to Mike's timber home on the beach. Resembling a house out of a cartoon, built with random timber on stilts, a tree house, but built on the beach. We were taken from room to room of the strange residence, which resembled the Doctor Who Tardis, at first glance but seemed enormous inside. Lovely open spaces with interesting, unusual objects and memorabilia, collected from his travels.

Magnificent massive tree roots carved with hundreds of elephants, as huge coffee tables. They were beautiful masterpieces, which he sold for big money, but carved by the locals for a mere pittance. Mike's creations were purchased by large corporations, banks, and private collectors. Mike was an extraordinary character, he fascinated us with strange and amusing stories of his life in the outback of Australia.

We drank his special hooch, Aussies home brew; it was delightful and potent. We sat on Mike's Funzi chairs on the old wooden veranda eating a spicy chicken meal, with the sound of the ocean waves washing the white sand. The ever-present nocturnal echoes in the still night, mesmerised by the crackling open fire burning in a sand pit on the beach.

Over the next week we made another trip down to Tiwi Beach and enjoyed more campfire stories with Mike. A week or so later Mike showed us how to make Funzi beds at his furniture exhibition in the car park of the shopping parade. Some of the boys at our factory had ideas how to do it and made a few samples which we kept for ourselves. They didn't match Mike's creations and we needed a Funzi seat outside the factory.

Aussie Mike went on a trip up country, and we never saw him or his Harley again.

TRIP TO SHIMBA HILLS

As the days passed, we realised that it was becoming increasingly difficult to purchase the timber we so desperately needed. We were advised to go up country to the Tanzanian border where we could buy from the local timber merchants. The route there would take us through some of the most difficult roads to pass, not only was there a distinct lack of signposts but also the dirt roads had become dangerously muddy from a heavy rainfall. Large boulders once covered in layers of earth had become exposed by the rains washing away the top surface, and huge potholes would make the journey treacherous. To reach these small timber mills we would have to go deep into the mountainous areas that were difficult to find when the roads were good. Now impossible to pass, we had to venture the long way around. The further inland we travelled the hotter it became, the truck struggling to keep in a straight line as it glided along the slippery mud. Bump after bump the trip was endless, and truly exhausting due the added time in travel, then finally in the distance we could just see stacks of timber and a small shed.

> *"Only a small safari mummy, you are not used to Kenyan roads, and it gets hotter inland, no breeze from the ocean here, pole sana, very sorry."*

Dylan began to inspect the timber with two of the merchants as I sat under the shade of a small tree drinking a very warm coke and smoking a much-needed cigarette. After a short time, a deal was made for a dozen split trees, the exact wood we required for the job, but they tried to cheat us by putting eleven on the truck. Kenyans always need to cheat you, either with shortchange or no change, but if it's goods there is always something missing. When they trade with mzungus they automatically assume you are very wealthy. Even after long explanations, they shake their heads in disbelief.

Now the truck was correctly loaded and secured with ropes we could make the long slow journey back to Diani Beach, at least it would be all downhill. An hour of careful driving down the muddy track we noticed another route to the main road. It looked safer than the one we arrived on. It turned out to be the road we were looking for originally but somehow missed due to the fallen trees near the entrance. They were only small young trees blown over by the recent storms, but they fell together blocking the view of the road. Dylan and Joseph had no problem in dragging them away to clear the path for us to reach the main road back to Diani Beach. We passed several small villages on route the women wore traditional colourful wrap around skirts, carrying baskets on their heads. It was a delightful scenic and peaceful journey home.

A few days passed when a farmer called at the factory with a large box of fruit and vegetables. He asked if we were interested in a tree, he had for sale in Shimba Hills. We purchased the box of fresh produce, shared it with everyone and agreed to visit his farm.

That week we visited the farmer.

Dylan and I travelled up to Shimba Hills to his farm it was very remote, so peaceful and tranquil. The scenery lush, as the hills and valleys displayed their crops. As we strolled through each area of the neatly kept farm we were given a very detailed summary of his produce.

Back at the farmhouse his young pretty wife waited with a large bag of mixed produce, for us to take home. It was a very informative tour, and the farmer a well-educated and knowledgeable man. The tree was purchased at a very reasonable price, loaded onto the truck.

We bid farewell to the farmer and his wife.

Mosquitoes were huge, like dragon flies.

THE SWISS LADY ARRIVES

One day a very odd character arrived at the factory in a dirty old green jeep, screeching brakes and noisy horn blowing, hoot! hoot! She looked in her mid-sixties, very thin, frail, and petite wearing safari clothes.

> *"Hello, I am looking for Janette, my German friend Maria sent me here, I am Helga."*

She wanted me to view some furniture and if I cared to purchase it. I told her we didn't buy furniture, but she insisted I go regardless. Dylan and I followed her in our pick-up along an endless bumpy dirt track. We passed several nice attractive properties and eventually she turned off into the bush and headed towards a rather big house, set in charming gardens. The spacious house looked inviting with whitewashed walls, black iron railings and gates, a somewhat colonial feel to it. Several pretty shrubs and plants lined a stone path, to an ornately carved wooden door.

> *"Come, welcome to my home would you like iced tea, cold beer or a glass of chilled wine?"*

Helga gave us a quick tour of the house; we noticed several strange objects hanging on the walls like trophies. A rather cluttered mix of souvenirs she had collected in Kenya and abroad. Helga was returning to Switzerland; she was terminally ill and needed medical treatment there, however she hoped to return later in the spring. Offering us more refreshments and directing our attention to two enormous hand carved and quite extraordinary bookcase units.

> *"I want to sell these if I can, and I need to close the house unless I can find anyone to rent it from me, for three or six months, would you care to rent it?"* She asked.

The house was very inexpensive for such a roomy space, so it was an interesting idea to contemplate. Within a few days we agreed to rent her house, starting on 18th December, and planned at Simba Village with Barbara to leave, with an option to return.

FRANCIS AT THE FACTORY

One day Francis appeared at the factory and started talking to the boys in Swahili. He was claiming his right to the business as a director.

> *"I'm a director of this African Oasis and I can prove it to you all. My name is on the Articles of Association; I will be keeping an eye on your progress, and I shall expect my share."*
>
> *"Up your fucking arse Francis, piss off!"* Shouted Dylan.

> *"You will have bigger problems from him I wanted something small. He wants something big,"* he pointed to Joseph Obetto.
>
> *"What would your church think about you conning money from a white woman Francis,"* I yelled.

Francis snarled in Swahili, looked very angry and made a hasty retreat across the road back to his home in Ukunda. I thought about Rose and the shop scenario, and now Francis with his name on the documents, more problems to deal with. Ngala suggested I should go to Mombasa to the advocates office where we created the company and find out if Francis was correct. They were aware that I had to have a Kenyan as a director to make it a legal document.

TRIP TO ADVOCATES

A few days passed by when Dylan, Joseph and I headed into Mombasa for some special timber to make a desk for a local office. We arrived at the timber merchants and bought the few pieces we needed and headed off to the Blue Moon Café for a snack and cold drink. We called in to see the advocate. It was a sweltering day, and several people were jammed into the elevator going up to his office. I couldn't breathe and became very dizzy. When we reached the top and the doors opened, a sudden rush of air prevented me from fainting. I felt so ill, but I thought it was the Blue Moon Café food. It was as if the elevator was getting smaller and smaller. Sweating and wanting to vomit.

Outside the office a clerk approached me, I couldn't understand what the man was mumbling, but he was concerned for my health. I was handed a much-needed bottle of chilled water. Only a few minutes passed when we were all called in to see the advocate who had formed the company. His assistant looked at me and muttered a few words about looking unwell. After a brief chat he explained that he was a witness to Francis offering his aid as a Kenyan citizen forming the company that day. Additionally, he would be only entitled to *one share*, as one Kenyan shilling.

We also discussed tax and insurance for the men at the factory. With a great sigh of relief, we left the office feeling satisfied and content.

JOURNEY HOME

On the journey home, we stopped for about ten minutes, I was sick. Finally, we reached the factory and dropped Joseph off. Dylan drove straight to our doctor's surgery in the shopping parade. After a blood test the doctor said it was a Kenyan virus, I needed to drink plenty of water and rest at home. The following day I had become terribly ill and returned to the doctor for more blood tests. He repeated what he said before, go home it's a Kenyan virus, but intuitively a knew different.

> *"You must come back tomorrow in the morning for another blood test."*

That night I became delirious, profusely sweating as my temperature soared. I needed the bathroom, but my legs gave way and I collapsed to the floor. I realised it was malaria, due to the massive dragonfly type mosquito bites in Shimba Hills. I could hear Dylan calling me and then.

> *"Jan, we need to go to the hospital. I'm fetching Joseph, it's too dangerous to go over the ferry this late at night,"* he panicked.

He wrapped me up in a blanket and carried me to the pick-up. We met Joseph outside the factory. In no time at all we were motoring down the Mombasa Road at full speed. This was a journey that I dreaded; no one wanted to be going to Mombasa late at night. No ferry, we had to wait for it to return. The wait seemed endless and then we boarded, whilst Joseph was yelling to people.

> *"Haraka mummy ni mgonjwa sana, hurry mummy is very sick."*

After a speedy drive through the quiet streets, we arrived at the gates of the hospital. I was promptly examined by a young well-spoken Asian doctor.

> *"I'm so ill and bitten by enormous mosquitos in Shimba Hills,"* I whimpered.

Hastily given the right injections and medication. The doctor spoke.

> *"Mummy you are very lucky to be here, just in time, another few hours and we would not be having this conversation. You would be here in a bag, not a blanket. You have malaria very bad. You need to take this medicine every two hours and your boyfriend must keep changing the sheets, you must keep her cool and dry. She is a very sick person."*

It was an expensive trip to the hospital, yet I was so grateful for the help, and I was going to recover.

Just another day in Kenya, I thought.

I was reminded how fortunate we are to have the National Health Service or NHS, in the UK.

Malaria comes in waves; your eyes burn and feel gritty. The top of your head like hot air blowing on it. Your body heavy, a constant pounding headache, fever with profuse sweating and insatiable thirst.

At home in bed for five days, I was seriously ill, fevered, and delirious, Dylan had to wake me up every two hours. Even the smell of water made me nauseous, yet I needed to drink and hydrate myself. Every sound echoed through my head like thunder.

DYLAN GETS MALARIA

Dylan was poorly. At first, I thought it was simply exhaustion from caring for me. Normally he panicked at the slightest ache or pain.

"I'm feeling so dizzy, I don't feel very well," he grunted.

"Sit with me."

He crawled into the bed and started shaking and sweating. We lay in each other's arms drifting off into a semi-conscious state, feverish for a few hours.

I realised he had malaria, but I couldn't give him my medication, nor get him to the doctors. I crawled out of the bed weak and feeble, with the notion of raising help from somewhere. I could barely stand; I shook from head to foot as I dressed. I struggled out the apartment but there was no-one around, not even askari guards. I had to shuffle along the drive and cross the main road to the hotel where we stayed on holiday. I was dragging myself along, so weak and exhausted. When I finally got to the hotel my energy was depleted, I fell onto the reception desk. I tried to explain I had malaria, I required Dr Assain. He needed to come to the apartment quickly because bwana Dylan is sick and it's an emergency.

I was helped back across the road to our apartment, by the hotel management. About thirty minutes later the doctor arrived at Simba Village extremely worried and at once checked Dylan.

> *"You are in no position to help each other Janette you were crazy crossing the road with malaria you could have been killed,"* he declared.

He gave Dylan an injection and pills for me to give him every two hours. This is not good you must both take care. Over the next week we gradually recovered and during that time our staff called in with plenty of food and water. Eventually we found enough strength to return to work, we tried our best to get back to normality. We were noticeably thin and frail.

Unfortunately for me the medication didn't completely kill the parasite; I was informed I would undoubtedly have malaria recurring.

MOVING TO THE BIG HOUSE

It was December 18th, and we were moving from Simba Village to the big house. Joseph and Ngala arrived at the apartment to help Dylan load the pick-up and drop me off at the factory. Everything went according to plan. However, it never occurred to me that we were out in the bush without the askari to protect our belongings and us. Now on our own with an old grumpy Kikuyu gardener for company. Over the next few days, we settled in and continued a busy schedule at the factory.

I invited the staff and their families to celebrate with us and have a party. Waltraud and Sonke, my old neighbours from Simba Village also came with the two yapping poodles. We had a great feast of roast chicken, baked potatoes, sausages, salads, cheese, and bread. Wine and beer flowed all night, along with nuts, crisps, and fruit. We danced and sang until after midnight, then one by one they left into the dark still night.

Over the Christmas holiday we simply relaxed in the garden with friends and soaked up the sun.

The idea of the big house was great, although it was roomier, but the reality was, the gardens were full of big ugly insects, and it never really felt like home. We moved from our apartment where friendly people lived. Now we were isolated in this big house in its own grounds up a long dirt track. I began to worry about security. Although it was closer to the factory it was more difficult to get to. When it rained, an awful muddy road to the house. The boys complained that they couldn't get to mummy in an emergency. They could always get a lift to the apartment, however.

I heard a local woman had her car burnt out then a month later her house was set on fire. I became a little nervous as strange things were going on. The lights would suddenly go out, it was very spooky with shields and spears on the wall. Then I'd see random people in the garden day and night. The water was cut off, eventually I became tired of locking the gates behind me. Every room had a big iron gate it was like being in prison, I missed my airy apartment, my European friends, the swimming pool, and my freedom.

REINER RETURNED AFTER CHRISTMAS BREAK

The New Year 1995.

I had been working very hard all day and totally exhausted. I just wanted to shower, eat, and relax watch a video. Dylan left me to meet up with Reiner.

I waved goodbye, oh my God it's pitch black out there, I thought. The path lights were not working, I wasn't normally afraid on my own or in the dark, but this night felt different. I snuggled up with a glass of red wine and felt very uneasy watching a video. Dylan returned after midnight, surprised to see me sitting up that late.

"What's up Jan are you ok?" he asked.

"No, I feel very uneasy tonight, no garden lights on and so dark out there."

My regretting leaving Simba Village grew after that strange spooky night.

WILLIE ARRIVES

Dylan was helping to build an outhouse for a couple nearby, they offered him a bush dog as company for me at night, a mongrel type of Jack Russell puppy.

"Oh, hello Willie."

In no time at all Willie was at home running around the gardens and making new friends at the factory. He loved hanging around the boys, especially jumping in the sawdust and getting under the work benches. Willie was a welcome addition to the group, everyone loved him.

He became a very good little guard dog.

ALICE ARRIVES

One day Willie was yapping and barking at a young local girl in the driveway of the house.

"Jambo mummy I am Alice, I am here to work, I'm a good housekeeper mummy, I only want to learn English and a little money, they sent me from the factory."

Alice was the next addition to the group. She was a small young woman neither attractive nor plain, quite an interesting face. She was a member of the Christian Church nearby, I liked her. Alice fitted in very well and kept the house spotlessly clean, did the shopping and washed everything by hand even our shoes would be drying on the lawn most days.

Then one morning we discovered the water pipes had been deliberately cut, I had to pay a man to renew them. A few weeks later they were cut again. I was getting tired of having showers with buckets full of cold water poured over me by Dylan and began wishing myself back to Simba Village. I felt restless staying in the house, even with Willie and Alice there.

I wasn't at all fond of the miserable old Kikuyu gardener either.

ANOTHER MEETING WITH REINER

We were invited to Walter's, there was quite a big circle of mzungu people drinking and having fun, like a party atmosphere. Reiner was sitting alone in one corner; he stood up and came over to greet me. I was sitting with John Bland and Bill Roberts and a few others.

> *"This is no longer your seat, you are moving. I'm sitting here next to Janette we are talking business,"* Reiner grunted.

Reiner leaned across me and whispered.

> *"I am imagining you having no panties on,"* and winked.

Reiner was a powerful energy; he seemed to get what he wanted; I was attracted to that side of him. I felt secure around his presence, safe and comfortable, he was like a big cosy sofa, or an old pair of slippers. He had a fatherly presence, aside of his flirtatious naughty nonsense.

NEW YEAR BACK TO WORK

The factory re-opened, and things were back on course with the workload. Everyone shared stories about what they did over the holiday period, and it felt good to be back at work. I was so much stronger after the break and the memories of malaria soon faded. I noticed a change in Joseph Obetto, he was very aloof and lazy. He had visited his home up country and returned a different man.

We became quite busy and required more staff, essentially someone to oversee the boys. Joseph was preoccupied getting work for us and not on site.

He made another trip home for a family funeral and to find his old friend another Joseph. They had reunited on the Christmas break and mentioned African Oasis. After the funeral he returned with his tall friend Joseph, I liked him immediately and he started work the following day.

FIRST MEETING WITH TALL JOSEPH

"Hello, I guess you're the man for the job."

Tall Joseph about 6'4" with a cheerful face and gentle disposition. He had worked for several different companies in places throughout Kenya. Especially in Msambweni for Italian and German construction, and he could speak six languages, German, French, Italian, English, Swahili, and Lua.

We were at the house with Alice preparing to wash clothes and introduced her to tall Joseph.

I didn't have many things left over from the shop stock, but certain I could fit tall Joseph out with some of the clothes. I explained to him, whenever a new person arrived, I gave them baggy pants, pair of shorts, two T-shirts and a little money for sandals, or shoes.

He had tears in his eyes.

"Oh, mummy, people don't do things like that for us.

"Well, I do."

That evening we had a meal of cold chicken, bread, and cheese outside on the veranda. He shared stories about different people that he worked for, I found him really endearing and delighted to have him as part of the team. I wanted him to oversee everything, the foreman or manager on site. Tall Joseph was very professional with obvious leadership qualities, unlike Joseph Obetto who caused chaos amongst the boys. I knew that tall Joseph would bring fresh ideas and manage the factory appropriately. We had a brilliant evening filled with joy and laughter.

BUILDING THE MAKUTI EXTENSION

We were expanding very quickly and discovered as the orders came in, there was little room to work. There was no space to store the timber to be used in the factory. An extension was urgently needed at the side of the building. I was introduced to a very cheerful old man who owned the small piece of land we used as the path to the toilet. After some negotiating, he agreed to rent it to us and moved the boundary for a small monthly fee. The extension an open space, was built very quickly, with a makuti roof on support poles.

Joseph Obetto suggested he would stay a few nights per week at the factory, to watch for anyone stealing our timber. People hanging around the factory at night, where they had a place to shelter under the new extension. Joseph Obetto moved his bed and some of his belongings into the factory. However, he began gradually moving in all his things at night, without our knowledge. Because he stayed a few nights, he began telling people he was a partner in African Oasis. Over time his attitude towards his work altered, he began to bully some of the younger boys, causing disruption and resentment.

He was also selling our timber to a local trader who would randomly arrive at the factory offering to sell me my own wood. I had marked the ends of the planks, however neither Joseph nor the trader was aware of it!

TALL JOSEPH AND THE BOYS

Tall Joseph would gather the boys around him, he'd sit on a bench outside, they would sit on the floor. They seemed to drift towards him, realising he was their new teacher. He was respected and foreman of the factory, however, under my supervision. I wanted Joseph Obetto off site because we found his energy very unsettling. His job was to find the contracts and tall Joseph was to organise everything else. However, he wanted to boss everyone and became unpleasant, indifferent, rather menacing at times.

I noticed he had several new shirts and shoes.

"You're rapidly increasing your wardrobe," I remarked.

"They are from my old house," he grinned.

"These are new Joseph, labels on them."

Tools, fixtures, and fittings were going missing, and new shirts were appearing. He was drinking several beers at night and leaving a mess everywhere. His personality had changed, no longer a happy guy, now he would aggravate the workers and stop the production. He was disruptive and annoying.

HIRING ASKARI

I hired a very charming young Samburu man as a part time askari, he would be keeping an eye on Joseph too. He mentioned his friends would also check in on the factory when he was on duty. I would leave firewood, food, and drink outside, for the askari and his friends.

Obetto was bringing outside work to our factory and finishing off in our time. He was moonlighting. The askari told me he noticed a young woman coming out of the factory with Joseph in the mornings.

TROUBLE BEGINS JOSEPH OBETTO'S GIRLFRIEND

Two young women chatting in Swahili and sitting outside my office. Behaving peculiar.

"Can I help you, what do you want?" I asked.

"We're looking for Joseph the owner."

I explained that he only worked for African Oasis, my company, when he casually sauntered in.

"Can Paula occasionally stay the night here," asked Joseph grinning.

"No, this is a factory, and you only work here."

A couple of days passed; I noticed her hanging around talking to the boys as they were working.

"Excuse me don't hang around the equipment you could get hurt and you're slowing the work down," I insisted.

Parading around with little shorts on, showing off and flaunting herself around the young men. I found her very disruptive and extremely irritating.

The following morning Joseph and Ngala were in the factory laughing.

> *"I just met Paula she was coming out of his room this morning naked,"* laughed Ngala.

I was furious.

I explained to Joseph he could no longer stay at the factory; it wasn't a hotel. He said they were seriously thinking about getting married. Again, my answer was no. If they had married and stayed in the room, they could have suggested they were much more involved in the business.

FINAL PAYMENT BOOTLEGGERS

Sadly, Bill had overlooked the fact he was in debt to my company. It was only a matter of days to the opening and Bill had yet another instalment to pay us. Unfortunately, this time he didn't make the dusty road to my door briefcase in hand.

> *"Bill this money is long overdue, and your big opening is at the end of the week?"*

For Bill to practically beg for the delivery was quite a show and with a promise of cash in two days. My immediate reaction was to refuse all the tables and chairs until the long overdue account was paid. However, he was a friend, but I reluctantly agreed.

As promised the money arrived on time. The delivery was arranged for the next morning and the grand opening event.

Bill was in such a panic, people from all over Kenya would attend, but more importantly his father Dr Omamo MP.

BOOTLEGGERS DELIVERY

We arrived there with all the furniture piled up on the pickup truck and Paula was waiting outside the building. I demanded she got off the work site. Dylan reluctantly asked her to leave. She seemed to appear from nowhere, it was so annoying.

The grand opening was a great success and we met Bill's brother Tom, father, and other members of his family.

Joseph Obetto was missing from work a couple of days and arriving late on others, or he would disappear for a few hours. He was behaving very strange and unpredictable. Everyone felt uncomfortable with him around doing little work or behaving erratic.

INVITED BACK TO BILL AND JACKIE'S HOUSE

We were invited to Bill and Jackie's house for a meal to thank us for the Bootleggers work and to meet some of their friends. I was chatting to Jackie outside, when she mentioned what a bully Bill was. He was cruel and would push her around. She wanted to leave him but was too afraid to go.

> *"What are you doing with him Jackie, he is big and ugly."*
>
> *"His family will never give me any piece if I leave him,"* she cried.

Jackie gave me insight into how things work in Kenya. She was no longer a person but a mere object or his belonging.

She was too afraid to tell her family how unhappy she was. I hugged and comforted her.

"I don't have answers for you, but there must be something you can do?"

"No, they will kill me," she cried.

I felt very sad for her ordeal, and whenever her and Bill popped in at the office, I gave her a hug and reassured her of my friendship and support. It was only a matter of days after the meal that we noticed them at Walter's Inn. Jackie didn't raise her head to look up and Bill was too busy showing off with friends. I did hear rumours that she left him and went up country, but I never saw either of them again.

THE RAVENS ARRIVE

I don't know if they were ravens or crows, but they were huge black birds I could see two of them, one on each post at the front of the property.

"We are being watched, mummy," Mohamed said.

All the workers were terrified of black magic.

"This magic will be the end of us mummy, what are we going to do? we won't come to work," Msambuku muttered.

The day finished in absolute chaos and confusion with all the boys in a state of fear.

SPEAKING TO TALL JOSEPH

"Obetto went up country and brought you down here. You have been friends for a very long time. What do you think I should do? He's your friend."

"Be prepared for anything now that Obetto is with that witch Paula, they are dangerous together mummy."

Joseph said with a concerned look on his face.

Joseph Obetto was demanding double wages, or he would create problems for us.

"If you give him a higher wage it is not done in Africa, he is not a partner. This is your company mummy, be very careful. You don't realise living in that room allows him to lay claim. They will get married, then you've got bigger problems."

I listened carefully to tall Joseph.

Joseph Obetto moved into a friend's house but continued to work at the factory. He was becoming very hostile towards everyone. Paula was hanging about at the top of the driveway talking to Joseph, he sauntered over to me.

"You know I am seriously thinking about getting married. I want more money. I would need more money as a partner, and I would have a wife."

I anticipated this conversation for a few days after the discussion with tall Joseph.

"You're not a partner in the business you're the factory manager."

"I am a partner in African Oasis!" he yelled.

"Joseph my papers state that I have a Kenyan director and it's not you!"

"I am not moving until you give me in writing my partnership of the company!!" he yelled at me.

This was going to be quite a fierce argument.

When I insisted that he go back to work and get on with his job he walked out the factory. The following day he returned.

I could see that he was angry as he marched into my office. He told me how he was going to plant drugs in the truck and a whole list of other things that he could do to ruin me if I didn't agree to the partnership.

Dylan and I drove to the police station, I had listened to enough of his madness.

Joseph moved out that day.

THE POLICE STATION

At the local police station, it was packed with people coming and going. We were directed to a small office with a desk and a few old chairs and the sergeant a tall heavy-set man, gazing out of the dirty window.

We enquired what was the average wage? And the maximum wage for a manager. I realised he was being over paid. After an hour of explaining the whole story about Joseph Obetto and the girlfriend, he said don't worry go back and carry on. We will warn him, he cannot be an employee and a partner then make demands.

I showed the policeman the company papers for African Oasis, with Francis named as a Kenyan with one share and not Joseph Obetto. They casually remarked mzungus are always getting into problems when they take on locals. We need to have written agreements with them and inform the employment office of the person's position. There can be no argument after that. They were very clear about moving him off the premises and advising Paula to keep away. They could both be arrested.

JOSEPH ON THE BOUNDARY

The following day Joseph Obetto appeared at the top of the driveway, waving, laughing, and shouting.

"Hahaha. You can't do anything!" he shouted.

"But I can Joseph."

Two days later, a rather tall overweight man arrived at the factory with Joseph's girlfriend Paula and told me to be careful, big magic is on its way. The following morning, we arrived at the factory to find all the boys sitting outside looking rather nervous.

"You're late getting into the workshop," I asked.

"We can't go in the factory mummy."

There was a large pool of water by the front door and a strange symbol drawn on the ground. They were very afraid, but James approached me saying.

"Don't cross over mummy, I will take you to my father," he smiled.

He explained that his father was a juju man, and he would help me if I could visit the next day. I agreed and everyone went home. The following day the boys worked outside the factory cleaning up and taking orders. They refused to enter the factory, however.

JAMES AND THE JUJU STORY

James met us at the factory the following day.

Dylan remained with the boys, keeping up their spirits.

It was a hot and dry afternoon when we arrived at the village. The old man was sitting outside the house on a broken wooden bench, poking at the embers of a small fire on the ground. He was wrapped in an orange and black robe, baggy brown trousers and wearing an interesting large black cloth hat with a colourful feather. He was singing; he seemed delighted to meet me.

"Habari mzungu," he said.

With his leathery hand he led me into his little house, like an old shed covered with dried mud. The roof was made of makuti. There were two small dark rooms inside, very little furniture only a battered broken table, chair, stool, and small tatty cupboard. On the dirt floor was an old sack bag, a few kitchen things.

James chatted, and the old man started to sing a magical song to me, he said a few strange words and began to sing again. He sat me on the small wooden stool in the centre of the room and picked up the old sack bag. He mumbled some Swahili, as he pulled out old twigs and stones, and then placed them all around me. He clapped his hands jumped up and down, patted me on the head said a few more mysterious words and mummy, mzungu, mummy.

He went to each corner of the room and muttered some more magical words. Then he sat down on the floor in front of me, he was holding a twig and sang another song and waved his hands in the air. I watched him going into a deep trance, his appearance quickly changed. His muscles became rigid, his teeth clenched, nostrils flared, and only the whites of his eyes showed. His arms outstretched in front of him, and fingers spread wide apart but still waving the twig around as if writing in the air. I could feel the atmosphere change. It became heavy humid and difficult to breathe. Suddenly he jerked. He glared at me, but it wasn't the old man anymore. Then a deep, gruff voice spoke gibberish, as if he was drunk and rambling on. It could have been any dialect of any of the many Kenyan languages or just some crazy made-up words, but James seemed to have no problem understanding him.

James explained that nothing would happen to me, the mzungu because his magic was greater than any other magic that's coming to me. The old man was panicky, and wild, he was fumbling for something to write with. James quickly gave him his carpenter's pencil, and he scribbled some things down on a scrap of paper. These were magical words, and he wanted me to chant them. I tried to say the words several times, but I couldn't understand the scribble or the sounds, I was tongue-tied. James explained that the words were just sounds, not meaningful words. I must make them in my mind first and feel them as I say them aloud.

"Sssss jojammaaa jaja eyo eya jaja mmaaajoja."

The old man was silent for a while just sitting and staring and then he became relaxed. Burst out laughing, jumped up and started spinning around like a child and clapping his hands. He asked James to fetch mummy a special drink that nearly blew my head off. It was awful but did the trick, it hit the spot. James explained a few things about his dad to me regarding the trance.

Then the old man told me what I needed to do to defeat the magic that was being sent. I needed to take some water from the well outside, put it in a pot and take it home. I needed to put the water into a stone dish or clay pot and imagine my thoughts moving into it. James said to imagine myself much bigger and grander and how powerful I was. When I had the feeling of great power I was to spit into the water, then take a deep breath and blow into it. Then thank the water. Wait a few moments and then tip the water at the base of a tree to feed the roots. I was to say some very long bizarre sounding magical words. Then clap my hands, jump up and down and laugh. Walk away and forget the magic. It was done.

"I will write a song about you that will make you more powerful."

We chatted a little, his English was poor, he was slightly hard of hearing too, but we could communicate well enough. I told him about the white man's magic. He already knew about auras and energy zones and seemed to understand our style of magic and healing, as I understood his. We both agreed that magic was about using fire and water internally and externally, and air too. And the art of magic was about causing these things to come together to work for you, through the medium of earth, a physical or material body.

"Yes, mummy all magic is in the air."

When we returned to the factory, we did what the old juju man had told me. We walked in backwards over the water, so we go in before it happened. We chanted and sang and burned incense in each corner of each room. We made a small fire in the yard, jumped up and down, shouted and screamed. I gathered everyone in one room for a short meditation.

James reassured the boys that everything was going to be alright.

WALTER'S INN

John Bland arrived.

I mentioned to Bill and John that Joseph was causing black magic at the factory. Several people at Walter's Inn said let's take him out of the scenario.

"I'll shoot the bastard. Remember the old days and the Mau Mau uprising we would shoot many of them."

"What shall I do, I can create magic myself, but this type is different, this is Africa," I asked.

Both Bill and John said fuck the magic Janette let's go and shoot the bastard and be done with it. The following day Joseph marched into the office. He pushed James against the door laughing and confronted me. Everyone was apprehensive of what he might do. He started shouting about the juju magic with James, and he was going to do it on me. I quickly reflected to him using a small hand mirror on my desk and said some magical words. I pointed to the patches of psoriasis on his arms.

"Surely you are different from your tribe look at your arms and hands."

I wanted to redirect his intention to do magic on me towards his own weakness. I reminded him of his dreadful skin allergy and took his attention there. And amplified it, connecting it to a greater fear of being abandoned by his tribe. I reminded him how bad his skin becomes when he is stressed. He will soon be covered in the skin disease. Suddenly his demeanour changed he became subdued and shaking his head. He admitted to the water magic attack and left the factory screaming and shouting at everyone like a mad man.

I discovered Joseph Obetto was accepting contracts under the name of African Oasis; however, the others were too afraid to tell me.

Facing fear sometimes means that all you need do is merely misdirect the other person's attention away from you and on to them, reflecting it back. Sleight of hand illusion, rabbit out the hat or card magic.

JUJU MAGIC IN AFRICA SOME OF THE SECRETS

I would always bring him a small gift of food and drink. Then we made a comfortable chair and stool for him.

When I arrived, he would be excited to see me, as I was equally eager to listen and watch him. The fire in us made us giggle and be very happy to be in this magical space together. We always had the dirty stale bread, drank water and the hooch, and sprayed it in the air to finish the rituals and the meetings. I would say mumbo vippi what's the story? and he would answer mumbo vitti the story is?

JAMES'S INTERPRETATION OF HIS FATHER'S WORDS

> *"Be quiet and be loud, be still and be moving. To laugh and to cry or to sing and chant all the same thing."*

He offered me a handful of dirt this is you. He spat in his hand; this is you too. He jumped up and down like a Masai, as he clapped his hands this is you? He drank water, then hooch this is you? Ate the stale old bread and lit a small fire. Gave me bark and leaves from a tree. Then some roots, a stone, this is you? He danced and spun around and around, jumped up and down then showed me how he would change state.

"In my country we have snow, that's me too," I smiled.

"But this snow I have never seen, will you capture some for me and let me see it."

"It melts, I can't bring it to you," I answered.

"But you can, in your eyes and in your heart, tears live in your eyes and that is water too, is it not?"

"So how does magic happen for you?" I said and laughed at him dancing and singing.

"Let the wind carry it to where it is meant to be," he smiled.

"Yes, as a spoken word then blow it into the wind."

James came to my office a week later.

"My father has been helping you understand African magic. He is so thankful for you teaching me English and working at the factory. I'm so grateful to you mummy Janette, for giving me this chance to learn more about life from you."

James was an interesting well spoken, polite young man I was very fond of him and his father. The magic experience had a positive impact on better understanding the ancient art of magic from a unique perspective. It made a positive impression on my comprehension of how we are coerced into fearing something. I understood the natural fears we are born with are loud noises and falling. All other fear is imposed by phobia and others controlling our minds.

I met with James' father another three times after that. He came to the factory twice to say habari, hello and talk magic. Then in Ukunda at a local meeting place, to teach me more secrets.

"You don't need me anymore mummy, you are complete."

I never saw my juju friend again.

THE TYSON STORY

The day began with the usual get together and blessings that I conducted as part of getting the boys into a routine. It was not so much a religious event just a few moments of connecting to the universe in a positive way. After the

Joseph Obetto experience, we would ward off any dark forces and negative energy.

"Someone is missing," I remarked counting them as they left my office to start work.

"Sorry mummy, I am not well."

A voice cried from the corner of the workshop.

"Lao jotto mingy sana," it's very hot today are you alright? I replied.

It was Tyson a very strong and muscular young man about twenty-five years old.

"Are you ok?"

I could clearly see he was in great pain.

I invited him into my office, he stood very awkwardly in front of my desk. Then he simply lifted his red cloth wrap around up to his chest exposing the absence of underwear. I was shocked by his action but after a closer inspection, I could see the terrible burns he had in the groin, thigh, and lower abdomen.

"Oh my God, look at you poor man!"

I yelled as he swiftly removed his wrap leaving him standing totally naked, as Dylan dashed through the doorway.

"Oh! Shit, what the hell is going on in here? Oh, dear poor bastard."

Realising that it was an innocent situation and Tyson was badly hurt. We rushed Tyson to our Asian doctor who praised us for bringing him in. I explained to the doctor when I was seventeen, I was badly burned. I had good sound knowledge of the best treatment for Tyson.

We headed straight for the beach with our patient feeling much more comfortable but still suffering. Tyson stood naked on the beach and slowly slipped into the warm ocean as we held him afloat. He was terrified of the water, but he trusted us with his life, and we cared very much for this poor young man's agony. Floating in the sea in my arms I continued reassuring him he was quite safe with me and that I could help heal him.

After a week of rest, some healing ointment and pain killers Tyson returned to work with a slight limp and a huge grin and wearing an orange wrap around.

> *"Mummy I forgot that I was naked in front of you and now I feel ashamed for you, but you have cured me, and my skin is better."*

I assured him that he would be okay in the men's department, and he would soon be indulging in sex with his girlfriend. He chuckled as he proudly lifted the wrap to display his manhood, in a semi active position.

> *"Oh yes!"* I gasped.

> *"That's just fine Tyson. It's much better now. Put some shorts on."*

He thanked me again and made a quick exit to tell the other boys about mummy's surprised expression. Dylan laughed and remarked sarcastically.

> *"Aren't you going to kiss it better then?"*

Tyson was an exceptionally well-endowed young man!

> *"No Dylan I am not."*

WHISPERING PALMS PROJECT

COMPARING THE BIG HOUSE TO THE APARTMENT

It was February and Reiner was moving in Simba Village within a few weeks.

At the apartment we would get up in the morning, sit on the veranda, walk around the garden. Swimming in the pool, I really missed the pool and walking to the shops. I was completely alone in this big house. Then a job came in from the Crismani family. They mentioned we could have a bigger apartment as part of the deal and move back in April. I was so excited because I would feel safe, and Reiner would be there.

One morning I received a phone call from Reiner to go ahead with Whispering Palms samples. The hotel was renovating in stages, twenty-six bedrooms first. We went ahead and created unique designs and different sizes of chest of drawers, bedside cabinets and small tables. A sample of everything we believed would work for the hotel renovation, based on the information supplied by Reiner.

I talked to Walter about Reiner and his projects.

> *"I'm glad I introduced you Janette, Reiner also mentioned the work for a Malindi hotel, Msambweni shopping parade he has lined up."*

THE DELIVERY DAY

It was a very hot day when we piled up all the furniture onto the truck. When we arrived at Whispering Palms Hotel, we were greeted by a mzungu woman with an odd accent who appeared rather puzzled but asked us to unload the furniture samples immediately.

After waiting an hour another woman arrived and simply instructed us to reload the samples saying.

"Sorry Mr Moser at ITA didn't sign the contract on time, another company has the contract."

We were so disappointed at the news and quickly reloaded the truck. On the way back to the factory we stopped for iced coke to quench our thirst, baffled, and lost for words just silently gazing at each other. When we arrived at the factory, everyone gathered in anticipation of the news and excited to begin the project. The boys unloaded the truck.

"Which one's did they choose mummy?"

I went straight to my office leaving Dylan to explain the scenario and sat quietly contemplating the day's events.

"He didn't sign the contract on time. They didn't want our samples to show the owner."

A gloomy atmosphere swept through the factory, with everyone feeling disappointed. Anticipation of work for the hotel now just wishful thinking. There would be no project to start the following day. As the sun went down that night in Ukunda I returned home somewhat pissed off at Reiner.

HIRING THE MASAI ASKARI LITIBIKWAN

Our Samburu askari was only part time, I really needed a full-time guard for the factory. Arriving one day a handsome young Masai called Litibikwan Lekararo.

"Me askari mummy," he declared.

"Yes, welcome to African Oasis, I will call you Liti is that Okay?"

He smiled and danced, so happy to join us.

Liti shared stories of life in the wilderness and with his Masai tribe. He was such a sweet temperament, an interesting character. When collecting his salary, he would sign SM, I asked for an explanation? He simply copied it from the man in front in the queue and thought that everyone's signature was SM. We were in hysterics and after showing him many times, how to write LL, he was so proud that finally he could do it. How their lifestyle had changed, once great and noble warriors that roamed freely and highly respected by other tribes, now reduced to selling beads on the beach to tourists.

MARCH 1995 – ELECTRICITY ARRIVED

Now the workshop had electricity the work became much easier, and jobs completed faster. I enjoyed standing outside in the warm air under the makuti roof, listening to the men chatter and laugh.

I had a good contract with a local hotel, they asked me to make sunlounges with adjustable back rests. They only ones they had were like a flat bed. All the quotes they had were too expensive. We made a sample, and the manager was so impressed he ordered garden tables and chairs, at a very good price.

REINER RETURNS TO THE FACTORY

Reiner returned and made excuses about the Whispering Palms contract. He apologised for the error on the date and casually remarked.

"So what? Fuck them! Plenty of work to come."

"It's not fuck them. All the work we have put into this, I'll still have to pay the boys."

> *"Don't worry Janette plenty of work is coming for us, you can sell off the samples that you made,"* he grinned.

I mentioned the black magic saga with Joseph Obetto and Reiner shrugged his shoulders huffed and spoke.

> *"Forget it. I'll sort it out if he comes back, I will shoot the fucker,"* he smirked.

I was very annoyed and frustrated at Reiner for messing up the dates for Whispering Palms contract however, I was grateful to have him around.

REINER AND MALINDI CONTRACT PAPERS

It was a drizzly wet morning when Reiner arrived banging his fist on the office door and shouting.

> *"Janette, I have something for you. We are really in business now!"*

A tatty old black cloth briefcase in one hand and grasping a rolled-up bunch of scruffy documents in the other waving them above his head. Perspiration pouring down his red puffed up face, as he tried to catch his breath.

> *"Look here just what I have been waiting for, the big contract with Malindi and a massive shopping complex."*

Kissing me on the cheek and then hugging Dylan he shouted.

> *"You are my partners now so; how does that feel?"* he declared.

Dylan was jumping up and down and ran out to tell the boys that African Oasis has a big contract with Malindi. I wasn't exactly sure how we were partners, and the bigger question was how on earth could we cope with such huge orders; surely this was something for Keystone factory.

"Let's celebrate tonight. It's on me, we can meet at Walter's, have a goodtime, and talk about this contract, okay?"

CELEBRATE AT WALTER'S

We met Reiner at Walter's, as the food and drink began to flow Walter's beautiful wife Sylvia made an appearance. Sylvia a tall slim beautiful lady, with very long blonde waist length hair and big sparkling blue eyes. She had trained as an operatic singer in Germany her homeland and she seemed completely out of place in this bar and the butcher shop in Diani Beach.

She joined us for a glass of wine and then with an impromptu and unrehearsed song entertained us with her amazing voice. Later we all chatted about the forthcoming shopping complex that was to be our big break. I didn't intend to dampen the excitement and celebrations, but no-one mentioned the fact we couldn't make the hundreds of door and window frames. How could we possibly cope with such an order with a few men. Professional equipment was required for this contract.

"Don't worry, I have a plan," Reiner said.

We enjoyed the evening of food and drinks with no more conversations about work. But we mentioned the weather getting unpredictable as the rainy season approached.

RAINY SEASON March April May

The rains increased and storms raged for days on end. The dirt track was now thick mud and dangerous. The big house was on the back side of Ukunda township and Indian Ocean Road which divided the small villages. Even though we had permission to use the pool at Simba Village it wasn't the same. Also, we would go to parties at Walter's, and Forty Thieves, and have the long drive back to the house.

REINER MOVES TO SIMBA VILLAGE

14th-16th APRIL

> *"If the wife wasn't pregnant, I would fucking leave her,"* Reiner snarled.

Reiner's wife Ngery (Jerry) and two children come down from Nairobi for Easter. When I was talking to Ngery she said she was deeply religious and wouldn't go anywhere without her bible, a very anxious disposition. Quite attractive and shy. Awful old fashioned chunky clumsy shoes, and a big white plastic handbag. Constantly looking down, I could sense she was unhappy and uncomfortable. She seemed emotionally unstable. I understood her father was something to do with the government, he held an important position. Reiner had to marry a Kenyan woman to keep him out of trouble. I guess a marriage of convenience.

Reiner needed to go somewhere with Ngery and asked me to look after the two girls.

> *"Yes, I'd love to."*

I entertained them with songs and drawing pictures. Then we went to the beach for an hour and returned for cold drinks fruit and biscuits. We watched a video.

After the Easter break Reiner with his wife and children went back to Nairobi and he returned alone the following weekend.

At the apartment complex lived a very flamboyant man called Rudi a friend to Reiner. His mother was South

American and a Swiss father. Rudi often held parties or barbeques we were always invited. An intelligent most interesting man with so many stories to share would keep us entertained for hours. We all became good friends in a short time and enjoyed our visits to Simba Village for gatherings by the pool.

The barbeques were always flowing with cold beers and wine, freshly made sausages from Walter's and Rudi's delicious impala fillet steaks marinated overnight, crispy garlic bread and fruit.

As the friendship blossomed between our group it became very clear that Reiner was more than interested in just me working with him. Often, I would catch a glimpse of his ever-roving eye, as it scanned my bikini-clad body. Bronzed and with a great figure I guess there was no harm in his looking.

A BUSINESS MEETING AT WALTER'S INN

Dylan's birthday.

Reiner and his business associates were meeting us at Walter's Inn, but he was delayed. After a long wait Dylan began feeling unwell, so we returned home. He became very anxious, sweating, shaking and seemed to be in great pain holding his stomach. I called Rudi my neighbour to help me get him to the nearby doctors. After a short time, Dylan was in agony and the doctor suggested he be taken to hospital immediately with a suspected appendicitis.

We made haste to the Mombasa hospital and informed that I should immediately pay a substantial fee before the operation. I explained we had no such funds at hand, but Rudi and I would leave Dylan there and return later with the doctor's fee. They reluctantly agreed but went ahead with the emergency operation. Rudi and I stopped off at Waters Inn for a beer, then to the apartment for my bankcard and to the bank, to get the cash.

REINER VISITS ME

That evening as I sat alone watching a video and worried about Dylan, a knock at the door. It was Reiner.

"Reiner, how are you?"

"What happened to Dylan today, Janette?"

With a concerned look on his face and bloodshot eyes Reiner spoke softly.

"Janette. How is Dylan?"

"He is okay, I guess, it was appendicitis."

Reiner wanted to take me out for a drink, but I wasn't in the mood and concerned for my love. He hugged me, kissed my cheek, and said goodnight. I closed the door and longed for my darling to come home.

Two days later Rudi and I made the trip back to the hospital to collect Dylan. He looked dreadful but so pleased to see us. We thanked the hospital staff and slowly drove back to Diani Beach.

After a few days rest Dylan was back to work, and all the staff wanted to see the scar.

"Poor bwana," the boys remarked.

Now that the workshop had electricity the jobs were moving along quickly.

THE GERMAN FACTORY TOUR

Reiner arrived at the factory, overly excited and almost hyperventilating as he gasped for air, in between smoking his cigarette.

> *"Come with me you two I want to show you something very special; this is a surprise."*

He grabbed my hand pulling me along out of the factory to his car and yelling.

> *"Dylan hurry up please, beeilen, kommen sie bitte we need to meet some-one who can help us. What is it with that boy that he must parade around showing off to the workmen, foolish idiot boy, you need a real man, Janette?"*

We travelled for about twenty minutes and turned off onto a dirt path with a metal gate leading to a huge factory. At the gate an askari assisted us to the factory where a German businessman greeted us. He was the man we missed on the day of the appendicitis operation. We were welcomed and given an in-depth tour and discussed why the furniture factory had closed. Apparently, it was personal issues.

It was an enormous place, filled with expensive up-to date equipment. Reiner said we would need it in anticipation of the forthcoming work in Malindi and other work he was securing in Diani and Msambweni.

THE DRAWING OFFICE

The drawing office was enormous with boxes full of paperwork, plans left lying about, timber and piles of design templates.

> *"These machines can automatically jigsaw designs in minutes that would take your boys over an hour to do, all they have to do is press a button,"* said Reiner.

I noticed there were still pieces of wood lying on plates of the machines as if it had been suddenly abandoned.

> *"We will need this place for the contract I have lined up with Teresa in Malindi."*

Malindi contract a petrol station, supermarket with a disco over the top would be a very profitable contract.

> *"You'll be making all the furniture and woodwork. And there's more work I'm getting for you in Diani and Msambweni,"* said Reiner.

Through another door an enormous timber storage area, shelved and stacked with seasoned wood. We could turn our African Oasis factory into a showroom and have a selection of samples there.

BACK AT WALTER'S INN

After the tour Reiner and I dropped Dylan off back at our factory and we continued onwards to Walter to share the news. I asked how we would acquire such a place as that, we didn't have sufficient funds only the business as it stood. Yet Reiner was adamant he could secure a loan for us to purchase it, as a partnership. I listened to other ideas from Walter and said I would sleep on it.

> *"Malindi is a huge contract. We will need to have such a place to produce the goods they need. I will get the money in Nairobi, I have Chiromo Garden Hotel as collateral, and we can say that African Oasis and ITA have the contract. I have connections. Don't worry,"* smiled Reiner.

Walter grinned, patted my hand, and winked at me.

"Good luck!"

Within a couple of days Reiner promptly returned to his home in Nairobi. We were instructed to wait for news.

WAITING FOR THREE WEEKS

During the time that Reiner was in Nairobi he would phone Walter to update me concerning any progress regarding the proposed loan. I seemed to be constantly thinking about the loan and Malindi, which diverted my attention away from the work in hand.

Dylan was working very hard with the men finishing the orders that we had before the mention of Malindi. I just couldn't concentrate on the factory at all. My heart was set on the forthcoming partnership and the big break that hopefully would set us up for life.

Meeting up with a few friends in the evening

While waiting for news from Reiner we met a wonderful, peaceful man called Rene from Switzerland at Walter's. Rene was in his fifties and retired, he was sitting on his own having a meal and Sylvia introduced us. At the time we didn't know he was Teresa's husband and the proposed project for Malindi.

Then German Joe arrived and gave us a good contract to replace some mosquito screens and repair a few doors on his properties. One of the houses was much bigger with a swimming pool, it was for a German associate (Andreas Koeltz) who wanted to buy the house, we could use the pool after work. Inside the property was some of Aussie Mike's Funzi furniture which looked fabulous with lush cream cushions. Other furniture made from enormous tree trunks and heavy varnished branches. It was a beautiful house with so much character and African luxury.

Walter waved to me, a call from Nairobi, Reiner wanted me to go up to Nairobi regarding the loan for the German factory.

Farewell to Rene and German Joe and headed back home.

PART 3

NAIROBI-1

CHIROMO EXPERIENCE STORY

I spoke with Dylan about having to travel up to Chiromo Garden Hotel at Reiner's request. I mentioned he must show respect to the boys because they're teaching him, their trade. They knew he was the boss, but he wasn't that smart! Dylan was either showing off dancing or parading around like a puffed-up peacock. Whenever we needed him, he was off at Walter's, or hanging about with the local white boys. He was acting like an idiot in front of the colonial Kenyan boys who thought he was very entertaining. I didn't, however.

He'd go off in the truck pretending to be busy not informing tall Joseph where he was going or what he was doing.

"I'm the boss and I don't answer to the boys."

His attitude gave me some concern regarding the German factory and his approach to work.

THE FLIGHT TO NAIROBI

It was only a small plane from Mombasa to Nairobi.

Rene the Swiss guy from Walter's Inn with a softly spoken voice, was sitting in the next seat to me on the plane. He was also heading for Chiromo Garden Hotel. What a strange happenstance I thought.

Rene spoke very broken English mixed with German and Swahili. I had much difficulty in understanding all he had to say, with exception that his purpose for going to visit Reiner was to acquire funds.

It was no coincidence that we were both on the same plane heading to Nairobi for business loans, arranged by Reiner.

Rene had savings in Switzerland that were held up and unable to be released in time for the construction to continue. Reiner would seize the moment and offer to arrange a large loan at a price that would suit everyone. A short-term loan with a big interest factored in. I told him the loan was for a German furniture factory and forthcoming Malindi contract, he grinned.

"What a coincidence Janette, I guess it's my contract with Reiner in Malindi, and the loan is the same banker?"

ARRIVING AT CHIROMO GARDEN HOTEL

Rene and I arrived safely at the hotel, yet I felt rather out of place and uncomfortable being away from Diani and my gypsy lover.

The hotel was a big ugly shabby looking building in need of renovation and obviously seen better days. A large carpark in front that swept around the side into a big garden. A paved area with open-air eating space, a few metal tables, and chairs with a BBQ under a broken shelter. An old sign hanging precariously and making a squeaky sound as a gentle breeze passed over it. A couple of taxis and a big black car at the bottom of the steps, which led up to the hotel. To the right a small reception with an old grey-haired man sitting on a small wooden stool in a corner reading a newspaper. We were greeted by a tall thin man wearing a red jacket at the reception desk.

"Habari, mummy and Mr Rene."

A door leading to a disco and bar in much need of renovation, with a few odd tables and chairs scattered around rather randomly. To the left a passage leading down a long dark hallway with several numbered rooms, mine was the last one. Rene was the other side of the hotel via the gardens. A nice bar area leading to a restaurant and massive kitchen with storerooms. Through the back the garden led to ten rooms, rather like a motel, all in great need of renovation. I was very surprised to find a wonderful welcoming swimming pool with a small bar and eating area hidden neatly under an enormous tree. Another huge tree that overshadowed the bar and a couple of wooden benches. An iron gate which led to the back entrance of the gardens and onto a quiet street. The gardens were tidy with shrubs and plants, a few pretty flowers but with odd random stone features. It didn't look very attractive with two strange metal and wood saunas pitched in the middle of the lawn area. I felt I was sent there to give it some life and to bring back the business it had obviously lost through neglect over the recent years. Plenty of staff running around like headless chickens, not really doing anything but appearing busy.

MEETING TERESA

I met Teresa Rene's wife, a very peculiar lady looking late sixties or seventies. Especially petite, flat chest and desperately skinny, her face was covered with deep lines and loose skin hanging from her long chin. She reminded me of a witch. Long shaggy, badly bleached uncombed hair with big staring eyes almost popping out of their sockets. She put out her thin bony hand to shake mine and grinned exposing dreadful black and broken teeth.

> *"Lovely to meet you Janette, you look remarkably young for a woman in her forties, I would say ten years younger, amazing!"*

Fumbling in her bag she pulled out her passport and asked me how old I thought she was? I didn't like to say because I thought Rene was early fifties and she looked seventy. What a shock I had when she revealed her age, younger than me and quite oblivious to the fact she had aged so.

"Oh, Rene is late sixties and me just over forty."

So, I revealed there was a nineteen-year gap between Dylan and myself. Teresa smiled. She went on to explain her house in Diani Beach was very beautiful, although they had separate bedrooms and no longer indulged in sex. No problem, she had an African toy boy called David a schoolteacher and she would introduce me to him later.

An odd mixture of unusual looking characters milling around at the bar or sprawled across the seating areas.

"Girls of the night, and local villains," remarked Rene.

Rene mentioned the prostitutes frequented Chiromo and well known to Reiner. As they pulled up skirts and dresses displaying their underwear, men wandered around inspecting what was on sale, a very unsettling feeling ran through my body.

MY GUEST ROOM AT CHIROMO

My room was small, dark, and uninviting with a musty damp smell. It was painted a dreadful shade of utility green, with torn rust brown faded patterned curtains hanging from a damaged railing. On the floor several broken cracked vinyl tiles with a dirty brown rug beside the bed. A door led to a bathroom with a cracked toilet seat and matching bowl. The old lead pipes hung from the wall constantly dripping created a large pool of brown water in the bath. It wasn't long before I was greeted by a swarm of scampering cockroaches that paid no attention to my presence, as they scurried across my feet. A very unpleasant uninviting place indeed, I could only hope my stay was a short one.

It was a long and sleepless night with people banging doors, drunken revellers shouting in the early hours and the constant hooting from the taxis outside.

The sweet sound of birds singing and an amber glow peeking through the curtains was a most welcome sight, dawn had arrived. There was little warm water as it drizzled out the shower making a dreadful hissing sound and a constant rattle. Peering through the cracked window I smudged enough dirt away to see the garden filled with flowers. My heart sank thinking of Dylan and the workshop, I prayed that everything would be alright and my stay in Chiromo would be successful.

At breakfast I sat alone contemplating all the reasons why I had made the journey, when my thoughts were interrupted by a young waiter.

"What do you want to eat mummy?"

Asked a charming young man neatly dressed and standing upright, like a soldier on parade.

I ordered a full breakfast and large pot of English tea.

REINER IS ABSENT FOR THREE DAYS

It was three days before Reiner appeared at the hotel and everyone's spirits were lifted. Apparently, we were all in a queue waiting for the elusive loans. As I sat daydreaming one late afternoon beside the pool a cool breeze swept over me, as a large heavy hand was placed on my shoulder. The tall figure of Reiner blocking out the sun, causing a shadow to cast over me. He was looking down at me smiling and spoke softly.

"Janette don't be so sad, your darling is waiting for you in Diani, and I am here."

"Are you just passing through?" I enquired.

"No, I am sitting here with you for the rest of the afternoon there is much to discuss."

We talked about Diani Beach and the workshop; he was constantly reassuring me that Dylan would be fine. I began to relax in his company as we drank wine and ate delicious snacks. Suddenly he blurted out we were going out that night and to be ready at seven in the bar.

I explained that since my arrival I had not left the hotel but watching other people eating, drinking, and playing cards all day. The conversations were in German, and I was very bored in the company.

NIGHT OUT WITH REINER

That evening, I was paraded around the nightspots of Nairobi meeting up with German friends. I was introduced to some important businessmen and government officials, mostly Kenyan. Everyone treated me with the utmost respect, boosting my confidence. We called into the Intercontinental Hotel to meet a colleague and then to a delightful Indian restaurant for a light meal. Moving on to Gypsies Bar situated underneath the Four Aces Casino. The music very loud, but I loved flamenco. Everywhere pictures of people dancing and bullfighters. All things Spanish, so, I was in wonderful surroundings, I simply loved Spain. A very good-looking well-dressed African government official was standing near me at the bar and smiled as he glanced at my bare thigh. I was wearing a slinky black dress with a slit at the side and backless. Reiner raised me up onto the shiny leather stool and glared at the man admiring my leg.

"Do I know you, you're in the Kanu party?" Reiner asked.

"In government my friend," the man replied.

"Are you looking at my woman?" Reiner growled.

"No," he said.

"This is my woman!" said Reiner and grabbed hold of my arm. He banged his hand on the counter.

"She is with me!" he yelled.

I belonged with him. Is that what he thought?

"It's too hot. I'm going to sit outside," I said.

I sat outside and Reiner followed.

"Get back in the bar Janette, I want people to see that you are with me," he snarled.

I wasn't happy with his random behaviour, he apologised with a kiss on my cheek, squeezed my hand then winked.

"You look so good with me, let me show you off to Amin Walji Janette," he chuckled.

MEET AMIN J WALJI MP AT THE CASINO

We arrived at the casino there was a long queue of people waiting to get in. Reiner manoeuvred his way forward, pulling me along by the arm. At the reception desk, a well-dressed rather attractive young Kenyan woman greeted us.

"I have an appointment with Amin Walji, my name is Reiner Moser."

A stairway leading to the next floor where a tall attentive older grey haired Asian man nodded and moved a red guard rope aside, allowing our entry.

> *"Welcome to The Four Aces Casino sir, madam, I hope you have a nice evening."*

A fantastic atmosphere on the gaming tables, I was amazed at how beautiful the place was. A recently built casino with wooden floors, with a deep piled patterned carpet in the centre of the floor. Enormous windows draped with colourful lavish curtains. To one side a small restaurant area with neatly covered tables. Overhead, hanging stained glass lampshades, beautifully designed to show the four aces from a pack of cards. The bar was rather unadorned and featureless with very few bottles on show, but a glorious selection of sparkling crystal drinking glasses.

The constant sound of the roulette wheel and ball that clanked into a space, with calls from the croupier on the blackjack table. I felt quite at home, I worked as a manager for Brian *Kiwi* Adamson, a nightclub casino called the Silhouette Club in England, in the early 80s.

I was one of *Kiwi's* many girlfriends and lived in a big apartment at the rear of the building. The familiar clatter of the ball dropping on the spinning wheel was no stranger to me.

An attractive middle aged Asian man dressed in a grey suit, white shirt, and silver tie, came in and wandered around for a while, then stood next to me at the bar.

He smiled and nodded.

> *"Hello, who are you here with?"*

Reiner noticed him and came over to the bar.

"Ah just the person I want to see. This is Amin Walji MP for Westlands; this is my very good friend Janette. She's up from Diani."

Reiner pulled me in closer to him; I shook Amin's hand.

"So, are you on holiday or what?"

"No on business," I answered.

Amin was called away to his office.

"He likes attractive blonde women."

"Oh, he does. What's that supposed to mean?"

Reiner said he was just introducing me to someone in government, the only Asian MP and he was a very good guy. Indicating that maybe later we could do business with him, or he could help us. In Kenya you need many friends, mostly in government or police. Amin returned chatting to Reiner, then he smiled at me.

"How long are you staying up here for?"

"I'm not quite sure, I have a partner in Diani."

"Come on we need to go somewhere else. I want to introduce you to another person," interrupted Reiner.

As I passed Amin by the bar, I thanked him for the drink.

He grabbed my hand.

"I need you to phone me, come and see me on your own. Will you do that?"

"Yes."

I didn't think I would have a reason to return on my own, and Reiner asked me what was said.

"He wants me to go back on my own sometime."

"That's great, you see, I knew he would like you, we can do business with Walji Janette, let's go to Impala now."

IMPALA HOTEL

It was very late, but he insisted I meet another person. An old white haired African man who owned the Impala Hotel. It was dark I couldn't see much of the place, and we sat outside on the veranda. He introduced me as a friend from Diani Beach. The old man came across as charming and amusing, he told me I could always come to visit him, if I needed help. We had a couple of drinks then left for Chiromo Hotel.

For the following few days Reiner would confide some of his many secrets, he seemed smitten with me and consumed in my presence. It was obvious to everyone at Chiromo that I was having special treatment, and their needs were not being met. I was given an alternative bigger room across the gardens, in a quiet area because the nightlife and hooting taxis kept me awake. A matter of days after the introduction to the old man from Impala, he was sitting with Reiner and another businessman in the bar.

"Janette come sit down and meet my business friend."

The old black man was looking carefully at me and listening to Reiner say-

"Janette could be up here helping us, and could be involved in this hotel, or another hotel together, anything is possible."

I found Reiner's statement rather odd, I was only there for a business loan for the German factory.

"You know the factory idea is just one of the many things we can do together Janette."

Reiner left to his office and the old man from Impala said.

"You must come and see me at Impala."

He looked and sounded very serious.

"You get a taxi."

"What?" I replied curiously.

"You come to Impala; I must talk with you."

TAXI TO IMPALA

Later that evening curiosity got the better of me, I wrote a note to say where I was going and left it on my bed in case I didn't return. I wasn't in least bit afraid to go, it was just a curtesy note for the police if anything happened to me. If you wanted a taxi you needed to wait on the steps outside, but I left by the side door and walked down the street. I took a taxi from there, so nobody knew I'd left. I arrived after ten minutes and looked for the owner, he was at the bar.

"Come on we must have a drink first you seem to be a very intelligent woman; you have style and class Reiner likes that; you are that type he goes after. You must never say this conversation took place, you must be careful because Mr Reiner is very professional and dangerous he's a well-known criminal, he spent time in prison. I don't know if you know that?"

"No, I didn't."

I was curious why he requested me to meet him.

"Well then you don't need to know the details, but it's all government connected. You be most careful of Mr Reiner mummy, he can be dangerous," he frowned and shook his head.

There much more to the tête-à-tête I was mindful of his warning, then someone called a taxi for me.
I simply wanted the loan for the factory and believed I could handle Reiner and his nefarious plans. At that time, I felt confidant Reiner was a true friend and naively believed he would be all I expected of him. Government issues and crimes were irrelevant to friends helping each other in business, I thought.

THE MEETING FOR A LOAN

The day came to meet Reiner's contact and discuss business. We were informed he was currently unavailable for over an hour; we sat alone having a few drinks. Unexpectedly Reiner confessed that he was falling in love with me and hoped to persuade me to become his girlfriend and manageress at Chiromo. The statement of affection and his admission of loving or lusting after me, didn't surprise me.

Over the months some of his remarks were obvious. He was often drunk and blurted out strange random comments, regardless of who was present. He was relatively elusive most of the time, what did he want from me? I missed my sweetheart so much, but Reiner would not hear such murmurings, he wanted to have a relationship with me. Not wanting to listen to my adoration for my gypsy lover.

The business contact arrived, a very attractive tall thin African man wearing a smart blue suit. Reiner and he chatted about money issues. It was too puzzling and after a while, I lost track of the conversation when they mentioned I would be manageress of Chiromo. They shook hands, Reiner smiled at me, and we parted company. Reiner took my hand and said let's walk together. I declared my concern regarding the manageress for Chiromo comment when I had come up for the German Factory and nothing else? He assured me all was well, and everything would be sorted out very soon. On our way back to Chiromo Reiner toyed with me and later pointed out a wooded area and sniggered.

> *"See over there Janette, it's a dumping ground for people who upset the government, there is a few other places a bit further out."*
>
> *"How do you know that?"*
>
> *"I have put a few in there myself, never upset me Janette, I'm a bastard when I don't get my own way,"* he scoffed.

We continued the journey in a strange uncomfortable silence. He didn't mention the loans for me or Teresa, so what exactly was he up to? Several days passed without seeing Reiner, then he resurfaced at Chiromo and suggested it was time for me to see his home, he needed to collect papers for Moses Kurgat the advocate.

INVITED TO REINER'S HOUSE

It was a warm breezy day when Reiner invited me to his home to see Ngery and the two girls. On the way through the busy streets of Nairobi we chatted about how to improve Chiromo and give it a face-lift. There was no mention of the German factory loan. In my mind I was expecting a grand house with iron gates and in an up-market area. I was quite shocked when we pulled up outside a small shabby house in a less popular part of town.

A broken picket gate that led to a small unkept garden with overgrown shrubs and broken clay pots. An abundance of dying plants crammed against a wooden fence. In one corner huge bushes, a child's swing, and toys scattered around on the patchy grass. It looked as run down as Chiromo Gardens.

A narrow dirt path leading to a green wooden door, where Reiner's wife Ngery and children greeted us.

"Jambo sana, habari Janette."

I was led through a small cluttered dull kitchen, to a gloomy damp living room cluttered with papers and a desk piled high with more of the same. Ngery made iced tea and offered homemade biscuits. Reiner gave me a quick tour of his awful home pointing out it needed a little work doing on it and he should make a start.

Ngery remarked.

"Yes, you have been saying that for years Reiner."

He glared angrily at her, Ngery seemed anxious and uneasy. Every dismal, room giving off an awful musty odour. It resembled a dwelling for poor people, not a businessman's abode. After looking around this insignificant unhappy home, Ngery asked if I was a Christian or another religion.

I was about to answer when Reiner butted in.

"She's not interested in anything you have to say. Shut up and get on with your work," he snarled.

"I am spiritual, no religion Ngery."

Ngery hurried the children into a small room at the back of the house and out of sight. I strolled around the garden whilst Reiner sorted out some documents and to my sheer delight the children nervously reappeared from the dim untidy room.

I took them by the hand and suggested we walk to the far corner amongst the dying shrubs and flowers.

"Let's look for the fairies and make special wishes, shall we?"

The two girls now happy searching for faeries, as I taught them English nursery rhymes. I couldn't help but wonder what the future held for these two little darlings. I hugged them both and left with mixed feelings. It was a very gloomy ramshackle house, with unfortunate discontented people in it.

As we slowly drove away Reiner said.

> *"So, you have seen where I live, and my wife in the house with the children. Now you can see we are unhappy and it's a marriage of convenience. You might not realise this Janette, but I know one day you will be with me."*
>
> *"Are you joking?"* I laughed.
>
> *"Hmm, what do you think? Don't you think it's possible?"*
>
> *"No Reiner!"*

Reiner intimidated his wife and children, he was a very angry man, why did he consider that an endearing quality? He would not have power over me I thought; no matter how he manipulated others, I would not be a victim. As we approached the driveway of Chiromo he suggested I should have an evening with his business friend David, who wanted to assist with the loan for the German factory.

DAVID ADVOCATE MEAL OUT

I was invited out to a very upmarket Indian restaurant with David, a very attractive well-dressed man in his forties. He arrived at Chiromo wearing a dark grey suit and white shirt, maroon tie. He wanted to discuss Chiromo and possible partnership with Reiner if they couldn't secure the German factory loan. He was delightfully charming, most entertaining, and wonderful company. A notably educated

Kenyan encouraging me to remain in Nairobi. David studied in London and from a well-connected background.

> *"There are more opportunities here for you with Reiner, because he will need your help with Chiromo and other projects in Nairobi,"* David suggested.

It was a very pleasant and informative evening.

MISSING DYLAN AND MY HOME IN DIANI

As the days passed my phone calls to Dylan become considerably longer. I wanted to be in his arms and touch his long silky hair. I loved and missed him so much. I couldn't bare it any longer this torturous nightmare without him, crying night after night.

Teresa and Rene were kind enough, they tried to keep my spirits up, but they too had become prisoners of Chiromo. Just waiting, day after day for some news. We heard a constant flow of bogus stories and excuses from Reiner. I began to feel sorry for Teresa and Rene; they were so frustrated waiting for the illusive loan. Most of the time playing cards with another odd German couple. The nervous tension began to show on their tired faces. We didn't see Reiner very often; he would breeze through the hotel like the east wind sending a chill down our spines. Always in a hurry, rushing around doing nothing, but coming and going without explanation of any progress. He would arrive late drunk or with rowdy friends, incapable of conveying any useful information. My concerns for African Oasis grew evermore; Dylan couldn't manage it without me? He was a young illiterate gypsy in a man's world, in a very corrupt country. I began to fear for his safety.

MEETING PAULA ENSELMO

It was a very busy night at the hotel. I was introduced to Major Paula Enselmo a round faced chubby American woman working at the embassy. Her young German husband Rolph was an ex-soldier. My partner Dylan was several years younger than me; this gave us a talking point.

Toy boys.

We connected very quickly, and our conversation continued metaphysical and theosophical subjects. Paula listened intently to my vast knowledge on spirituality and especially magic. She was a very bubbly and compelling character, pleasant looking and a little overweight. Rolph, tall, slim quiet good looking with light brown floppy hair and pale blue eyes.

Paula was very interesting to talk to, yet rather loud at times. However, we shared a similar sense of humour and enjoyed each other's company.

INVITED TO TEA AND CATS

I was picked up by Rolph in his black jeep and taken the short ride to their charming but cluttered apartment and two scruffy unsociable cats.

> *"Gee Janette you're the only person that my cats will respond to, now that's kind of spooky don't you think?"*
>
> *"No, I am a very spiritual person, and animals have a sixth sense, I can communicate with them at a very subtle level."*

We chatted about hypnosis and higher states of awareness, agreeing that energy is expressing itself through different planes of consciousness. We shared some interesting, strange phenomena stories, drank three large Cognacs, ate delicious sandwiches, then it was time to continue the waiting game at Chiromo.

THE NEXT EVENING PAULA AND ROLPH

The following evening Reiner turned up in a humorous mood and chatted with Paula, Rolf, an African man, and me. During the night I noticed that Paula and Reiner were very close whispering to each other. I detected a special bond between them, so I asked Reiner what the link was, he said money and laughed. Then he hugged me tight and whispered that I was his favourite woman, and Paula fancied me too! Earlier she had asked him if I was a bisexual, because she fancied a romp with me, he chuckled and told her good luck with her. The following day Paula had invited me for a few drinks at her place whilst Rolph hit the bars in Nairobi, as per norm. After a few glasses of wine Paula confessed a strong desire for our relationship to be more than just friends. I asked for an explanation, and she remarked warmly.

> *"I have never felt like this about another woman before, I've been in the army a long time, but I am so attracted to you, I think I am falling for you Janette."*

I wasn't shocked or disturbed by her statement and simply informed her, I was not bi-sexual and very much in love with Dylan.

> *"Gee I'm sorry, I don't know what made me think you were, it's just you're so attractive and very sexy, I would love to experience a relationship with you,"* she uttered.
>
> *"Thank you for the compliments, Paula, I'm not offended."*

I cut short the visit and returned to the hotel rather flattered and curiously intrigued.

TALK TO INGA AND KLAUS THE GERMANS

The next day I waited for Reiner to emerge from his office. The odd Germans that played cards with Rene and Teresa beckoned me over to their table. In broken English, they introduced themselves as Inga and Klaus. Inga a short fat rounded woman in her fifties with enormous bosoms, dressed in tatty worn-out vintage clothing. Her hair was badly rinsed with a deep red tone that didn't cover all the grey, was swept over her head with a green plastic clip. Reminding me of a cartoon character, from World War 2.

As she rushed around the restaurant, she looked like a clucking mother hen about to lay an egg. Klaus quite tall, stooping hunched and overweight. With thin light brown hair curled on his forehead, rather a *gay* or entertainer appearance. Huge bloodshot watery eyes and thick slobbery lips, he reminded me of a big slug. These two rather ugly people, with loud voices, explained in broken English they once were partners with Reiner, in this hotel. They were just waiting for the outcome of a court case against him, for money owing. Reiner declined to pay them back, so, they refused to leave the hotel, until the matter was legally sorted out. Hence, their constant presence in the hotel was primarily to annoy Reiner. Reminding him of the agreement he had broken with them.

Inga, thoroughly interrogating me and Klaus nodding as he repeated the same questions.

> *"So, Janette what exactly is your connection to Reiner and is it business or personal?"*

"Oh, it's business I have a partner in Diani."

Explaining in detail they had been given a managerial position with another German friend called Wolfgang. Hopefully they would soon be off to the bush to run his safari lodge Kindani, in the Meru National Park region.

"That sounds marvellous, I would rather be back at the coast than here, anywhere but here," I said.

"Vee don't pay, Vhy should Vee, he owes us a great deal of money, so, you are in Diani you must know our friends Walter and Sylvia," muttered Inga.

"Yes, of course."

"Your business is furniture Janette, this is good, you can make some for us when we go to Kindani. There will be plenty of work for you, I'm sure. That's right eh Klaus?"

"Yaa, Inga lots of vork for Janette to do for us, good, good," mumbled Klaus.

Although I wanted the safari-lodge contract; however, it might be too difficult and very expensive to transport all the way to Kindani? It was unrealistic.

"Let us wait and see, all we do is wait Janette and you will too ha!"

TERESA EVENING DRINKS

Teresa invited me for a drink at the bar and chatted about her great disappointment not receiving the loan. I remarked.

"I'm getting worried about this loan for the German factory in Diani, what do you think Teresa?"

"Janette, you will not get this money. But don't be concerned too much, I will give you all the carpentry work on my building in Msambweni, you and Dylan can make all the furniture also, don't worry it will be alright."

What a marvellous opportunity this was for us, at last there was something positive. If I didn't secure a loan for the German factory, I could continue with our work regardless. Reiner arrived and I discussed Teresa's dream home which he helped to build, she explained to him her plan to help African Oasis with work. However, I was unaware it was not his objective for me to have work in Diani, Reiner had other plans.

He wanted me at his side in Chiromo.

DELAYED PHONE CALL FROM DYLAN

It was Sunday and Dylan's call didn't come at the agreed time, it wasn't like him to be late, I was worried. Did he have an accident at work or on the roads or perhaps Walter was too busy to make the call. Eventually the call came, he explained that he was out all night at a disco in Mombasa with Roy a local white boy. I wasn't worried he went out, but I didn't feel happy knowing he travelled on the ferry late at night. It was too dangerous. He was at Roy's house and apparently got bitten by an insect. The bite was so bad he needed medical attention from the doctor, and he could barely walk. I thought it was strange he was unable to walk but went dancing that evening?

"What are you doing going across the ferry late at night? You are an idiot."

"We went to German Joe's restaurant and nightclub."

Roy's family were close friends with German Joe and apparently, they went late at night to the nightclub. Then in the morning they were snake hunting and Dylan got bitten by a sandfly. Later Walter called me, he was concerned for Dylan out with the white boys and black girls from Shakatak night club, all the time. This news was very worrying.

GOING HOME TO DIANI

My plane ticket was booked, and I eagerly left the madness of Chiromo and Nairobi, for my home and lover in Diani Beach and Simba Village. Leaving behind Reiner and waiting for money that would never manifest. On the plane looking down on the open plains, mesmerised by nothingness, no buildings, no people I drifted into a trance. Amin came into my mind. He would be the only person I could trust if I needed him.

Amin's face and voice haunted me.

DYLAN AT THE AIRPORT

Only one hour from Nairobi and the plane touched down with Dylan waiting for me. Dropping my bag, as I rushed towards him, I missed him and longed for this moment. We hugged and kissed each other and cried with joy, the separation was over.

> *"Jan, I love you so much, don't leave me again, please promise me?"*

We would spend the night together making passionate love, as we had so many times before. However, I noticed a strange dark mark on his neck and asked him what it was.

> *"Oh, just a mosquito bite I scratched it."*

As we approached the driveway to our home, it felt different somehow, but I was just glad to be back. I was home at last and Chiromo was well and truly behind me. I showered then changed into loose baggy clothes and sat on the bed listening to romantic music playing softly in the background. Dylan poured two cold beers into iced glasses.

"Jan, please don't leave me ever again, I nearly went crazy without you here, lonely nights no one to talk to when I came home from work. Only Alice jabbering away about nonsense housework, she also missed your fun and laughter, the apartment felt so empty, just look at Willie he's really grown."

"Much bigger, what have you fed him?"

"Sorry I can't wait any longer, I'm so bloody frustrated Jan, I'm having a shower."

He returned wrapped in a towel; he dropped it in a very seductive manner. Water running down his back, dripping from his long-wet hair. Dylan paraded around the room showing off his beautiful, tanned body I reached out for him to come closer, I touched his soft warm skin.

Holding his cock, he moved towards me, as I removed my clothes, eagerly waiting for this moment. Our bodies melted together as we kissed and caressed each other. Touching, kissing every inch of our bodies, until we could no longer wait to fuck. We made love repeatedly until exhausted and satisfied. The only sound in the room was the large fan spinning around above us creating a cool breeze, which swept over our hot sweaty bodies. Sleep came very easily to me that evening.

The following day we made love repeatedly, not leaving the compound, only for a swim in the cool inviting pool. We sat outside under the African stars, and nothing seemed more remote than Chiromo with only the Germans and Reiner for company. Amin was the one memory I reflected upon. He made such an impact on me, his soft voice, his handsome face, and the sheer sense of mystery about him.

WALTER'S ISLAND

The next morning a surprise boat trip had been arranged, to take me on a day's outing with my friends in Diani. Everyone met at Walter's Inn and just as were about to leave, Reiner unexpectedly arrived with two Germans, wanting to join the adventure. With Walter at the helm, we set sail for Kilifi Bay, but we called it Walter's Island off the coast at Msambweni. On board the boat was a young English woman who worked for a travel company in Diani. She seemed overly friendly to Dylan and ignored my presence. I queried her strange manner but was met with a cold silence. I left it at that, I had no intention of spoiling this glorious day.

I took a few photos with a disposable camera of the stunning scenery and then faced my camera towards Reiner and clicked away. He promptly jumped up and tossed the camera into the sea, swearing and grunting in German.

"No, no Janette."

Everyone looked horrified but kept silent, as did I.

Pictures of German Mafia was obviously out of the question!

Arriving at the bay some of us headed towards the small shack which had The Bar, painted on a piece of driftwood hanging from a rusty old chain and swinging in the breeze. Then others were seeking refuge in shaded areas, out of the scorching sun. Reiner was heading to the makeshift toilet at the end of a sandy path and soon returned laughing at the experience. Eventually we all sat together and shared the food Walter supplied for the outing, the drinks were purchased at his honky-tonk open-air bar.

Sylvia entertaining us with Puccini, Tosca vissi d'arte, Walter with German beer drinking songs and *lederhosen* frolicking. With moments of madness and classy opera, it was a memorable day filled with fun and laughter. The amber glow of sundown appearing on the vast horizon, we gathered our things and boarded the boat. As we clambered on the boat waving farewell to Kilifi, memories of Nairobi quickly began to fade, with the setting of the sun. I would never have such a glorious day as this again, I thought.

Paradise in Kenya.

BACK TO THE WORKSHOP

> *"Karibu karibu sana."*

Welcome home mummy they all shouted as I stepped from the pick-up truck, everyone rushing around to greet me.

> *"We have missed mummy, it wasn't the same without you, please don't go away again."*

I was very touched by this unexpected outburst by the staff; it was very easy to see they cared for me. They mentioned Dylan wasn't around very much but did stay odd nights at the office. What were they trying to tell me?

FURNITURE FOR POLICE CHIEF

Dylan had made furniture for the chief of police without putting it through the books and out with his daughter. Ngala informed me of the work not being part of the business, because bwana Dylan didn't want me to know about it. A very nice dining table and six chairs.

An order came in to create ten chairs for a restaurant.

> *"Shall we use the same templates as Dylan used for the policeman?"* asked Ngala.

> *"What policeman order is that there's nothing in the books?"*

When I questioned Dylan, he looked guilty.

> *"I did it to keep them off our backs."*

He apparently met him at Walter's and asked Dylan to make the dining set as a gift, as a *pesa kidogo.*

> *"I can explain at home."*

Something about this story felt wrong and why was he hanging around with the policeman's daughter?

TRIP FOR TIMBER AND FARM

Within a couple of days, we had a trip up to Shimba Hills, for timber and visit the farmer. We met with our friend the farmer, and he asked why bwana Dylan was limping, his foot had a big lump on it.

> *"Oh, I know what that is."*

He cut a large fruit in half, then wrapped Dylan's foot with a cloth and told him to sit there for about twenty minutes.

> *"You must keep putting it on your foot it draws out all the poison."*

We were handed more fruit to take home, so that we could continue the process. I took Dylan back to the doctors for another check-up, and explained what the farmer gave us.

"Your medicine didn't work, but the local remedy did."

He laughed and remarked.

"That's often the case, nature is a wonderful healer."

MARIA STORY

Reiner was back in Diani to sort out Teresa's building in Msambweni, he was renting an apartment next to mine. Teresa mentioned a mutual friend wanted a new house built in Diani, her name was Maria.

It was a sunny morning when a loud bang on the door to my apartment, it was Reiner.

"Come on Janette, let us go to visit your friend Maria for a contract," he shouted.

We travelled along the Mombasa Road until we came to a dirt track leading to a complex of elegant houses. Each one individual, with swimming pool and beautiful gardens.

"Hello lovely lady, come in for some cool drinks."

'Maria this is Reiner, he is German a good friend and colleague."

Maria was tall, average weight with light brown wavy shoulder length hair. Neatly dressed in a plain pale blue cotton blouse and floral cotton flowing skirt. She was radiant and beaming with gorgeous expressive blue eyes that sparkled. Originally from Austria but now very settled in Diani Beach. Reiner went into the house to look at building plans Maria had organised for his inspection; she was to build a bigger house nearby, no shortage of money. Whilst he scanned over the documents Maria, and I walked in the tidy flowered gardens.

She mentioned that my aura and energy field was so mystical and charismatic. She understood I had extensive knowledge of healing energy and psychic powers.

"I do understand these things, I was very privileged to have had mentors when I was much younger, I seem to have a special gift."

We chatted for some time whilst Reiner was busy contemplating the plans and then he abruptly left to meet someone at Walter's Inn.

"I must go it's important that I see someone at Walter's, be back in a couple of hours, or you can come Janette?"

"No, I want to stay with Maria."

Maria asked if I had heard of Reiki healing.

"What is it?"

It's a Japanese form of hands-on healing developed by a man called Mikao Usui at the beginning of the century. Maria was a Reiki Master and offered to teach me. I was shown books, as she chatted explaining the concept of this ancient healing method. We found so much to share, talking about consciousness, spiritual concepts, healing, magic, and angels. She was indeed a very special lady.

After a light snack Maria began to tell me a story concerning a lady who lived close to Simba Village who owned a shop in the parade. Apparently two men followed her home one night and broke into her house. She was terrified and locked herself in the bathroom behind an iron gate and bars on the window. The two men were trying to attack her with spears as they poked them through the bars. An askari heard the woman's screams and came to help her. As he yelled at the two men other locals came running to assist. The robber's fled empty handed, and the woman was treated for shock. She sold up and left Diani Beach.

What was the purpose of the story I asked Maria? She replied the two men had worked for the shopkeeper she sacked them for stealing.

> *"Janette you must be so careful with these locals, don't trust them please. Be careful who you employ. They will turn on you just like Joseph Obetto and Francis did,"* expressed Maria.

The two men had worked for the lady at the shop painting her house and stole goods from her. She informed the police, so they retaliated by trying to rob and kill her.

> *"Maria that's so terrible."*

> *"Yes, Janette those two men killed my dog and burnt out my jeep, you must be careful who you employ it is a very dangerous place Africa."*

> *"I don't fear things and I always protect myself with positive energy and spirit guides,"* I assured her.

> *"Ah, indeed such an angel as you, you are well and truly guarded."*

Reiner returned and we said farewell and took a slow and pensive drive back to Diani Beach.

REINER RETURNS TO NAIROBI

FLY UP URGENTLY

This time I was to leave my sweetheart for only a few days, and Dylan seemed very eager for me to go. Not for one second did I think anything suspicious but that he was very excited with the new challenge that awaited us. He had his own circle of friends his own age and would frequent the local bars and discos. Obviously, he met several people when he was out, but I never gave too much thought to it. After a few months at the workshop, I found it too tiring after a long day in the scorching sun. I would be more than satisfied with a couple of cold beers at Walter's Inn and quite content to read a book or watch a video at home.

THE KWALE TRIP

I collected documents from Walter on behalf of Teresa that required stamping and signing at the local district planning and government office in Kwale. I was asked to take them to an Advocate in Mombasa, to be counter signed. We set out for Mombasa with tall Joseph in the back of the truck with my suitcase. Dylan was driving quite fast through Mombasa as a bus swerved. Dylan pulled out of the way just in time but hit on the side door and bumper. As we came to a stop Joseph was looking across at the bus, when a man appeared from nowhere and grabbed my suitcase. Joseph jumped out and ran after him, unfortunately he got away.

Dylan shouted.

> *"Oh, shit I guess you're not going now."*

We eventually made our way over the other side of Mombasa to the advocates house, and he signed the papers for us but wasn't happy about something.

> *"Why is this woman Teresa not here with you?"*

I must investigate these documents and call Reiner in Nairobi. He called Reiner and I spoke to him about the truck accident and my bag was stolen, I would be going back home to Simba Village, but fly up late the following day…

I did fly up late the next day and Rene met me at the airport. I handed over the documents to him we chatted about his projects on the way to the hotel. Reiner was away up coast somewhere, so I stayed for two nights. Nothing much happened however, I met some new Europeans frequenting the bar, chatted with the Asians, drank wine with Rachid and Betty Kenyatta. I stayed in the hotel grounds then flew back home to Diani.

NIGHT CLUB WITH DYLAN

Dylan met me at the airport but appeared aloof and rather miserable.

"Let's go up to Shakatak, I want to take you for a drink."

I didn't like Shakatak nightclub, it was for tourists and prostitutes. Walter's Inn and Forty Thieves were my preferred social and drinking places. But he insisted.

I was asked to sit in a dark corner, he was behaving very strange. Sipped his drink, then on to the dance floor showing off as per norm. He began dancing with a small Kenyan girl in a bright coloured short skirt and flimsy red top. I thought he seemed too familiar with her.

"Let's go home Dylan, I am tired from the trip."

"No, I'm staying on dancing."

"Well, how am I supposed to get home?"

Another girl was hiding behind a pillar and waving at him, she was beckoning him to go to her. Dylan jumped up, grabbed my arm, and forcefully pulled me out the club saying let's go. He didn't speak on the way home and acted very odd when we arrived at the apartment.

"What's going on Dylan?"

He stayed quiet and indifferent, sulking.

TWO NIGHTS LATER

Another night club with a young white Kenyan friend of Dylan's as we walked toward the entrance he remarked.

"I can't do this, you're such a lovely lady, I'm off."

"What was that all about?" I asked Dylan.

"You're always fucking tired you don't want to come out."

"What are you hanging around these clubs for, we've got a business to run, we're not on holiday now."

An uneasy feeling came between us, and I sensed that he was up to something no good.

SHAKATAK OUTING WITH REINER

At Simba Village Reiner called in for a chat and invited us to meet some German friends in Shakatak. Reiner asked us to follow him to the owner's office, he was sitting behind a large desk chatting to a young barman.

"Hi, come in, please to meet you guys, call me Foxy okay, if you come back tomorrow, we can discuss a contract for tables and chairs for my nightclub, but for now enjoy yourselves with my buddy Reiner."

It was very crowded, smoky and the music too loud. However, Reiner chatted to me about taking Dylan back with him to Nairobi for a *male bonding* experience. I was very sceptical and made it quite clear. I was concerned about Dylan going. Finally, I agreed he could see Chiromo where I was contemplating the partnership with Reiner, in a month or so. He would be given the opportunity to visit the numerous nightspots that lured the mzungu man to investigate. Reiner promised no harm would come to him.

DYLAN LEAVING FOR NAIROBI

A glorious sunny morning and Dylan excited to leave, as they packed the car with their bags, I felt a sickening sensation of impending doom. Now the situation was reversed I would me alone at the apartment, watching videos with only Willie to cuddle at night.

I couldn't drive the pick-up truck, so Rudi drove me to Shakatak to discuss the contract with the owner Foxy. We were there for thirty minutes and agreed to make a few sample tables and chairs ready for when Dylan returned from Nairobi.

Rudi also drove me to the factory and picked me up at night. The time passed quickly working all day, and I remained at home in the evenings. All communication between Nairobi and Diani Beach was made via Walter's Inn. One lunchtime Walter presented me with an outstanding bill, I was shocked at the number of beers and Bacardi. I asked Walter if he was sure, it was Dylan's? He looked at me with raised eyebrows and peering over his black rimmed glasses.

> *"You might like to see these, Janette; you must bring him here when he returns then we can discuss it together."*

I thought it wise to leave it at that.

Walter mentioned Dylan was out each night with Roy, Marco and the Crismani boy frequenting casinos, nightclubs, and bars.

DYLAN RETURNED TO DIANI

I waited for Dylan to arrive home; I had already prepared a special meal for his return. I was absolutely thrilled to see him, and we kissed and cuddled just so happy to be together once more. He told me he would like to take the opportunity to manage Chiromo Hotel with me and felt positive we would soon be making a lot of money there. He said he was with Reiner most evenings at nightclubs and danced with the local girls.

"Manage Chiromo?" I asked.

I thought you were staying in Diani to run the factory with tall Joseph and the boys, with Reiner dropping in regularly. There was no mention of him managing Chiromo with me at this point. Even I wasn't exactly sure what was unfolding. I surmised a trial run with the option to return to Diani Beach if it didn't work out well for me.

ALICE POINTS TO LIPSTICK

After work Dylan dropped me off and went to see tall Joseph. I noticed that Alice my maid had laid Dylan's shirt out on the edge of the bed with a business card next to it. I called her through.

"What's this Alice?"

She told me it was Dylan's best shirt from his trip to Nairobi and pointed out a very bright red lipstick stain on the collar. Looking puzzled, she added, this is not your colour mummy, it belongs to another lady. My heart sank; I felt sick but refused to believe the worst.

"I suppose this is someone who he's met that's given him a card mummy."

She was being very diplomatic, and she handed me the business card. Then she removed more cards from his jacket and left them on the kitchen counter. They were prostitute calling cards and massage parlours. I tore them up.

CONFRONTING DYLAN

When I questioned him later, he looked embarrassed.

"You know what these girls are like, I only danced with them."

"Actually, I don't like you dancing up close with these young women."

I pointed out to him they were all Nairobi massage parlours and prostitutes.

"Some girls at Chiromo gave them to me," he grunted.

"I'm not happy, I've torn them up."

I had a shower.

"What are you going to have to eat?"

"I'm not very hungry and meeting a guy down at the shopping parade."

Dylan was changing from the beautiful gentle soul I fell madly in love with. I started to blame myself for bringing him to Africa. No longer the fun-loving gypsy lover but developing into a stranger and behaving indifferently. He started regular outings with the white boys. I began to get very suspicious of his behaviour, I noticed he lied several times and didn't even care about it. One evening Dylan showed a different persona, unexpectedly very smug and self-assured, put on a new shirt, and started to do his Michael Jackson dance.

"Where are you going?"

"Oh, one of the hotels."

Suddenly changed his hairstyle wearing it down loose, it was waist length and normally tied up in a ponytail or rolled up in a bun.

"You're behaving peculiar. What's going on?"

"No, I'm working hard so I'm going out with the boys."

"You never used to go anywhere without me."

"Well, now I am."

Another lonely night for me, he came home at 3am.

MY BIRTHDAY WALTER'S AND FORTY THIEVES

May 12th strolling along the beach hand in hand to Forty Thieves with friends, then other people joined us later. I got a little bit tipsy and sat on the beach and overheard local people talking.

"Look it is that guy from Shakatak? The one who is always dancing like Michael Jackson and showing off with the black girls, he sure enjoyed himself when she was away."

I did not mention anything to Dylan because he was entering the Michael Jackson dancing competition and I wanted to enjoy it too. However, I stayed home and watched videos, drank wine, and fell asleep. Nothing really happened until midnight at Shakatak, but Dylan arrived back at 2am.

Another time at Walter's.

"Are you all right Dylan, is everything okay are you going out tonight with the girls and Marco?" asked Walter.

A deathly silence as Dylan turned into a complete mess trying to rearrange itself. Walter found the appropriate time to spill the beans on him.

TERESA ARRIVED FROM NAIROBI

It was only a few days later Teresa returned with part payment of the much overdue loan; however, Rene remained behind in Chiromo waiting for a bank transfer from Switzerland.

That evening Dylan and I made a marvellous spicy chicken curry dinner for six. Teresa with David the Kenyan teacher lover making up the party with my wonderful German neighbours Sonke and Waltraud. They had two yapping sandy coloured poodles that played in the compound with Willie our Jack Russell bush dog. It was a glorious warm night as the stars shone overhead, we enjoyed the food and drink with friends, and nothing would disturb our joy. Tales from Germany, Switzerland, Kenya, and England with everyone in fits of laughter, at some of the hilarious stories we all revealed. There could be no greater joy than sharing with friends, under the vast African sky.

REINER LOAN MONEY IN DIANI

Reiner could not secure the German factory loan.

He was desperate to pay off a contractor and he wanted me to be his business partner in Chiromo.

> *"Come on Janette you must give this to me I need it right now, urgently. You and I are partners, you will have shares in Chiromo hotel, it is a small amount I am asking for considering what we will make together I'll give it back to you."*

"I don't have this kind of money to give to you."

"Of course, you do because your lover has already told me."

After some thought, and much persuasion from Reiner, I went to the bank to withdraw the Kenyan shillings he requested. The friendly manager came over and asked why such a big amount of money was being withdrawn. I explained I was purchasing a share of Chiromo Garden Hotel in Nairobi; this was apart cash payment.

"Well, be careful my dear, remember the other nonsense you had to resolve with me?" he smiled and kwaheri, goodbye.

Reiner requested more cash, but I refused and suggested a bank transfer so there was evidence. He nodded and agreed because he needed me at Chiromo for five days to help organise and sort out his rundown hotel.

"You are standing in as manager and shareholder, my partner, be happy Janette," he quipped.

BACK TO CHIROMO NOW PARTNERS

A marvellous welcome at the hotel with cheers from the staff. I was fully aware of the many problems I needed to overcome; it was too late to turn back.

Three thoughtful Asian businessmen I knew, invited me to dine out with them, I was totally spoiled, the feeling was wonderful. Perhaps things might get better after all.

One evening Paula Enselmo remarked how fond she was of Reiner. She had given him a large sum of money to help him out on a business deal. However, he paid her back eventually. I mentioned I had given him an even larger amount in Diani, he repaid a token amount of 20,000 KS, the outstanding debt was much more.

Previously Reiner gave me a tour of the hotel, pointing out that he wanted me to manage it for him. He had lost so much money and no longer trusted his manager.

I was taken to his office to discuss ideas.

> *"Janette, I understand you have wasted your time at Chiromo, but you have put some of your many skills to good use."*

During the three-week waiting for the loan, I had become very bored hanging around the hotel waiting for news. Uninterested in playing cards all day with the Germans, I busied myself with the hotel staff. I had plenty of clever ideas to run the hotel more efficiently and improve their working conditions.

The bar began to function properly and without the huge loss it normally incurred, cleaner and operated with efficiency. The staff were motivated by my enthusiasm to assist and share the secrets of hotel management with them. Nonetheless, Reiner ever elusive I thought he was ignorant of my efforts, to help save his run-down business.

Still unable to deliver the German factory loan, he chased after his tail like a dog on heat. One day as he sat behind his desk lighting up another cigarette.

> *"Janette you are well suited to Chiromo. You have told me you have years of catering experience and owned a hotel in Ireland. Sell Diani and be partners with me? You are perfect for this hotel; you have the experience we can make it work. I promise you; this is a better opportunity than the factory, and I have tried several people to get the loan but nothing yet. I will buy the business from you myself, when I have my finances sorted out and Dylan can come here too or work in the factory and here."*

"I don't know Reiner I have wasted so much time here; my factory isn't operating as it should. Why would I give up the coast for the city, there's too much to consider."

BACK TO DIANI AFTER FIVE DAY TRIP

Upon my return to Diani, I discovered Dylan had spent most of his free time out until early morning with friends. The workshop was taking a back seat as he revelled in the night life. An order of forty safari chairs and ten tables, were almost completed for the Crismani restaurant. Payments due for that contract were long overdue and I became increasingly concerned about cash flow of the business. Other accounts were also late, so the business had been neglected.

However, I made it very clear to Dylan that he needed to call upon the customers for the overdue accounts, or we would not supply the remaining furniture. He was reluctant to approach the Crismani family because he was frequenting bars with them in my absence.

However, Reiner took charge and called the unwilling customers in debt to African Oasis, offering to settle within the month. I felt satisfied with the progress, but unhappy with Dylan's reluctance to put business before pleasure.

When you're being conned by a friend you don't see it until it's too late. Even though there's some feelings of doubt concerning the situation, you continue to believe in them, pushing aside those important questions you ask yourself about the arrangement.

I needed evidence that Reiner received two payments of £5,000 as my investment share into the hotel, rather than a loan idea. We reached an agreement with the proposed partnership. Everything in motion and just waiting to be signed by Kurgat the advocate and a judge. I departed from Simba Village and didn't have the heart to bid farewell to the boys at African Oasis.

I left African Oasis and Diani Beach for Chiromo Garden Hotel Nairobi.

A new experience unfolds.

PART 4

NAIROBI-2

CHIROMO GARDEN HOTEL STORY

Udo was a friend to Inga's son. I knew nothing about Udo, he knew nothing about me. A very thin scrawny and sickly-looking German in his mid-thirties. Although quite handsome with badly cut light brown hair, he was married to an estranged Kenyan woman.

> *"What's going on, I didn't know anything about this. Just because I'm sick sometimes, is this how Reiner is going to treat me. Push me out."*

After a long discussion with Udo, I discovered he was the hotel manager. We decided to work together.

> *"Now you're here Janette you'll get drawn into all sorts of shit you nothing about. You don't know the real Reiner he can be evil."*

How bad can it get, I thought.

THE FIGHT AT CHIROMO

That evening the bar was packed, the usual mixture of crooks and villains. Regular undesirable faces getting very drunk and exchanging stories alongside the customary fulltime prostitutes. A small group of Asians also gathered in one corner. There was a sudden uproar when two men began fighting outside in the car park. I ran outside to see what was going on to stop the punch up, with staff yelling.

> *"Don't go mummy it's too dangerous!"*

I leapt between the two angry men not thinking about my own safety! One was a Sikh; his turban went flying across the car park like a big orange ball. The other man much smaller I recognised as a bodyguard called Rachid. Blood poured down the face of the Sikh, as Rachid lashed out again, and again. Hitting his target with every blow. A much older bigger Kenyan man pushed and pulled me, landing a mighty punch on the Sikh. My long hair was tangled in his hand, he abruptly stopped, realising he might hurt me. I managed to shove him aside and stood between the fighting men.

"Stop this madness, you idiots!"

Instantly they backed away, the Sikh ran to collect his orange turban, then rushed over to his old battered green car. Unexpectedly he came rushing back through the crowds that gathered, waving an iron golf club, and screaming.

"I will kill you, you bastard!"

Once again without thought for my own safety I surged forward grabbing the golf club. At the same time desperately trying to push a big angry man away. No one came forward to assist me, as I tried in vain to tackle with a crazed man.

"Please stop this madness!"

Suddenly he withdrew but insisted he would have his revenge another day. Sirens echoed in the gardens, as several police arrived, pushing through the ever-increasing mob, and arrested both men on the spot.

No questions asked.

> *"It's ok mummy, go in the hotel and shut the door."* remarked a small thin police officer.

The two angry men were released after a couple of hours and made their way to Chiromo to apologise.

> *"We are very sorry, can we sit at the bar for a quiet drink, we want to buy you one please, we are very sorry for the trouble."*

I accepted the apology and the two large vodkas with ice and lemon. Both men were to become my friends after this strange event, and I was seen as a hero by everyone.

GOING OUT WITH ASIANS

After the fight in the car park incident the Asian community bought me free drinks.

> *"You need a break from here,"* suggested an Asian friend.

> *"I can't leave."*

> *"Yes, you can leave you can do anything you want to do. We have known Reiner years, we can take care of him, you come with us."*

I asked Udo for permission to leave the hotel and have lunch out with my new friends.

> *"Yah, Janette you go, that's fine no problem."*

A delightful Indian restaurant only minutes away from Chiromo, the food delicious and the company so uplifting. They told me they watch out for each other all the time and are not afraid of Reiner. The silent ones you cannot see coming, are the ones to worry about.

> *"Our culture is quiet; you do not know when we are coming, Reiner is like a bull and very loud."*

I respected their company.

INGA AND KLAUS CRAZY STORY

> *"Inga and Klaus told me a crazy story about them in court with Reiner, is it true Udo?"*

"Yes, and so much more Janette, I told you you're going to get dragged into all kinds of shit."

I questioned Reiner concerning Inga and Klaus.

"Reiner what about Inga and Klaus taking you to court for their partnership with you, you never mentioned this to me. So, who am I in partnership with?"

"The lying bastards, I could have them killed."

I returned with Reiner's answer as Inga and Klaus huddled in a dark corner puffing cigarettes and creating a cloud of smoke.

"He says you're lying bastards, and he could have you killed," I giggled.

"Are you not afraid of Reiner Janette?"

"No, you can only die once so that's a bonus!"

"Reiner is terrified of ghosts and spirits anything he cannot control. We had such good times with him once Janette, I love him, but I hate him too," Inga replied.

Reiner would merely ignore them. Yet would two strangers be eating, smoking, and drinking in his hotel for free? It was a very peculiar situation.

"You should have told Janette our story, why are you telling her lies and we are nothing to do with Chiromo," Inga demanded.

Reiner laughed and turned his back on the odd German couple. Nothing was what it appeared to be in Chiromo.

Nothing was what it appeared to be… in Kenya!

BEN PONT

A regular customer at Chiromo was an interesting character called Ben Pont.

He was passing through after meeting up with a friend at Esperia or Impala Hotel. Ben was chatting to Wolfgang, Inga, and Klaus, a gathering of the Germans and beckoned me over.

"Come have a drink with us Janette."

They chatted about Reiner as per norm. The following week I met Jenny his beautiful English wife.

"Have you met Jenny, she's English," Inga asked.

"Please to meet you Jenny, so good to hear an English voice."

Apparently living in the bush for several years, Ben particularly good looking, an actor and film producer of Dutch origin, especially charming and educated. I enjoyed his company very much. Jenny also a film director, enchanting, attractive and softly spoken with a quaint English accent. Her brother a famous wildlife artist called Simon Combes.

"What's going on Janette? You look like you need a break from Chiromo."

"Your right Ben, I'm tired and it's all work."

"Come out for tea tomorrow we can get a friend to pick you up. Would you like that?" asked Jenny.

"Thanks, I'd love that, I'm free after 11am."

The next morning, a driver arrived to take me out of Nairobi to Ben's house. On route I observed the shocking poverty on the outskirts of the township. It was quite appalling and upsetting to see people living in such dreadful conditions. Nevertheless, I had witnessed similar conditions in Cape

Town South Africa many years back, when working on ships in the Merchant Navy.

We arrived at the property, an old colonial style house, surrounded with mature shrubs and flowers. I was greeted at the door.

> *"Hey, welcome Janette, come in, come in."*

A very curious house filled with an abundance of paintings, framed photographs, and fascinating collectables. Jenny served up a delightful variety of small sandwiches and an assortment of tasty cakes on a silver tray. A large pot of hot tea, poured into bone China delicate cups with saucers and stirred with a silver spoon.

Very colonial I thought.

> *"Oh, this is nice to have female company for a change,"* giggled Jenny.

Jenny and I chatted about her brother's incredible wildlife artwork, and intriguing stories of Ben's exploits. Then some conversation about Dylan my Romany gypsy lover, how we met and the romance that brought us out to Africa. Later Ben arrived with his oriental dish of the day an Indonesian meal called *nasi goreng*. We sipped chilled white wine and listened to great classical music. Followed by a brief viewing of a Kenyan film with Ben starring as a Rambo type hero. It seemed quite surreal with him sitting in the room giving a running commentary on the movie, as he killed people in the bush. More wine and food, as they delighted in talking about the big break they just secured. It was to film Michael Jackson's new video here in Kenya. They were very excited about it. I was too.

> *"Oh, please get a signed photograph for Dylan he is a great fan of Michael Jackson, and dances like him too."*

> *"Yeah, sure."*

Recently they thought a burglar was attempting to enter via a window. Ben shot a few rounds through the shutters and hit the guard checking on the security that night. It was a terrible accident, but life was like that in the bush. Just another day in Kenya.

They thought I was crazy to ever contemplate making a life in Kenya, without having the right connections.

> *"You will be betrayed, robbed, conned, or killed unless the gods are on your side. Or you have bigger magic than the Africans,"* Ben chuckled.

They thought I was a very courageous woman to work with Reiner, saying he was not a good man, and I should be very watchful and cautious of him.

> *"You need to give people a chance and trusting is good."*

> *"You trust him? I wouldn't trust him. He's a notorious criminal, the Moser is Mafia," laughed Ben.*

I was increasingly learning more and more about my friend and new partner Reiner Moser. We finished the day with fun and laughter, then I bid them farewell. I would return to Chiromo for more of the madness and Reiner.

MISSED MEETING WITH NGENGI MUNGAI

Reiner arrived in an exceptionally aggressive mood and a most unpleasant aspect of his nature. He was out drinking all day with business friends and now yelling in German at everyone and glaring at me.

"You were supposed to meet my other partner Ngengi Mungai. If you leave the hotel I want to know exactly where you are and who you are with, do you hear me."

"Am I a prisoner, must I ask your permission to go out, besides you were not here, and I left word with Udo."

"Where were you?"

"Having tea with Ben and Jenny Pont, it was a lovely break from the hotel Reiner."

He began shouting demanding I do exactly what he wanted and should report to him if leaving the hotel.

"I get people killed Janette."

"I have no doubt, but I will return and haunt you. I will appear in your dreams, you will hear my voice in your head, because I am not afraid of you," I snapped.

"Do as I say woman, I always get my own way."

"You're not getting your own way with me Reiner."

"I will." he yelled.

"Only with physical force, you are a tyrant, or you'll pay someone else to do it for you Reiner?"

"Well Janette in the case of me wanting to fuck you, I think I'll be doing it myself. Not paying someone else to do it for me," he laughed.

"Fuck you! I'm going back to Diani Beach."

"Let's look at it this way, we can keep everything going in Diani. Sort out this hotel. There will be plenty of money for us," Reiner ranted.

STANDING UP TO REINER

The Germans and Asians were fascinated by my courage in standing up to Reiner, he was just a drunken bully at times. He was unpredictable, arrogant, and challenging.

I was aware he loved me in his own peculiar way and therefore able to manage him when sober and drunk.

> *"You're not afraid of this man, this is incredible, he gives us the shits. I have never seen Reiner behave like this; hey Janette, you can shut him up,"* Wolfgang remarked.
>
> *"I'll shut him up permanently,"* remarked an Asian friend.

GOING OUT WITH THE ASIANS

In between work I would go out with my new Asian Sikh friends, another day out with Udo and listening to Inga and Klaus crazy stories of life in Germany, on safari and Reiner. The Sikhs were keeping a closer eye on me. They didn't like Reiner but frequented Chiromo for entertainment, watching police, government officials, drug and arms dealers, and half naked prostitutes.

They were all interesting businessmen, but one guy was noticeable, he was Gurdial. He stood out, so handsome with big brown eyes, in his mid-forties. Medium height and build, strong and dynamic.

One day I asked him about his orange turban.

> *"Do you have long hair Gurdial, is it tied up in a knot?"*
>
> *"I will show you one day in private,"* laughing at my inquisitive mind.

Gurdial was married to a short overweight unfriendly lady; she was always yelling at him. Hence his constant visits to

Chiromo and fascination with me. I was impressed by the Asian men, always complimenting me, I would feel safe, and treated with kindness and consideration.

DATE WITH GURDIAL

Another day out with Gurdial and an old Sikh. Do you believe in the unseen world? I asked him.

> *"Yes, and this unseen world must be respected."*
>
> *"Yes, it must be more respected than the physical world, because of that unseen dimension, we come into this one,"* I stated.
>
> *"We like that you want to have a deeper understanding of this, you know this otherworldliness, and you look like an angel,"* Gurdial smiled.
>
> *"Thank you, and do you call upon the gods or those energies to enter this reality."*
>
> *"This is all part of ancient culture. Yes, and it is a pity that modern culture does not understand, isn't it? Like Reiner he is a big bully, and you can see him coming, he is not a god, but thinks he is. He has no conscience, he must understand what is right, what is wrong or good and bad,"* remarked Gurdial.

Old man Sikh said.

> *"We all think you are beautiful. You are like an angel floating around Chiromo. You make us want to come back. Reiner makes us want to come back just to annoy him. Our people have waited a long time to get him. You help us, and we'll help you."*

But I don't betray my friends.

> *"He is not your friend. He's using you,"* retorted Gurdial.

I'm hearing this same story from Inga, Klaus, Ben and Jenny, aside of the Asians. Yet, I do not betray my friends, I am loyal to them.

Later, Reiner came to the hotel and took my hand.

> *"I heard a crazy story about you Janette and the fight with the Asians. My fearless little angel. So, you had a meal out with the handsome Sikh fellow with the beard and turban. He's going to hang around you more now, so that's going to really piss me off, I don't want you seeing him,"* He grunted.

SENT ON AN ERRAND

> *"Udo pay this electricity bill and take Janette with you for safety,"* Reiner yelled.

We paid the electricity bill and decided to enjoy time away from the hotel at Gypsies Bar. When we returned to Chiromo Reiner was still there, we thought it strange because he mentioned an urgent meeting?

> *"Oh, fuck he is still here,"* gasped Udo.

> *"I told you to be here at one o'clock, why did you take so long?"*

> *"Went for a drink, but we've paid the bill, here is the receipt,"* replied Udo.

> *"You were supposed to pay at the court not the electricity company you fucking idiot Udo!"*

> *"I've had enough of your screaming and shouting, you're such a tyrant,"* I said and went to my office across the garden.

REINER ATTACKS UDO IN THE GARDEN

Udo and I had worked long shifts, the hotel was open for twenty-four hours, I was so tired and needed to rest. Walking through the gardens to my room, I heard yelling and shouting and staff running around like headless chickens. I approached the scene, where Reiner had Udo by the throat, strangling him. He was lifting him off the ground, and against the kitchen wall. Udo desperately grabbing at him and trying to get his breath. He was frothing at the mouth.

Reiner was fuming mad and relentless, a crazed animal.

"Reiner stop you're going to kill him."

"Fucking kill him, yes I will kill the fucking bastard," Reiner yelled.

I lunged at Reiner, grabbed his arm but he was demented. I started punching him on his back and arms.

"Reiner please stop, don't hurt him, please!!!"

I moved to the side and hit his face quite hard, he turned and glared at me. The most horrifying stare with bulging eyes and his face purple with rage.

"Hit me you bastard, not Udo!"

He dropped Udo like a rag doll and stomped the ground. Poor Udo fell into a bush utterly breathless and red-faced. Dreadful marks around his throat where he was grabbed. Reiner pulled back his arm with a clenched fist, ready to punch me, but stopped mid-air.

"Fuck you! get away from me! I will fucking kill you; I will kill that bastard and you, and anyone who upsets me now!!!" he screamed in my face.

"You fucking animal I hate you!!" I yelled.

I pulled Udo up from the bush, he couldn't speak and made his way to his room. I departed to mine and left the Bavarian bully to sort out the hotel. Later in the day I visited Udo, he looked dreadful. His face scratched and bruises over his neck and his eyes puffed from crying, he could barely talk.

"Don't ask me about it please, I cannot tell you Janette," he whimpered.

"Udo please tell me, I'm not afraid of his madness."

"If I am killed tomorrow at least you will know it was Reiner, don't ask me anything, or you will end up hanging from the wall too Janette."

Early evening Udo and I sat quietly contemplating what will happen next, then Reiner walked in.

"Ignore him Janette, he will pick on you,"

He strutted over to us, ignoring Udo and clutched my hand.

"Come Janette."

He slowly guided me to his office, opened the cupboard grabbed a bottle of vodka and poured two large drinks.

"Here you will need this, what you have seen today is how I get when I don't get what I want. You're just seeing the result. Remember what it looked like. Now drink up and let us continue… I am going to take you somewhere very nice and show you there is another side of me, that is more attractive. My nature, I am German, and I want things in order, when I ask someone to do something, and they don't, it makes me go crazy. The last thing I want is for you to see me ugly."

I talked to Udo about Reiner's conversation and taking me out to make amends. Udo looked relieved, we hugged.

MAYFAIR HOTEL

We left Chiromo and headed to the Mayfair Hotel. On the way through the restaurant my Asian friends commented on my black dress and blonde wavy hair.

"You are an angel Janette, so beautiful."

"Yes, she is my angel," grunted Reiner.

The Mayfair was extremely busy we had to wait twenty minutes to be served. We sat quietly and apart from the occasional uncomfortable gaze, I enjoyed the meal of steak and vegetables, with red wine. I spotted Bill and Tom Omamo sitting in a corner with two other men, they didn't notice me, however. After a couple more drinks I found the courage to speak about Udo.

"How could you be so unkind and cruel?"

"You think I am unkind, I'm the one paying for his treatment."

"What treatment?"

"He'll be dead soon with Aids, people misunderstand me Janette, I get crazy. I scare people and then I get what I want."

"But you get what you want through force, you bully, torment and hurt people, why?"

"Because that's all I know," he said.

"No, I have seen a very charming Reiner, that's the man I can relate to and love as my friend. Not the lunatic."

He smiled and touched my hand.

"You bring out the best and the worst in me. You are a big mystery to me, Janette the enigma, let us forget about the Udo story, it was his own fault, he knows it and so do I."

"But one day it could be my fault and you would strangle me too," I said.

"No not strangle you, have you shot, ha-ha! No Janette, I love you."

ANOTHER DAY OUT WITH UDO

Udo wanted to take me out for a few hours around Nairobi. The idea was good but as we were traveling through the city, we witnessed a white jeep drive over a young man who had collapsed in the road.

As the jeep bumped its way over the body people stood motionless for that moment, then carried on their routine of trying to survive another day in Nairobi. Life holds little value; people are surviving day by day with no regard to anyone else.

Stop! Stop! Yelled a small odd-looking white man, with a baldhead, wearing grey shorts and a fancy pink shirt. Waving a walking stick in the air as he pointed in the opposite direction. Udo and I rushed to the old gentleman as he tried to steady himself against a shop window.

"Bloody bastard took my bag and pushed me over," he shouted.

I rushed into the busy street to stop the young boy getting away with the robbery. As I pushed passed a small group of street kids, a scruffy man in his twenties jumped out waving a huge knife at me. The thief ran up an alley and disappeared. It happened so quickly, I never thought of endangering myself, I simply wanted to help the old man get his bag back. Quickly realising my vulnerability, I pushed my way through the group and made a dash over to Udo.

After a few minutes we pacified the shaken victim.

"Sorry we couldn't get your bag back."

We hastily returned to the car to continue our day out.

The irritated man in a truck behind, kept his hand on the horn continually honking, we slowly made our way through Nairobi. It was bedlam, no one would give way, the traffic came to a complete standstill.

It was far too hot and dusty to be stuck in traffic, so we pulled over near Gypsies Bar for a cold beer. Before we had a chance to shut the car doors, a band of street kids encircled us, yelling and screaming for money. About ten of them pushing, shoving, and kicking. We were surrounded like a pack of wolves, it was terrifying. Luckily, friends nearby Gypsies Bar could see our plight and scared them off with sticks. The long cold beer quenched my thirst, as the sweat rolled down my dusty face, I began to wish I had stayed at work that day. It couldn't get any worse I thought.

THE ROAD ACCIDENT

Driving back to Chiromo a terrible road accident and all hell had let loose. It was ghastly, as crowds of people shouting, trying to drag two men out from their car. They looked petrified, as the manic crowd pulled at their shirts and began hitting them. The lifeless body of a young woman lying in the filthy street. Police arrived waving batons and beating people over the head, as they forced the hungry mob back behind the police vehicles. Suddenly a woman lunged forward brandishing a knife and began attacking the two men in the car. She was promptly brought down to the ground and severely kicked and punched numerous times, by the police officer. We were waved on by other officials gathered to witness the furore and gradually made our way safely back to Chiromo.

"Thanks for a lovely day out, Udo, we must do it again," I laughed.

"Hold me please, I have Aids… who cares?"

"I do," and held him in my arms.

Udo sobbed and thanked me. We hugged for a while.

"Janette Reiner is mad about you, he wants you, be very careful he is a very dangerous man as you can see, he turns crazy for nothing," he remarked.

"We will look after each other Udo, he has too much pressure on him and he can't handle it at the moment, aside of me trying to fit in as a manager and partner, he wants sex with me, I know it."

A few days later Reiner handed over a file of official documents, with title to the Chiromo Garden Hotel in joint names and signed by a judge.

"You see Janette here it is the partnership agreement; I will get a copy for you.

TERESA HAS GOSSIP ABOUT DYLAN THE PLAYBOY

Teresa informed me Dylan was out at night spending our business money in Diani casinos, with her son Marco and a black girl. Evidently often out with other local girls. She said Dylan would be visiting Chiromo with Marco. She understood Dylan's companion was introduced by Bill Omamo and working at Indian Ocean Hotel.

[*The police chiefs' daughter from Ukunda*].

How extraordinary I thought.

DYLAN SURPRISE VISIT

Marco and Dylan were arriving at the weekend. I was excited but a little apprehensive due to the casino story that Teresa revealed. Was it true? I would soon find out.

Dylan was sitting with Marco and Reiner, Teresa arrived shortly after. Both boys looked very dishevelled, untidy, and tired, Dylan appeared rather sheepish and Marco basically awkward.

"What's this on your lips Dylan?"

"I had mosquito bites; I've been scratching them."

I had heard that same excuse before. There was an uncomfortable distance between us. I could detect the lies and see the guilt in his eyes, there was no emotional connection. I'll deal with it later; I have more important things to attend to.

Reiner made a comment.

"Those scabby lips are from kissing pussy with black girls."

Dylan alarmed by the comment, and I could sense Reiner was playing games with him and exposing his lies in front of everyone. Reiner was always seeking a way to unmask Dylan's behaviour, but I was too blind to see it or accept it was even a possibility. I didn't enjoy Dylan's company nor want to be near him, I was embarrassed and angry. I joined Rachid and Betty for a drink. Rachid from the fight with the Sikh and Betty Kenyatta were two regulars at the bar who I liked very much. He was tall fit and particularly good looking, her bodyguard yes, but there was more to the story, it was Kenya. She was a chubby-faced well-dressed girl, always giggling and cheerful. I understood her to be a great granddaughter of Jomo Kenyatta. She brought a little class to Chiromo, with Rachid at her side. They both agreed the prostitutes must vacate the rooms above the restaurant and renovate the whole place to attract a higher-class clientele.

TAKING RESPONSIBILITY FOR INGA AND KLAUS

I approached Inga and Klaus.

> *"Reiner wants you to leave Chiromo, he's angry at you constantly eating and drinking. You could do some work in the hotel; it will be good for you."*
>
> *"Janette, if we must leave… we're easy pickings… our goose is cooked,"* remarked Klaus.

Reiner ordered me to convey to Inga and Klaus, he wanted them to leave the hotel, but I had become relatively fond of the odd couple. After a short chat with Inga, it was decided she would assist with the bedrooms and me. Klaus general maintenance and gardens. I reported back to Reiner the latest development. He grabbed my arm and pulled me towards him with a tight grip.

> *"You upset me with Udo and other people will suffer for it now, I said get rid of the two Germans they are in the fucking way!"*
>
> *"You put them in this situation. You are responsible for them,"* I replied.
>
> *"I am not responsible for anyone,"* he huffed.
>
> *"They will be my responsibility, I'll get them working, it's better than having them sit around all day eating and drinking the profits."*
>
> *"Good idea Janette, make the lazy bastards work,"* he laughed.

HOTEL UPGRADE IDEA

We thought we'd get it up and running and looking lovely, Reiner just wanted to bleed it dry and dump it, and then move onto the next scenario, instead of cleaning up the place and attracting more business. I suggested to Reiner shutting the disco, it was always empty and a magnet for criminal activity.

> *"Nobody wants to come here, prostitutes living upstairs, arguments being aired. Police and criminals rubbing shoulders it's a den of iniquity."*

I mentioned sprucing up the front garden and advertise a big BBQ (nyama choma) and have an event, perhaps with some live music?

> *"Yes, let's promote that for a while. That brings in families,"* said Inga.

There were numerous outstanding debts, I needed to settle them immediately. Staff salaries were overdue for months. Cash from the bar, restaurant, and hotel rooms were retained for the court and advocate fees. I hadn't received any payment as manageress either.

Udo was given another cheque for the electricity bill, it bounced. It was becoming a nightmare trying to juggle everything, as further court action letters, and the impending bailiffs notice arrived.

Meanwhile the madness at Chiromo Garden continued.

THE MAJOR ENSELMO SAGA

Major Paula Enselmo's unfaithful husband Rolph was having a secret affair with a local prostitute called Mary. Rolph fooled Paula into believing he was giving swimming lessons to Mary's daughter, at the hotel. This he revealed to me after a wild drunken afternoon in one of the guest rooms. Uproar across the gardens that disturbed my concentration. Suddenly a gun shot fired followed by more yelling and another shot. Mary rushed from the scene with Rolph stumbling through the door waving a gun in his hand. I dashed to the room with Inga who was yelling in German at Rolph, as he roared obscenities at both of us. In the room on the floor, I found an empty cartridge, I placed in my pocket and gave instructions to the cleaners to make good the room.

> *"Please don't tell Paula she will go crazy, please don't tell her Janette, she will leave me,"* mumbled Rolph.

I demanded an explanation, but he was too incoherent to understand, but Inga chatted in German to him. I understood that he had taken Mary to Kindani with Klaus, Inga's slobbery husband on the invitation of Wolfgang the owner. We believed it was a male only trip, they needed a few days away to get drunk in the bush and bond. Kindani was approximately six hours drive away from Nairobi and Paula new nothing of the female company. She was delighted that the boys were having a male bonding long weekend. A couple of days later Paula popped in to invite me for dinner, when she spotted Rolph with Mary. Asking for my opinion on what was going on I remained silent. I did not want to lie to her, and I was in an uncomfortable situation. An argument erupted with Paula she began yelling and blaming me for throwing Mary and Rolph out of the hotel.

> *"How dare you treat my husband so disrespectfully; I know he's younger than me and likes Mary's company but that's no reason to send them packing from Chiromo?"*

I tried to explain amicably they were both drunk and disorderly shouting and upsetting the guests. She refused to listen to me and became overly aggressive.

"You will not like it Paula, do not force me to tell you the whole story!"

Paula insisted Rolph did nothing wrong but get a little drunk. However, I explained with reference to the gunshots, but remained silent about Mary in the room. She refused to believe her husband's stupid and reckless behaviour. Constantly insulting me as a dumb foolish woman, until I produced the cartridge. After seeing it she at once asked that I hand it over to her, I refused to.

"I will pay you Janette please hand it over."

She continued to offer me a generous sum of money.

"No thank you I'll keep it a bit longer."

After she had calmed down, she explained in detail how on various occasions she helped Rolph out of trouble when he was a soldier in Germany. But this incident could cost her expected promotion and transfer to America. Rolph could not enter the USA, she repeated anxiously.

I handed the shell to Inga. I was no longer involved. Paula promised to make my life hell, she was a US Major and carried a gun? Yes, I was fully aware she packed a pistol she had shown me often. However, I was not troubled or endangered by her threats, even after reminding me she threatened to shoot Reiner if he did not return the loan she made to him. We never spoke again, and although it upset me, I was not too unhappy we parted ways. Just another day in Nairobi I thought.

EVENING OF GHOSTS AND SPIRITS WITH REINER

Inga, Klaus, and a few other people were sitting together and laughing when they spotted me.

> *"Kommen hier schnell, come here quickly, we are talking about the mad dog Reiner yelling at everyone and especially you Janette."*
>
> *"Inga, I am not afraid of him and he's just a big bully who can't get his own way, he must be afraid of something?"*
>
> *"Well, Janette we were just laughing about him shitting himself when he thought he saw a poltergeist, ha-ha, he went white and shook, it was funny, eh Klaus. He isn't afraid of people he's terrified of spirits."*
>
> *"Thanks Inga now I know what to do?"*
>
> *"What can you do, where can you conjure up a ghost from to scare the shit out of him again. I want to see it don't you Klaus?"*
>
> *"Aye, Inga he is a bastard, he wants putting down like a mad dog,"* Klaus said.

The conversation continued for an hour or so, as we chatted about local people creating magic spells, juju men and witch doctors. The conversation abruptly ended, as Reiner came charging over to our table demanding to know what we were giggling about.

> *"I'm not bothered about what you call magic, witch doctors or juju men. Just shoot the bastards, the quickest magic is shooting somebody,"* he grunted.
>
> *"What? That's not magic at all, it's just killing somebody, what would you know about real magic, you are just bloody ignorant of this type of invisible power."* I replied.
>
> *"No, shoot them, I'm more afraid of them when they are dead. I can handle the living. You can be dead if I choose,"* he laughed.

"I will die once as Janette, and I understand magic before my death, I'll come back and haunt you until I find another body to reincarnate."

He went white and his pupils dilated. Beads of sweat developed on his forehead; his breathing altered.

"I can't deal with things I can't see!" he grumbled.

"Oh, I am in my element with spirits and ghosts, they like me, yet you're afraid of ghosts, a big man like you."

Someone else remarked.

"You'll give me the shivers talking about ghosts he doesn't like them do you Reiner."

"So, what are you afraid of Janette?" asked Reiner.

I knew he was trying to find my weakness; I would not reveal spiders or big moths; they are a phobia at times, but not always. I didn't want him to have anything on me.

"I don't seem to have any sense of fear I guess it's because I know what awaits me on the other side. If I should die by your hand or by your doing, I'd come back and haunt you. Especially now that I know you're afraid of ghosts. Yes, I will appear in your dreams and in your mind, you will hear my voice a constant whisper in your head. When you close your eyes tonight you will see me, my spirit will be watching you."

ANOTHER CRAZY NIGHT

A terribly busy lively night packed with the Asian community. Reiner was entertaining a Kenyan businessman in the restaurant. I walked by the bar and greeted my Sikh friends.

"Good evening, everyone, how are you?"

I always made a fuss of them, I kissed Gurdial on the cheek and he squeezed my hand, by the time I approached Reiner, he was seething.

"How dare you not come to me first."

"Good evening, Reiner. How are you?"

Visibly frustrated he yelled.

"How am I?"

BANG! His glass banged down on the table, grunting in German, as the Kenyan businessman hastily departed.

"You are nothing without my say so Janette."

"But I am your partner, am I not?"

Gurdial and another Sikh rushed over to defend me.

"Hey, hey, Janette is indeed very special, she has made Chiromo come to life, it's nice having such a beautiful woman here. We are tired of the angry Germans. We prefer the beautiful English rose."

"So now everybody is in love with Janette?"

"Yes Reiner, of course we love her!"

Gurdial nodded reassuringly.

"But darlings I'm only doing my job as best I can, I am nothing without all you beautiful men," I smiled.

He puffed up like a peacock, mumbling in German.

"I will say what I will say in my own language in my own place!"

"I thought I was your partner Reiner?" I asked.

Thumping on the table to make his point.

"Do you have to do that? I can understand what you are saying without you having to bang on the table."

"I'm not afraid of anyone," he hollered.

I reached across the table and gently touched him.

"Nor am I Reiner."

MORE REINER ENTERTAINMENT

The following evening.

Reiner arrived seeming exhausted, unshaven a complete wreck.

"You look dreadful, have you been up all night?" I asked him.

"Shit that was scary! every time I closed my eyes, I could see you. In fact, I had to drink more and more because every time I closed my eyes you were getting bigger. You were in my dreams; I close my eyes and you're there."

"That's right."

I agreed with him, seizing the opportunity to reinforce I will visit him in his dreams.

"Imagine that Reiner imagine it now."

He closed his eyes.

"I'm right there with you, can you see me and feel my spirit there now?"

I touched his hand to embed the suggestion, an old hypnosis trick.

"You're being haunted, and I am not dead."

He opened his eyes; I grinned and turned my head.

"You know paranormal Janette; you know these things."

"You prefer to shoot people that's easy, I send my spirit self in a dream to disturb them."

"Don't Janette! it makes me crazy; I am tired."

"You are afraid of spirits and ghosts the big brave Bavarian, what a laugh that is."

ANOTHER SCARY TIME

Wolfgang arrived a couple of nights later with another German called Hacky, he was a news reporter for a German TV company. We had great pleasure telling the ghost story.

"Reiner is shitting himself because Janette has frightened him with her spirit and ghost stories. He said she keeps popping into his mind and when he closes his eyes, so now he can't sleep," laughed Wolfgang.

"You must be careful of him, he is fucking crazy," said Hacky.

A few uneventful days passed and no sign of Reiner, he was keeping his distance. The Germans were fascinated by the story they had seen him drinking in Impala Hotel and telling the story to the old African man. He couldn't understand this strange power that you have and why he is dubious of you now.

"I have never seen Reiner behave like this. You have a special ability to shut him up, the mad dog is quiet," Wolfgang laughed.

"Come let us shut him up too!" yelled Inga.

"I'll shut him up permanently!" hollered Klaus.

"You are not afraid of him Janette, this is incredible. He gives us the shits!"

Wolfgang sniggered and shook his head.

"Hey, get Janette another very large vodka bitte, anyone that can put the shits up Reiner Moser is a friend of mine hahaha."

Creating a diversion, an illusion, like a rabbit out of the hat, is only one type of magic. There is also *Real Magic.*

Reiner departed Chiromo for the coast.

THE CAMEROONS' STORY

The chilled air on a dark night in Nairobi brought two very peculiar characters to the door of the Chiromo Hotel.

"We booked three days ago, why don't you have any record of us, where is the manager?"

A tall smartly dressed man, with a full round face and chubby hands fumbling around in a colourful cloth bag for his passport. Quietly standing beside him was a short thin odd-looking fellow with bushy eyebrows and a matching moustache, which looked fake. Both men were wearing flamboyant traditional African clothes and behaving nervously. This attracted the attention of the night porter Morris, who was intensely scrutinising them, but did not interfere.

"It's ok, I'm the manager what can I do for you?" I asked them.

They seemed incredibly surprised to see a mzungu blonde woman, as the hotel manager. I explained there was no record of them booking in, but we had rooms available.

"Hakuna matata," no problem.

"Follow me, but leave your passports at the desk, I will return them to you later, after I have taken your details."

The week that followed Chiromo drama increased with these two strange Cameroons playing the main characters. I discovered they were drug dealers. A couple of days passed with them both making phone calls and mysterious Africans coming and going at all hours. Late nights and taxis fetching more people from the nightclubs. The Cameroons mentioned they were going away for a day or so and would return late at night. The following morning Inga and Klaus came rushing into my office puffing and panting, with sweat pouring down their faces and both trying to speak, at the same time.

"Janette, you will never believe this; we were cleaning the Cameroons' room when water started pouring out of the toilet. Look, we found this stuff in the cistern. Look it is full, full of cash in this plastic bag. Let us keep it, let us hide it and pretend we know nothing!"

Inga's face was bright red and matching her badly dyed hair, as she vigorously shook the wet plastic bag at me and yelled.

"I can't believe it, our prayers are answered, there is so much money we are going to be alright Janette, don't let Reiner know about this, eh my friend?"

"We can't touch this money you fool, its drug money, they will kill us," I shouted back.

Inga and Klaus were extremely disappointed with me; I ordered them to put it back before the Cameroons returned, afraid for all of us.

"Don't open it Inga, we will never have any luck, please put it back right now."

> *"You fool Janette! this is our big break, our chance to get out of the shit, you will regret it."*

The package returned to its hiding place in the toilet and the water wiped up, leaving the room spic and span for the mysterious Cameroons. Eventually returning to Chiromo and none the wiser, however, someone informed the police Cameroon drug dealers were staying in the hotel. Later revealed to me by a friendly police officer, the money removed from the toilet to a crooked police officer's home and shared by the three who arrested the drug dealers. The mysterious package of money did not get mentioned in court, and the passports turned out to be fakes. Just another day in Kenya, I thought.

I was not getting coerced by Inga into keeping the drug money nor did I regret it. Kenya was so corrupt; the police were either taking bribes or paid off for turning a blind eye. Who to trust was a big issue, certainly not the local police force, government officials, or strangers in the night.

THE ANDREAS KOELTZ STORY

A phone call from Dylan, a brief account concerning a notably top secret and especially important mission for Reiner. He would only say it was essential for him to help a German friend of Reiner's, no details given. I should not worry he will arrive in Nairobi within the next few weeks. I was concerned about his involvement, but Reiner had good connections in the government and no harm could come to him.

If only I had the full story, I could have prevented the terrifying nightmare that was to follow.

The man Reiner and Dylan were helping was a wanted criminal; he had obtained a fortune from the largest security company in Germany by hacking a computer system. He discovered a way to open the safe and steal over 2million Deutsche Marks. Sending these newly gotten funds to different countries around the world. Also arriving in Kenya with bags of cash from the haul. He bought a beautiful house in Diani Beach from German Joe the wealthy *Mafia* businessman, married to Narima for cash. Narima a wealthy Asian beauty often seen in the company of the eccentric English John Bland.

The man in question was Andreas Koeltz and Interpol were in hot pursuit. He was to appear in court in Mombasa and Reiner his new criminal friend, would arrange bail, for a large fee, it was Kenya. Who else would be involved in this costly ordeal would be Moses Kurgat the crooked advocate, Matua the sleazy bent police officer, and later a corrupt judge. Bail arranged with a prominent government official heading the shady group, with Reiner dishing out their proper *pesa kidogo.* The stolen cash was handed over to Reiner in a plastic shopping bag, under the table in Walter's Inn, and Dylan was witness to the whole sordid affair. Naively drawn into this web of deception, it would later almost cost us our lives!

What might have seemed like a game of cops and robbers at the time, would later have drastic repercussions. Reiner decided to book Koeltz, Dylan and himself in the Mombasa Beach Hotel. Dylan would function as a bodyguard for Andreas. At the same time Reiner suggested to Dylan if he knew any local girl from Ukunda that would be prepared to stay a couple of days with Koeltz, at a price. Dylan promptly suggested a miss Jessie Mwkali who he had met at Shakatak nightclub. Reiner promptly registered her to stay in Koeltz room, Kurgat and the sleazy Matua also booked in, on the same floor. Meanwhile urgent steps to hastily produce a second passport for Koeltz and a secret hideaway for him in the suburbs of Nairobi. Whilst all this cloak and dagger was going on in Mombasa, I continued dealing with the events unfolding at Chiromo.

Top insurance agents and other secret police flew in to seize property and apply for an extradition. Reiner was rapidly making an escape route for his incarcerated new friend and could only see making a fast buck in doing so. Kurgat and Matua returned to Nairobi with cash in hand, and the Mombasa judge received his share. Following shortly after, would be the mastermind of the unlawful plan, Reiner himself, leaving Dylan alone to guard Koeltz. Finally, briefed on the situation by Reiner, my reaction was sheer horror!

"You idiot! what the bloody hell have you done?"

Not only jeopardising Dylan by losing his residency and work permit, but also placing him in a life-threatening scenario. I screamed at Reiner as he tried to calm the explosive situation down, by holding my hand assuring me there was nothing to be concerned about.

"How could you Reiner?"

I sobbed uncontrollably, police involvement was bad enough, but this was a genuine problem. We argued and fought for twenty minutes or so, as I drank large vodkas to ease the stress, then called the Mombasa hotel to air my opinion to Dylan, he could only reply with.

"I thought it was a clever idea, as Koeltz has given me a Harley Davidson motorbike and a speed jet. They are at the apartment, and he has promised to give me money too."

"What a fool you are. This is extremely dangerous and illegal."

I yelled as he begged me not to worry. I was furious that Dylan would be involved and implicated in this tangled web of deception. At the same time Koeltz began to fear for his life and heard it was all a setup for Reiner to obtain yet more money from his heist. Two plain clothed policemen arrived at the Mombasa hotel and demanded money from Dylan; they both feared the worst was yet to come. They vacated the hotel after receiving a warning phone call and headed for the centre of Mombasa. On route, they needed to change vehicles, and later discovered two mysterious men had fired shots at that car.

During Dylan's stay with Koeltz he had offered him money various times, but he always refused to take it. Koeltz believed this young Englishman was the only person with whom he was safe. He offered his heavy gold ring and chain to Dylan, but he refused the gifts. Matua the sleazy police officer summoned to return to Mombasa and ease the pressure from the two anxious men, now in hiding.

Reiner requested Udo and I should look for a safe house in the Nairobi suburbs, to hide Andreas, he offered two addresses, it was an emergency plan and to pick up a forged passport from his German Mafia contacts, Udo and I refused to get involved. He was furious!

RETURN TO CHIROMO AND REINER SAGA

Whilst the saga continued in Mombasa, the events to follow at Chiromo were equally alarming and very unsettling. Reiner charged into my office, I was reprimanded for going out with Udo to collect something, without telling anyone at Chiromo. He discussed the Andreas saga at Mombasa Beach Hotel; I listened with great concern for Dylan's welfare. I left and sat at the bar; he followed me. Reiner bluntly expressed his desire to have an affair with me.

> *"Don't be so ridiculous Reiner."*

Dropping my drink over my clothes.

> *"I love you as a friend, but I would never have an affair with you Reiner. Why would I want to sleep with another man when in love with Dylan? Why would I ever want to hurt him? I would never betray him. You are a fool if you think I would."*

> *"Fool, you're the fool, Janette what do you think he is doing at the Hotel in Mombasa? Just a bodyguard!"* he shouted into my face…

> *"You are over forty years old, don't think he is faithful to you, he is a hot-blooded young man of twenty-five, the women are all over him in the discos. He is surrounded by beautiful girls in Mombasa, as he was in Nairobi. Don't you think for one moment he has not cheated on you? He is doing that right now in Mombasa. You are the bloody fool!"*

He grabbed my arm and pulled me from the seat shoved me out of the bar. As I tried to pull away, he repeated.

> *"I tell you on my children's lives, I swear to you it is true!"* he hollered.

Then marched me back to the office.

Intuitively I believed Reiner, then another thought, no it's not possible he wouldn't hurt me, I tried to compose myself as we sat glaring at each other. There was plenty to drink in the cabinet, so I poured two vodkas, as Reiner lit the cigarettes, in silence.

> *"Janette, you know how I feel, I would love an affair with you. You are the woman of my dreams, beautiful, intelligent; you*

would look far better by my side. Dylan is much too young for you; this boy is an idiot. Okay you look good together, but what about in five years' time, you will be too old for this silly boy. Sweet Janette, I didn't want to hurt you, it's so easy for me to remove him from the equation, in fact, I could do it with one phone call," he smirked.

There was no point in arguing with him, I kept silent.

"Do you think I would not do this? The idiot could go missing in the bush and never found. Remember there are places where the government dump bodies, people disappear every day in Kenya. What about the English lady in the Mara, she was in the way and removed?"

"What are you saying, do you know something about this story?"

"This is Kenya Janette, it's who you know that counts," he boasted.

Yes, I had known the Julie Ward story, she was from Suffolk England, it was an unsolved mystery, and I might be the next victim?

"You are hurting I know because your baby is fucking a younger woman, I understand how you must feel, especially as she is a black girl too. I could satisfy you much more than a boy can, I have a big cock and very experienced. Well at my age I should be, ha-ha," he was taunting me.

I sobbed uncontrollably at the thought of my gypsy lover in that hotel with another woman, a young black girl, my whole world fell apart. There was a deathly silence for about five minutes, then I cried silently into my folded arms as Reiner looked on.

"I asked you and Udo to do something very important for me, but you refused to help out why?" He asked.

"You coerced Dylan into this nightmare Andreas story, but I'm not helping you Reiner, you've gone too far."

RETREAT TO MY ROOM

I left the office and rushed back to my room across the gardens, the last room of an empty block. Fumbling with the key and dropping my bag on the grass, I was very confused and troubled.

I wanted to shower and change my clothes. The cool water gushing out over my head as I wept for my lover. After drying, I slipped into a fine cream lace dressing gown. The bedside light dimly lit the dark room; it was peaceful, only the sound of my beating heart. Sitting on the bed I reflected upon every word that was spoken. In a state of uncertainty, I began to question the possibility of Dylan's betrayal, a reality.

It can't be, Dylan would never hurt me; we made a solemn oath, when I gave him a gold gypsy ring before leaving England. He promised to always be faithful and loyal to me. All these random conflicting thoughts churning around in my mind, I was going crazy. Smoking, drinking, crying then laughing, yes, I must be crazy to consider what Reiner said could be true.

It was effortless to eliminate people in Kenya who stood in the way. If he turned me against Dylan, it would serve his agenda to have me! My God he is a monster just as Inga and Klaus said a few weeks earlier. He poisoned one partner, and then another was killed in an unexplained car accident. Another friend told me he shot people.

I was aware he served years in a Nairobi prison for a big money scandal, that involved the government. He transferred a fortune via his bank in Kenya to his brother in

Germany. However, not realising how stupid his brother was, when the fortune suddenly appeared in his account, he panicked and promptly refused to accept it. The German bank hastily returned the funds back to Kenya. Thus, confusing the newly acquired computer system and ringing alarm bells of fraud.

Arrested, charged, and sentenced to prison for ten years Reiner, remained silent about the whole affair. For keeping quiet, the other shady top government officials involved, remained loyal to Reiner. Thereby, living a good life inside the murky prison and eventually released after serving four years. Having made his mark in government circles, by not spilling the beans on the other villains who were running the country, he could move about freely. Now he was a good asset to those corrupt men in government. It was more a jungle in Nairobi, than out in the bush.

I tossed and turned-on top of the sheets punching the pillows in anger and frustration. It was past one o'clock in the morning, when suddenly the door burst open and the dim light casting a shadow across Reiner's face.

There stood the big Bavarian proudly sticking out his huge chest, as he performed a peculiar twitch with his arm, when angered. His red face puffed up, his piercing bloodshot eyes glaring at me. Waving his arms in the air as he stomped the ground with a tremendous thud, he declared.

> *"Tonight, my dear you will be mine; I will have you regardless!"*

He slammed the door shut.

> *"There is more to tell you, then you will realise the whole truth my dear,"* in a very determined voice.

I was startled and alarmed, he was an exceptionally strong man, and my room was too far away if I screamed. Who would come anyway, he was the boss? No one would respond, everyone was afraid of him. This oversized big-mouthed bully, how dare he barge his way into my room. His jacket removed, his tie in one hand he was undoing the buttons of his shirt with difficulty.

"Reiner please go, I beg you please leave now we will still be friends. I will never talk about this to anyone. Just go!"

He stepped towards me.

"Get me a drink."

"You have had enough."

Reaching out he grabbed the bottle of vodka on my table and gulped. He was my friend, my business partner; he had taken a great deal of money from me what should I do? I stood to lose everything. I had lost my sweetheart if it was true. I was anxious, and confused, whatever was about to happen, it would change our future forever. Should I give in and let him have his way, perhaps it would simplify this intense situation. I couldn't possibly fight him off; he was too powerful. Maybe if we talked awhile, I could distract his attention from what he wanted, but inwardly I was screaming, what he wanted was me!

I would never betray Dylan. No matter what I decided the consequences would be insurmountable. How ever did it come to this? Where did I go wrong, was I giving out the wrong signals and unaware of it. For now, I would keep calm and try to convince Reiner not to pursue this insane act of lust. He slumped down on the bed, his massive weight causing the mattress to spring up and down. With a deep sigh, he mumbled.

"Oh fuck! let's talk."

"Yes, Reiner let us talk," I answered with relief.

His thin white hair ruffled and huge bulging stomach bursting over the top of his grey trousers, he sighed.

He was more relaxed and not so threatening.

"I want you so much, you are driving me insane. I love you Janette, I really love you, I want nothing more than to have you by my side. Someday I want you for my wife. I know you only love me as a friend, it's not enough! But who knows one day you may feel the same way about me?"

His bloodshot eyes were glazed and watery, and as he spoke, I began to feel compassion for my friend.

"What next Janette? Look I've told you before Ngery and I don't make love anymore and I have a big appetite for sex, I can't help it. She would prefer to read the bible."

There was some truth in what he said. She was deeply religious, but had he driven her to the comfort of the church.

"Look, you think I am just a crook, yes, I have served time in prison, I've conned plenty of people here and other countries too. What Dylan is doing for me he will be well rewarded. I will pay back the money I owe you at the same time. This is a very risky deal, I cannot afford to miss out on making money like this, Andreas can afford it, he siphoned a fortune out of Germany, and I intend to milk him of every penny. Don't worry Janette Dylan is safe, I swear he will come to no harm!"

"He idolises you Reiner, just look at yourself about to violate his partner."

"You are so wrong Janette, I want to make love, not to take you like an animal," he was indignant.

"I don't know you Reiner, who are you really? I heard your last two business partners were killed, is this true?"

"Who told you that story Inga, and Klaus? Anyway, yes so what, they were in the way… Ha, ha, it's Kenya," he smirked.

Brushing his thin hair in place, as he gulped from the vodka bottle.

"Anyway, it's very easy to get rid of someone here; you can get someone disposed of for a bottle of whisky, so don't ever think you are safe in Kenya without good connections and if government people want someone killed, they end up in the bush."

He snapped his fingers and threw back his head.

"That simple Janette! it happens all the time and I know there are many people out there that would like to hurt me too, but I have top police and officials looking out for me. I cannot be touched I am owed a very big favour so let's stop this talk, look I am sorry I hurt you about Dylan, but you must face the truth."

Once again, my heart sank, I refused to believe him.

"Janette we all make promises we don't keep, and is it so awful really? The boy does love you very much, but this is the animal in him, it is in all men, we can't help it, no other feelings, just for fucking."

Reiner held my face in his cupped hands and asked me to forgive him for hurting me with the Dylan affair story. He could see the pain I was going through, if it was true I would never trust him again, I couldn't bare him to touch me.

"Tomorrow, you must prove it for yourself, just ask him who Jessie is. Andreas is paying the hotel bill; Dylan would not stay there without her. Mind you I didn't like it, so Dylan booked her into Andreas's room to cover up the affair. She means nothing to

him it is only sex Janette; he has been fucking around since you first came to Chiromo back in June. Men are selfish, we want a faithful wife, yet we cheat on them, it is only sex nothing else," he insisted.

He kissed my cheek and left the room.

It was past three o'clock, yet sleep was beyond me; I buried myself under the sheets. I lie quite still filled with awful imaginings, lost in the lies, and tormented by the thought of it all.

THE MORNING CALL

There was a loud knock on the door, I looked at my watch it was 8.30am.

"Hello mummy, telephone call from Mr. Dylan."

Someone shouted.

"Tell him to call back at 10 please, I am going to take a shower."

What would I say to him and why was he calling so early in the morning? I arrived at my office after checking the staff, and the deliveries. As I sipped a cup of hot sweet tea, I waited anxiously for the call. Exactly 10am the phone rang, I was startled spilling the tea over some paperwork.

"I miss you Jan, I can't stand it here anymore."

"Is there anyone with you? Who is the girl that booked into the hotel with you and Reiner?"

"What girl, what do you mean there is no girl here?" he panicked.

I put the phone down on him, now I was unsure, by the tone of his voice I knew something was wrong. I waited for him to call again. Ten minutes waiting for the call to come.

"Hello, hello Jan it's me."

He spoke very anxiously.

"Yes, what have you to tell me?" I asked.

Trying to compose myself and afraid of what he might say.

"Okay there is a girl here, but she is with Andreas, I didn't want you to know in case you got the wrong idea."

So, she does exist, I thought maybe he was innocent. I'll let him tell me the whole story. After a long in-depth report of who she was and where she came from, I began to sense he was telling the truth after all.

"I love you Jan, I would never hurt you, why would I risk losing everything for a quick fuck?"

"Men do it all the time Dylan."

The girl Jessie did exist, it did sound feasible that she was there to cover up Andreas's hideaway. I set aside my emotions, cleared my mind, and continued working in my office until lunchtime.

INGA AND KLAUS CONCERNED

"You look tired and upset Janette are you ok?"

"Oh, Inga I am so tired, I couldn't sleep last night."

I decided to call the Mombasa Hotel and find out more about Jessie the mystery girl. I was informed she was booked into Andreas's room and was given her last name, after some persuasion. Later in the afternoon Reiner waltzed in my office, smiling and in a very jovial mood. He asked if I slept and how was I feeling? I let him know I had spoken to Dylan about Jessie, I double-checked with the hotel; his story was verified, so that was the end of it.

"No, no, Janette, I have told you she is sleeping in Dylan's room, but I booked her in Andreas's room. If you want proof, then call Teresa, she will tell you about her. Marco and Dylan were in the casinos with her in Diani, Teresa and I saw them together."

"Stop, Stop!... I don't want to hear it please Reiner, I can't cope with this, I swear I will kill myself!"

Then he reached into his jacket pocket and took out some receipts from the Mombasa hotel.

"This is Dylan's signature, he is signing for a Miss Jessie Mwkali, if she was with Andreas don't you think he would sign for her himself, you fool?"

He was getting angry, his eyes flashing.

"Take them look for yourself, wake up woman he's cheating!"

I composed myself, Reiner could see that it was pointless to continue. He was leaving for Mombasa and would arrange for Dylan to leave the hotel.

That evening a few of my Asian friends arrived and I joined their company for a drink, hoping to forget the day's events. Reiner had left the hotel for Mombasa, and I received a call from Dylan, we talked for over twenty minutes, there was no mentioning the mysterious Jessie. He was delighted to hear he would soon be coming to join me in Nairobi. Although news travels extremely fast in Kenya, telephone communication at times was extremely poor.

NEWS FROM WORKSHOP

To my horror Reiner had urged Dylan to sign for timber and other building materials on African Oasis accounts. Reiner's company ITA was based in Nairobi, he had difficulty with credit in Diani, causing a problem with his workload. Dylan innocently allowed him access to our account, and ignorant that most traders in Diani refused Reiner credit. The smaller traders were anxious to receive their overdue payments from Reiner, and my company was also under financial pressure. No payments from customers, cash flow non-existent with large sums of money still outstanding from the Crismani family. While I was in Chiromo my company had made timber screens for Indian Ocean Hotel, they too were slow to settle their account. Seemingly this was normal for Kenya.

THINGS GO FROM BAD TO WORSE

Gurdial Singh was sitting at the bar with an African man who had his back to me. I greeted him and he grasped my hand.

"Janette, stay for a while."

The stranger turned around and spoke.

"Ah ha, you must be the famous Janette of Chiromo, I was supposed to meet you, but you didn't arrive, I'm very pleased to meet the woman who owns my share of Chiromo Garden Hotel, I think I need to buy you a drink my dear, my name is Ngengi Mungai, Kenyatta family."

"I'll leave you both alone," whispered Gurdial.

"Oh, dear Reiner, Reiner what can we do with my dear friend Reiner, he has a dreadful habit of making money by selling my share of this hotel to the Germans and now you my dear."

He pointed to Inga and Klaus sitting by the window eating and shook his head.

"But he showed me official documents."

"My dear, you can acquire any document in Kenya, a birth, death or marriage certificate or property titles, you just name it," he remarked.

Ngengi tapped me on the shoulder and offered me a drink.

"But he has to go back to court, because it needs to be officially stamped, it's in process," I replied.

"You'll be in process for the rest of your life with Reiner," he chuckled.

Reaching into his black briefcase he pulled out various official paperwork.

"Do you have something like this?"

Several documents signed by Reiner, Kurgat the crooked advocate and a judge.

Reality hit me!

"Oh!… I didn't know, this is awful, how stupid of me."

"Look he's done this sort of thing many times before, I am so sorry, but you have nothing sweetheart. I'm very sorry all the papers are forged; he's just taken your money and that's what he does."

He was very blasé about the whole affair because that's the way it is in Kenya.

"You know Reiner will be left with absolutely nothing, once all the debts are cleared."

"All the debts are cleared?"

"You need to go and investigate my dear, that's all I can say."

He shook my hand, smiled, and pointed to the Chiromo accountant Mungai's office. I thought what else can go wrong, I will investigate tomorrow.

REINER RETURNED TO CHIROMO

Reiner returned after two days away and stated that Dylan would be arriving within a week or so. I was delighted; I couldn't wait to see him; this news cheered me up immensely. I began to feel more relaxed with the good news, so the financial situation was discussed. He seemed unconcerned about it, but I was very apprehensive. The fake hotel *share partnership* documents and Ngengi Mungai were not discussed at this point.

"Let's see what happens tomorrow, Janette, I am waiting to hear some news from a colleague, for now I must visit my wife so goodnight."

WALKING IN ON THE STOLEN MONEY

It was late in the afternoon the next day when I returned to my office. Reiner and Mungai the accountant were standing by my desk looking shocked at my sudden appearance. On the desk was a small brown suitcase full to the brim with German Deutsche Marks. My attention was drawn to the money, as Reiner quickly shut the case.

"Sorry to use your office Janette, but I still keep papers and private things in the safe, so I needed to be here today."

Reiner glared at me menacingly, as they scurried out the office, banging the door shut. However, I could hear Reiner's loud voice in the next room, discussing the hoard of money. It was from the Andreas Koeltz heist. Some twenty minutes passed and Mungai returned to my office.

> *"Janette please, please forget what you have just seen, it could be a big problem for you."*
>
> *"What on earth are you talking about Mungai?"*
>
> *"Oh, Janette I fear trouble will come; now you have seen all this money, Mr. Reiner didn't want you to see it. He is very angry, banging on the doors and tables shouting abuse in German. This is not good for us."*
>
> *"Mungai, stop it! Please don't worry, I know nothing ok?"*

CALLING DYLAN

Later I called Dylan to ask if he knew anything about the suitcase full of money.

> *"Yes of course, it's a big payment from Andreas. Jan I'm worried for Andreas, he wants to leave the hotel and go into hiding. He really is terrified they will get him. He's afraid for his life."*

Later that afternoon Dylan was ordered to drive Andreas to a safe house in Mombasa, where two professional bodyguards were waiting to transfer him up country, and out of Kenya. Everything was arranged Dylan took Andreas to the safe house. They were uncertain what was happening. Andreas discreetly passed a phone number to Dylan and made it very clear he didn't want to be parted from him. However, according to instructions from the bodyguards Dylan was to return to the Mombasa hotel and wait a further forty-eight hours, anticipating a call from Reiner. The mysterious Jessie had departed and returned to Ukunda. Matua the sleazy cop was still hanging around at the hotel waiting for instructions, Dylan was very relieved to see him there.

CONFRONT REINER

Ngengi Mungai informed me that you had sold his share of Chiromo to me, and you've done it before. He mentioned you sold it to Inga and Klaus and that's why they took you to court, and now refuse to leave.

> *"Don't be a fool and listen to other people, sometimes you are so gullible Janette."*

I confronted Reiner again, he made countless excuses about the debts and the shares, it became tiresome to listen to. He said he was in the process of buying another bigger hotel.

> *"What can I do to make it up to you?"*

> *"What makes you think, I would ever want to work with you again, I've seen the debts and court papers Reiner. There is no money in this hotel."*

He banged his fist on the desk and stormed out the office, slamming the door behind him.

NO CASH FLOW IN DIANI

There was no cash flow at the workshop, or the money Reiner owed me. My salary was non-existent and Chiromo was now in debt to me. Foolishly I paid some outstanding bills from my own capital to keep things going. At the time I didn't think too much about it, after all I was the manager and would retrieve it later. Dylan was to receive a lump sum of cash for his part in the Andreas affair.

I missed my home in Diani by the beach, with the inviting swimming pool and beautiful gardens. I missed the workshop and the boys too. Our life there was simple and without complications, only those arising from the actual work, quite normal in any business. Now it became one long succession of problems, that grew daily, and I couldn't see any possible way out of it.

Reiner arranged for a hired car, so that Dylan could guard Andreas. Dylan previously sold our pick-up in preparation of coming to Nairobi, I thought that was stupid! He needed to be mobile. Reiner was to pay the hired car from his own funds. I became increasingly concerned at the length of time Dylan was using the car. Something just didn't feel right for me. Intuitively I began to search through documents relating to Chiromo accounts. Because Reiner was abusing African Oasis account with the traders in Diani, I decided to check through references of outstanding financial records. Chiromo was in appalling debt to several people. To my astonishment I discovered a file containing legal papers, a forthcoming court case. Documents and several court orders, for payments long overdue.

MUNGAI REVEALS ALL

My immediate reaction was to call Mungai, I promptly requested a full and detailed explanation, regarding the papers. Mungai a very soft-spoken, quite reticent man had worked for Reiner for several years. He was good looking, thin with a nervous disposition. Understandably he had access to everything, I demanded he bring all the books to my office, and we would systematically go through them.

Mungai was always very reluctant to comply, I could sense that he was anxious.

> *"Janette there are many books and papers only I have access to, I fear the worse could happen if I were to show them to you."*
>
> *"Don't be afraid, bring them to me, I will take full responsibility."*

I persuaded him to reveal the books, I assured him it would be alright.

> *"Let's sit here and go through them together."*

After a couple of hours inspection, it came to light that the hotel was in debt to over ten million KS. I was absolutely astonished by the huge debt. I was troubled when Mungai disclosed the books never balanced from day one. The money outstanding to my company African Oasis was not included in the debt, and other traders accounts were not up to date. Mungai spoke very softly.

> *"It has always been like this, Reiner spends more than he earns, he orders goods and doesn't pay for them, he knows the current financial situation we are in and still he continues."*
>
> *"Mungai, do you know I paid Reiner a big sum of money for a partnership share in Chiromo? and I have paid out over 250,000 KS."*

Mungai and I hugged and sensed impending doom.

Udo hid away in his small dark room or stayed at a friend's house during this alarming scenario. Getting involved in the Andreas story wasn't an option for him.

Inga and Klaus rallied and were very supportive.

KIDNAPPED AND TAKEN TO THE BUSH

Reiner was drinking large vodkas at the bar, too early in the day, he beckoned and waved his arms around above his head, in a hurried fashion. I refused to acknowledge him and walked out of the hotel, and through the gardens. Unexpectedly from a side door he appeared and started yelling abuse. I was in no mood to fight with him especially now, he was quite drunk. I quickly dashed towards my room. He chased after me grabbing my arm with his huge hand, lifting me up and began marching me in the opposite direction. He was heading towards the car park; my feet were almost off the ground.

"Reiner stop this madness!" I yelled.

He continued dragging me along at his side and shoved me into his car. Extremely angry, almost breathless as he sped hastily out of the car park and along the main road. He was driving erratically, and there was nothing I could do about it. With a clenched fist heavy blows smashed down on my knee. I thought to myself this is it, he is behaving crazy, am I going to die?

"I am taking you to your grave, this is where you and Dylan will end up!"

We seemed to be miles away from the city. Approaching a wooded area, he slowed down laughed and shouted.

"You see, it is so easy to die here in Kenya!"

Laughing hysterically like a mad man almost frenzied, manic, swerving the car uncontrollably up onto the embankment.

"Oh, do it then, do it you're such a fucking maniac!" I screamed.

Unexpectedly he pulled over onto a dirt road and sped along it like a racing track, creating a huge dust storm. I couldn't see through the window, it was covered in dust, but I could hear the crunching sound of branches breaking on the side of the car. Crashing thumping noise on the sunroof as we gradually reached an open area of bushland and came to an abrupt stop.

"Get out!" he yelled.

Then shouted in German, he leaned across to open the door, his elbow digging into my ribs, then fiercely shoved me out onto the dirt road. Frantically struggling to get out of his side he began yelling more abuse. Finally, he grabbed something from the dashboard, or door pocket and stumbled out heading towards me. His face was red with anger, sweat dripping from his forehead; he looked like a raging bull about to attack. Yet even so, I wasn't frightened of him and only felt pity for his foolishness.

I believed his passion became an obsession, which had driven him to this crazy action. I wouldn't give myself freely, therefore he would impose force to satisfy his desires. Grabbing my hair pushing me down on my knees he demanded I look directly at him. The sun was behind him, all I could see was a shadowy blur. Enraged, beside himself and holding a handgun he pushed it very hard against my face.

> *"You see you can die right here right now; do you understand me Janette, fischsten (understand) Janette? I love you, and now you think I am an animal, don't you? Well, you are right I am a fucking animal!"*

His entire body shaking with rage, his face distorted with madness, yelling in German. With his other hand he fiddled and opened his zip and pulled out his big limp cock waving it in my face, the cold metal of the gun rubbing against my cheek. His cock pushing on my closed mouth. I shut my eyes, and just wanted to bite his cock and be done with it…

"Open your fucking mouth, I will shoot you if you don't, open it!"

There was no point in resisting, either way I was going to suffer.

"Shoot me then, you fucking pig," I screamed.

He pushed his limp cock in my mouth, and then smashed the gun on the top of my head.

"I will shoot with my cock first, and then with the gun, ha, ha, open your fucking mouth wider!"

I pulled my head back, gagging, and shoved very hard on both of his knees, he stepped back just a little, I struggled to stand up, yet he stood quite still glaring into space. I started screaming and waving my arms.

"Fucking shoot, do it, do it you fucking German dog I hate you. Kill me Reiner and I will come back and haunt you, look at my face remember it when you go to sleep, I will haunt you, you evil bastard, fucking do it!"

I was fighting back with words and frantically waving my arms around to confuse him. I could sense the adrenaline rushing through my body. There was a moment when he seemed reasonably calm and he stepped back and slightly off balance, surprised; he was rather dazed and dropped his arm holding the gun and fumbling to put away his big limp cock.

"What have you made me do, you fucking stupid woman, I loved you now look at me I am going crazy, get in the fucking car and shut up!" he bellowed.

BACK IN THE CAR

We stumbled back into the car; he continued fumbling with his clothes and smoothing his hair down. The gun returned to the dashboard. Yelling continuously, fuck you woman! and frothing at the mouth. As we slowly journeyed back down the dirt track, a fine spray of water splashing on the windscreen, the wipers turned the dust to slush. The car steadily moving away from the scene where it all took place, I glanced back over my shoulder in disbelief. The crashing gun on my head causing a lump and throbbing, my entire body shaking from shock. I realised just how close I had come to dying at the hand of my dear friend Reiner. It all happened so quickly there was no time to really understand what was unfolding. I didn't see my death occurring that way, I believed I would die an old woman, not now, and not this way.

> *"I will never forgive you for that, never, never you evil pig, I hate you!"* I hollered at him.

I felt sick, I was retching, but by now adrenalin had kicked in and rushing through my body. My hands were shaking and trembling, my confused mind racing with random thoughts. What the hell had just happened out there? It was tolerable now, but I couldn't bring myself to look at him as he adjusted his clothes and wiped the dust and sweat from his face. He was drenched in perspiration, breathing heavy and grunting in German.

Unexpectedly he grabbed my hair yanking it very hard and screamed.

> *"This is not what I wanted to happen, I'm sorry, so sorry. I'm a fucking bastard I know!"*

JOURNEY BACK TO CHIROMO

The journey back was silent, with only the sound of traffic passing and the occasional deep sigh from Reiner. As the car turned off the main road into the hotel car park, he made one final grunting noise slamming his hands on the steering wheel. I was about to get out when he grabbed my arm and glaring in a most hateful manner.

> *"Keep your mouth shut and you will not get hurt, you will live longer and so will your foolish boy!"*

Reiner returned to his office yelling abuse on the way.

I hurried to my room exhausted and collapsed on the bed in floods of tears. The horror had suddenly hit me, I realised how close to death I had come. Exactly what had happened in the bush? It was so disgusting and terrifying, yet somehow, I found incredible courage and strength to overcome the fear of dying. I wasn't meant to die that way; it simply wasn't my time to go. I am here, safe for now, to live another day.

His penis stuffed into my mouth was far more threatening than the gun he held to my head. I certainly did not want to choke to death on a big limp cock! Yes, one bullet and it was over, but not in that way, not with his cock in my mouth. I could have bitten off his knob in a reflex action, as I died. Killing me that way and losing his knob was not an option, I guess! It wasn't worth the risk. It wasn't worth his cock. My mind raced with different scenarios that might have turned out differently. I tried desperately to come to terms with the day's events. What could possibly be worse than a bullet in your head, and a big German cock in your mouth?

REINER WAITING IN MY ROOM

Late that night after work, as I made my way back to my room, I noticed the dim light through the curtains.

I called out.

"Is someone there?"

There was no answer, so I eased open the door to see Reiner lying on the bed dozing.

"What are you doing here?" I shouted.

Slowly he moved and opened his eyes.

"I thought I would wait here for you. Do you mind Janette?" Laughing sarcastically.

"Yes, I do, get out you pig."

"Well, it's too fucking bad I own the hotel!" he snarled, in a slurred voice.

"What do you want Reiner?"

"What do you think I want?"

He replied reaching out and pulling me towards him.

"I have waited long enough for you, and I am taking you, ha-ha. I have a big contract with Crismani in Diani, I have been paid my deposit and I have money from Andreas Koeltz too."

"There's no way I will continue here in this hotel, you conned me Reiner. The fucking crazy gun episode was the end for me, I want my money back, I want to go home, my head is thumping!!"

He lunged forward and yanked me on the bed, gripping me tightly with his big hand.

"You may or may not get your money back, your business in Diani is well and truly fucked, I may or may not kill you, but I will fuck you, what about that Janette."

Laughing at me and pulling his trouser zip down.

"I have had your money, now I'll have you, ha! ha!"

I struggled with him, but he had such a tight grip on me, he was overpowering. He slipped one hand up my dress and pulled down my underwear, ripping and mauling, then grabbed the flesh of my bare bottom.

"Lovely, lovely," he groaned.

I tried in vain to move away, I knew it was hopeless, I was totally drained from the previous event in the bush. I started to yell at him.

"Get off you pig, get off me, and let me go!"

Amid the struggling his big hard cock was poking out through his open zip pressing firmly against my leg. Like an animal he groped at me and pulled me underneath his big heavy sweaty body. The more I tried to struggle free it seemed the heavier he became; I was getting crushed by the sheer weight of him. As he rolled and manoeuvred himself in position I couldn't breathe. Grunting in German as his big fat hands mauled my thighs and bottom, his thick fingers poked around inside me.

"Lovely, lovely Janette I'm going to fuck you, not kill you."

His heavy leg squeezed between mine forcing them apart. I couldn't move. One hand covered my face and the other gripping my bottom, he lifted me up slightly and began forcing his hard cock inside me. Pushing harder as I gasped for breath, he was like an animal.

"Yes! yes," he was shouting.

He withdrew and began masturbating over my thighs puffing almost breathlessly. Unexpectedly, there was a power cut the lights went off! it was totally dark. Reiner heaved his body away just enough to shove him off me and manoeuvre myself from underneath his heavy body. I eased away and rolled off the bed. Stumbling around trying to get my balance and focus on the darkness, then dashed out the door into the blackness of the night.

No lights on to show the way, just the flickering candles in the distance from the kitchen and bar. As I staggered my way along the edge of the path heading towards the restaurant, I could hear him ranting in German. I paused for a moment to tidy my clothes and compose myself before entering the side door through the kitchen for bottled water and headed to my office. Not more than fifteen minutes past when car head lights suddenly lit up the dark driveway where Reiner had parked his white car. Off he sped into the night!

I felt empty; I couldn't feel anger, only repulsion at his vulgarity. How loathsome, evil, and cruel could he get?

I didn't return to my room that night but rested on the sofa in my office with the door bolted. Sleep avoided me. The morning call of birds singing and dawn breaking. A new day appeared as beams of sunlight shone through the window creating a rainbow of colour on the white wall. I realised I needed to continue the day focused on work and try my very best to overcome the terrible events that changed my life forever.

I returned to my own room to change. Reiner had tipped the bed over on its side and pulled things around, it looked a mess. After a long warm shower crying and confused, I dressed and tidied up my room, reliving the events of the night before, moment to moment. I was betrayed, I felt so alone and helpless.

I had to get back to work, carry on with the job and show a brave face, as if nothing had happened. For now, I would block it out of my mind. Perhaps later when I had figured it all out, I would feel the pain, humiliation, and horror. Maybe I might understand how to deal with my emotions. But for now, I convinced myself it was nothing, just a passing moment in time.

AFTER THE RAPE

Back to normal, whatever normal is in Chiromo?

Inga and Klaus were sitting in the restaurant eating an enormous breakfast, they were always hungry. Both plates were piled high with sausages, eggs, bacon with tomatoes, four slices of toast and huge chunks of cheese. This was followed by bread, jam, and several pots of coffee. After every meal complaining it was too cold, or too little, not cooked enough or over cooked. They complained, even when the meal was perfect.

Chain smoking cheap cigarettes with a constant haze around them, but strangely enough I grew fond of this odd couple. Inga a very domineering woman, a typical German frau. Klaus chilled out, terribly lazy and offensively uncouth. He was uncultivated, coarse, and ill mannered. His broken English effectively impossible to understand. I found it easier to answer yes, to almost everything he had to say. A strange mixture of German, English and Swahili, a cocktail of meaningless words, which splattered out of his thick slobbery lips, forever spitting and dribbling.

Inga mentioned Reiner was drinking with strangers and had pockets bulging with Deutsche Marks the previous evening? He was boasting about it to her. Reiner had promised me to clear his debt; I was very concerned for the financial situation at the hotel. I put aside my own personal problems.

"What's going on Janette, you look dreadful my dear, have you been crying or not sleeping? Janette, he does not like me working here with you, because of the court case we have against him, it really bothers him," Inga said.

"How ever did I get conned into this crazy idea, Inga. People say the hotel has changed so much since my arrival, but I am beginning to hate Reiner."

"Yes Janette, I know exactly what you mean, because there was a time I could have killed him, I have even thought of ways to get rid of the evil bastard," Inga said bitterly.

"You know Inga, I think I have lost my money, I don't think he will return the loan, there is no partnership, it's all fake."

"Yes, I think you are right!" she nodded.

The remainder of the day was talking to staff and listening to the many complaints about not getting paid. It was just awful for me when a member of staff requested wages that were three months overdue.

"I'm so sorry, but not today."

A dispute with the department of employment continued, concerning the company's delay in payment of wages and insurance contributions. This was a profoundly serious situation. At the same time African Oasis workshop in Diani was badly neglected by Dylan.

More and more problems, I needed to seek some advice urgently, from someone? But who could I trust was the question? I thought about my dear Sikh friend Gurdial then later decided to approach another Asian man.

SEEKING HELP AMIN WALJI FOUR ACES CASINO

The person I decided to seek help from was the man that Reiner had introduced me to at The Four Aces casino, Amin Walji an Asian MP, for Westlands.

It was late at night; I took the short ride to the casino by local taxi without informing anyone. I felt quite nervous, but I found the courage to walk into the crowded casino. Amin spotted me immediately and beckoned me over to his table. He was amongst his fellow MPs, and other prominent government officials.

Dressed smartly in a silver-grey suit and white shirt, red tie. His thick grey hair dishevelled, smiling as he pushed it away from his handsome face, and peering over silver rimmed glasses. I approached the group with hesitation, he was aware of my awkwardness.

> *"Welcome Janette how is your hotel management working out and are you well?"* he asked.
>
> *"Hello Amin, it's so nice to see you again, when you have some free time, can I speak with you please, it's very urgent!"*
>
> *"Yes of course, oh, please take Janette over there and give her some food and drink,*
>
> *I will join you in a short time,"* he asked the short jolly waiter.

Members of Parliament, wealthy businessmen chatting in a casino, quite normal in Nairobi, I thought.

THE CASINO

I chatted with the casino staff and other customers as I waited for Amin to come over. It seemed like hours had passed, but it was only forty minutes when Amin came rushing over to sit with me.

> *"You are hungry, you want more to drink?"* he asked and patted my hand.

I drank vodka and tonic as Amin sipped tea. A Muslim, married with two sons and a daughter he only consumed soft drinks.

> *"Do you mind if I smoke?"* I asked him.
>
> *"Not at all my dear, you must relax and tell me what the urgency is of this meeting."*
>
> *"Well, to be honest I desperately need to talk to someone. There's no one I trust Amin, please, I need your help!"*
>
> *"Janette, whatever you tell me is in the strictest confidence, I give you my word,"* he smiled, held my hand, and put me at ease.

He was looking into my eyes, deep into my heart, my soul; I simply knew everything would be all right.

> *"Don't look so worried, we can do something to make it better can we not?"*
>
> *"Yes, we can, so where do I start from,"* I said.
>
> *"The beginning of course, we have all night."*

REVEALING MY STORY TO AMIN

Amin listened very intently, occasionally nodding, sometimes shaking his head in disbelief as the extraordinary story unravelled. I could scarcely believe it myself, was this entire story mine own, or imaginings?

Occasionally a member of the security staff would interrupt Amin, but the saga continued into the early hours. Pausing now and again for another drink.

> *"I want you to listen very carefully, I will tell you what to do okay? So, all of you must get out of Chiromo, it's too dangerous, but wait a week or so until I know the right time for you to leave. You have no idea of the danger you have put yourselves in. Reiner is a dangerous criminal, he is Mafia, always in trouble and a damn nuisance to everyone, and he gets away with it every time. This Andreas Koeltz business is another story; this is very serious because Interpol are now involved. Later, I can try to help you get your money back, but it will be very difficult indeed, what to do first? Now let me think, you return to Chiromo for now. You will wait for your boyfriend to arrive, and then you both come up and see me. I will think of something, I am so sorry about the horrendous abuse this awful man has put on you, such a beautiful woman."*

He shook my hand smiled and made his way to his office, then waved. It was now 2am, the taxi arrived. On my return to Chiromo I thought to myself, this would never happen in England. Chatting all night with an MP telling him all my most intimate problems, yet it felt so natural with Amin. He was an extraordinary man, so composed, a gentleman.

I was informed he helped the poor and always fighting for a lost cause. Beggars would chat with him; he was greatly respected. Now he was my friend too, and for the first time in Kenya, I sensed some normalcy and hope. I believed that no matter what transpired, and if anything, serious happened to me, he was aware of my story.

BACK TO CHIROMO GARDEN

Amin arranged for a driver to take be back to Chiromo. I noticed Reiner's car and decided to hurry across the gardens to my room. The cool air and stillness of the night eased my racing mind. I entered my room, it was dark, I paused for a moment before putting on the light.

I lay on my bed fully clothed thinking about what I shared with Amin. The sheer horror of it, this nightmare situation I found myself in, but at least today Dylan would arrive, and Amin my guardian angel.

Sleep avoided me; I was exhausted in the morning.

After breakfast I became feverish, I didn't waste any time and took a taxi to the hospital for a check-up. After blood tests and filling in forms I became nauseous, so I waited outside in the shade. A charming nurse called me in for the results, I was delighted to hear it.

"No malaria my dear, a mystery virus, plenty of them in Kenya."

A prescription for antibiotics, that I collected at the clinic and returned by taxi to the hotel, within the hour.

"Any calls for me?" I asked the receptionist.

"Yes, Mr Dylan he is arriving about 2pm Janette you must be very happy?" he grinned.

Inga appeared at the doorway of Mungai's office.

"Are you alright Janette?" she asked.

"Yes, just a virus, I have come from the hospital, no malaria."

"Come sit in your office my dear, I will bring some coffee, Dylan is coming up at last, you must be very excited?"

I began to feel faint; I couldn't stop thinking about my meeting with Amin. The Reiner kidnap story, the rape, and the mysterious Jessie. There is so much to talk about apart from who this girl is. When Inga returned with the coffee I told her that we were unable to pay wages, and the bills that were piling up. There was no money for my salary either.

"Reiner is aware, but no sense of urgency, I guess when the bailiffs arrive, he will dip into his pocket. If you want the truth Janette, I think that he may lose the hotel, or at least the courts will remove everything they can. The bailiffs have already taken some office equipment, tables, and chairs from the main garden. Normally I am not too worried, I have known Reiner a long time he always manages to come up smiling," Inga muttered.

"Yes, and it's with money that he conned from us that he smiles!"

"You are so right, you know I would have gone to Kindani a long time ago, but Wolfgang has messed that up now with all his drinking and other nonsense."

"Well Inga, we are here together, if I get my money back from Reiner I would return to Diani and pick up the business again."

It was past 2.30pm in the afternoon I sat at my desk daydreaming about Diani Beach when I heard.

"He is here, tell Mummy Mr. Dylan is here at last."

My body was shaking, I felt very anxious about seeing him again. With a sudden thud the door opened, and Dylan was standing there holding an enormous bunch of beautiful flowers. He looked dreadful, with sweat pouring down his face, he could barely speak.

"Hi sweetheart I'm so glad you are here, but you are ill, what is it?" I asked.

He placed the flowers on the desk, he was trembling and crying as he threw his arms around me.

"Jan, I have missed you so much, let's get married please!"

We held each other tightly and cuddled, I could not believe the waiting was finally over.

"Sit down what's wrong you look terrible; you have a fever."

He collapsed on the floor; it was imperative to get him to hospital as soon as possible. A six-hour drive, how did he manage it from Mombasa to Nairobi in this dreadful condition? He was totally drenched with sweat, as if he had run a marathon. I phoned through to the reception to get help to lift him to the taxi waiting at the main entrance.

SICK WITH MALARIA

I had taken that very taxi to the same hospital earlier. We arrived and Dylan was helped into a small cubical, I sat the other side of the curtain. A smiling petite slim female Asian doctor arrived. She greeted me, and then asked if we were related.

"Are you a big sister or mummy?"

Looking down at his young face.

"No, I am his wife."

"Oh, very sorry, it's just this one is looking like a young boy, I thought you can't be wife you are much older, very sorry indeed."

She looked very uncomfortable, but it didn't bother me at all. After examining him she took a blood sample.

"He is not looking very well is he, but don't worry it is malaria, but also another virus on top of it, oh deary me."

Ten minutes later, I was handed tablets, the doctor gave him an injection and we were asked to move along for the next person to be seen. The hospital was very busy that day. After the injection he seemed to stabilise, we struggled to the taxi and returned to Chiromo. Inga and Klaus helped Dylan into my room.

After washing him down in cold water he laid on the bed somewhat delirious, a very sick man. He could not talk, he was still as if in a coma, sweating profusely and with a high fever. He slept for over four hours, I returned to change the sheets and wash him again. His medication was every two hours after that rest; it would be a long night for both of us.

Inga and Klaus helped with nursing him and prepared a little light food. I was worried about the malaria and the aftereffects too; he would be very weak for some time and unable to work. Tomorrow would be another day; and all that mattered was that he rested. Over and over, I whispered to him, I love you. I'd kiss his sweating brow and assure him that nothing would hurt him now that he was safe home with me.

It was a long night; Inga and Klaus would pop in now and again with fresh orange juice, iced water and flannels dipped in vinegar to wrap around his ankles. Inga said it was to keep the fever from going to his head. When dawn finally broke the sound of the birds singing lifted my spirit, Dylan was much better. After washing and brushing his hair I put clean sheets on the bed again, then took a much-needed shower. He was able to talk without slurring and it was apparent the medicine was working, there was a big improvement in his condition. I was delighted to see him perking up. I called in the office, gathered up the day's paperwork collected a tray of breakfast and made my way back to the sick room. Dylan was smiling as I waltzed in with food and drink.

> *"It's strange Jan, when I left Nairobi, I felt tired and very hot, but not shivering like when I arrived, I thought it was just a cold coming. Can you believe its malaria again?"* he muttered.

I told him to just rest and not think about anything. I returned to my office and checked on the staff.

THE BAILIFFS ARRIVE AT CHIROMO

The day began with two big gruff African bailiffs knocking fiercely on my office door.

Bailiffs, open the door shouting.

> *"Haraka sana, ambapo ni bosi, hurry where is the boss?"*

They looked rather indignant as they entered my office waving a rolled-up piece of paper. A legal document, a list of items thereon. My immediate reaction was to call the lawyer Kurgat, which proved pointless.

> *"Reiner has told me nothing of this, besides, I'm unavailable just now,"* he grumbled.

No one at the hotel had any idea what was going on, as the bailiffs loaded up their lorry with more office equipment, and furniture from the garden restaurant. Mungai was running around like a headless chicken in a blind panic, desperately trying to resolve the problem. Other members of staff gazed on nonchalantly and complacent at the strange scenario.

Eventually Reiner arrived waving his arms and shouting, bellowing all kinds of abuse at everyone. Another phone call came from Kurgat the lawyer to advise us the bailiffs would return the next day.

Reiner dashed passed me almost knocking me over and heading towards Mungai's office. The poor man looked terrified and frozen to the spot. Screaming in German and English at the top of his voice that echoed in the gardens like thunder, he demanded a full explanation.

> *"You knew they were coming Reiner, we called Kurgat he couldn't speak. I could not bribe them to go, I did not have enough money,"* Mungai pleaded.

They exchanged words for ten minutes or so; Reiner's arms waving in the air, retrieved a bunch of documents and left in hurry. He was yelling abuse out of the car and speeding down the driveway, a huge cloud of dust creating a hazy atmosphere over the hotel.

> *"There's only so much a man can tolerate Janette, I can't take much more of this abuse and no wages, enough is enough,"* sighed Mungai.

I understood how he felt; I had my belly full of it too.

What a mockery and farce it was all becoming. This must be the only place where the police, MPs, and government official's drink in the same company as the criminal fraternity. Crooks, villains, and prostitutes rubbing shoulders with the law, Chiromo Garden Hotel was infamous, and I was getting sucked into the den of iniquity. Mungai reminded me Reiner rented out rooms as a massage parlour. People would complain about these girls sitting on steps outside the restaurant with their legs wide apart advertising their goods. It was ludicrous to allow them to parade outside the restaurant windows. I tried to stop the prostitutes, but Reiner seemed to have his own ideas.

From the day I met Reiner, I was doomed with bad luck.

Nothing ever went as planned, all his promises were futile. All those stories and the lies that I listened to; this was going to be the last time for me.

DYLAN IN HIS SICK ROOM

Dylan was better and sitting up smiling, I would not burden him with any problems, nor would I ever mention Reiner raping me and taking me to the woods.

I chatted to him briefly about my meeting with Amin Walji, then we discussed the money that was owed to me by Reiner. Dylan was to receive a big sum of money for helping Andreas Koeltz, apart from that we were now in dire straits. I thought if we had all the money again, could we return to Diani and continue with the workshop?

Fully aware so much cash had slipped through our fingers, we must try our best to get back all outstanding debts from Reiner as soon as possible. Amin mentioned not to worry about the money, that somehow, he would find a way to help us. Upon reflection at times, I couldn't believe my own stupidity and how I ever got myself into this mess. But first things first my lover was back with me, and his health was the most important issue to deal with. He needed to rest and regain his strength if we were to escape this nightmare.

Reiner didn't call in to see how Dylan was, far too busy with the bailiffs and courtroom visits.

> *"You will discover for yourself Dylan what a bastard he really is, I know you look up to him as I once did, but we must face the facts, he is a professional criminal. We are not his friends; he is simply using us like he does with everyone."*

A MEETING WITH INGA

> *"Janette hier habenal einen Wodka, you will need it, you know Reiner and I have been friends for many years. And until this partnership episode when he conned us out of our money, we always spoke honestly to each other. I mentioned to him about the*

Jessie story, because I know it really upset you. I also know that Reiner is very calculating, (was ich meine) get my meaning?"

Inga explained to me Reiner needed a girl to come to the hotel with Andreas to stay in the room together. This way those who were looking for him would not suspect a couple. Dylan was asked if he knew any girls who could come that very day and she would receive a payment for her time involved. Dylan said yes, and this girl Jessie was picked up from Indian Ocean hotel by Andreas and Dylan. She was taken to the hotel and the plan was now in action. But Reiner was informed she did not want to sleep in the same room as Andreas but would sleep in Dylan's room, on the spare bed, as she knew him.

Reiner asked Matua, the sleazy cop, to speak to Jessie in his or her own tongue and find out exactly how well she knew Dylan. Matua questioned her for over an hour while the others drank beer by the pool. Reiner was duly informed that Jessie had sex with Dylan in the pickup truck a few times when his wife (Janette) was away.

They met at Shakatak one night and Dylan took her out for dinner and to the casino followed by a quick fuck in the back of the truck. Reiner began to ask Dylan questions about her, and he admitted he had fucked her a few times, when he got pissed. He felt bad about cheating, but it just happened, there was nothing in it just a fuck. But this situation did worry him because he genuinely believed she was to sleep in Andreas's room where she was booked in. But unexpectedly she wasn't having that she didn't like Andreas, she wanted to be with Dylan.

"Janette, Matua and Reiner have both told me the same story, now it's up to you to find out what Dylan has to add, okay."

I couldn't stop crying I was sobbing my heart out; Inga was so bloody matter of fact, and I was devastated. He had betrayed me in June, when I first came to Chiromo, if I had known then I would have made better choices, like not parting with my capital. Nor would I have accepted the management position leading to the proposed partnership.

What about when he came to Nairobi with Reiner, what did he get up to then? There was lipstick on his collar; Alice the maid pointed it out and those business cards in his pocket. As more and more vodkas disappeared in our thirsty mouths smoking one cigarette after another my in-love world had fallen apart.

INGA TRIES TO HELP

Inga tried to console and placate me, occasionally patted me gently on the head.

> *"Oh Janette, I'm so sorry, but you will only know the truth when you speak with Dylan, mind you, I could call Teresa or even Walter they know everything that is going on at the coast."*
>
> *'Do you mean to tell me they might know of this too and no one told me, I don't believe it!"* I sobbed.
>
> *"It's a very delicate situation when you know a couple and one of them is cheating how do tell the other one, you hurt them both regardless,"* she uttered with a sorrowful look.

How could I even contemplate returning to the coast now, after this it was impossible I would be so humiliated? My so-called friends knew he was cheating on me, and I foolishly bought into a partnership that wasn't worth the paper it was written on.

"Inga what a mess, all this has happened since Reiner came into our lives."

"Janette, Klaus cheated on me with a young black woman too and I went crazy, but I had to forgive him because I love him so much. I could not walk away from Klaus for one moment of weakness for sex, after all what the bloody hell is all the fuss about."

"For me Inga it's about trust, it's the commitment we made to each other."

I explained to her that I left my husband for a man nineteen years my junior; I walked away from my family, loyal friends, financial security, businesses and two beautiful homes. Dylan was unemployed, no money only a few clothes no possessions, a typical gypsy boy. I helped him from unemployment to running his own business. I bought him clothes, jewellery, a three-week holiday, before coming to live here. I have been honest and loyal. Is this the way you repay the person you love? If he's guilty our relationship could never be the same again, how could it be? I trusted him with my life; I cannot believe he has acted so shamefully, bad enough to have an affair, but a girl from Ukunda. I cannot go home to England because I will have no capital to start again.

"Janette, you don't know the truth yet, so be calm. You told me about this Asian man Amin Walji, he would help you. People say he is a very good man."

It was getting late I needed to fetch some food for Dylan from the kitchen and prepared it myself. I cannot remember ever crying so much in my life.

Dylan smiled and welcomed me to his arms as I placed the tray next to him.

"I missed you babe; have you been drinking?" he asked.

> *"Yes, I have had a few with Inga and talking about you in Mombasa."*

I wanted to know the truth about the mystery girl Jessie, when he met her and everything they did together. After much arguing, I explained to him, I knew the sordid details about her, but I wanted him to just admit the truth himself. Dylan remained adamant he had not slept with this girl, until I told him Reiner had tried to force himself on me, I didn't have the heart or the strength to tell him the whole story.

> *"He tried to rape you, the bastard, I know how he feels about you, the son of a bitch. So that's why he grassed on me was it, Jan I'm so sorry, yes, I did cheat on you with this girl when you first came to Chiromo. But I swear to you on my mother's life, I never touched her at the hotel. I told Reiner she was not staying in my room, but he just laughed and said you fucked in the truck, now you have a nice bed, and you don't want her, what's wrong with you? I didn't want her in my room, I never touched her, please believe me!"* he begged.

No more lies not now I thought, I felt deadened and empty, I was betrayed by him and Reiner.

We both wept as he begged forgiveness. Searching each other's dampened eyes for a sign, uncontrollably weeping. Why did you need to fuck her, I thought and turned away into the cool of the night.

MY SUICIDE IDEA

Walking towards the swimming pool, with a bottle of vodka and a packet of cigarettes, and a box of pain killer pills. I would feel sorry for myself alone. In the distance a faint cry as Dylan wept, his guilty conscience reminding him of his behaviour.

The full moon shone brightly against the dark sky, a gentle cool breeze, as I slumped into one of the remaining garden chairs. A very sorrowful woman, sobbing, drinking, and smoking, with everything rushing around in my restless mind. Impossible to concentrate on any one thing at a time and did I even want to. Eventually an entire jumble of meaningless questions and no answers. What was I to do now? I loved him so much; if I were to leave him, I would miss him greatly. Besides, I couldn't just walk out on him here in Kenya, I promised his mother I would take care of him. I didn't want to go back to England without getting my money first. No answers popping into my mind, I just wanted to switch my brain off and die. It was the simplest way out for me, I can't trust him anymore, I would never feel the same. Will he be thinking of Jessie when he's making love to me?

Crazy thoughts swimming around in my head. Drinking a bottle of vodka and taking pills. Reiner had betrayed my trust, he refused to repay the money and he grassed on Dylan. Reiner had threatened to kill me in the woodland, and then he raped me in my room. Dylan will never be paid for the Andreas work he did, but then, I don't really give a damn! He has destroyed our relationship so to hell with them all. I drank and cried and then I swallowed a handful of pills, I just didn't want to live. I felt so wretched and sorry for myself. I loved and hated Dylan. I loved and hated Reiner too. It seemed like hours had passed when someone pulled at my arm quite fiercely and I slipped through time. I was very drunk and incoherent.

> *"Go away I want to die; I want to die do you hear me,"* I mumbled.

It was Inga; she had called in to check on Dylan, he told her I was very upset and drinking by the pool. She yanked me up with a firm grip almost crushing my arms, and her enormous bosoms pressing against my face.

> *"Komm schon aufstehen, aufstehen Sie auf Janette kommen fool, come on get up, get up you fool come on Janette!"*

I stumbled about trying to get up and attempted to walk in a straight line, I was very drunk. Unable to coordinate, I constantly tripped over. However, Inga managed to get me back to my room safely, where Dylan waited anxiously for me.

> *"She will be okay now, but you will have to keep an eye on her. I think she has taken some pills and a bottle of vodka. Call me if you want help okay, goodnight, Gute Nacht."*

Dylan hauled me into the shower with my clothes on, the icy cold-water cascading over my head so fast; I was slipping around and gasping for breath.

> *"Jan don't leave me, please don't leave me, I love you so much, oh God, what have I done!"*

We held onto each other in a loving embrace as the ice-cold water gushed over our heads and bodies, shivering, shaking, and crying. He lifted me out of the shower onto a chair and began to wipe me with a towel.

> *"Jan don't do this to me please, I'm so sorry please forgive me. I don't have an answer why I did it; I guess, I was so lonely for you. I can't live without you, please, forgive me, give me another chance I beg you."*

I pushed him away; I couldn't bring myself to look into his eyes. Those beautiful big brown sparkling eyes once filled with love for only me. I needed to sleep to escape the world of pain I was suffering. I was dizzy, the room spinning around; I needed to close my eyes. Where did it all go wrong? maybe tomorrow it will be different.

I curled up with a blanket and eventually fell asleep.

THE NEXT DAY

Dawn broke, birds were singing, a warm breeze drifting through the open window, and it was good to be alive.

No glancing at each other as we passed from bedroom to bathroom, both afraid to look into each other's eyes for different reasons. I couldn't endure facing the truth, but he did have sex with another woman. He knew I was suffering; therefore, he didn't look into my unhappy eyes. I was leaving the room; he grabbed my arm, fell to his knees, and cried.

> *"Forgive me please, I beg you, please give me another chance, I promise it will never happen again, I can't live without you Jan, you are my life!"*

Although the anguish I felt was overwhelming, my love for this young gypsy man was beyond all understanding. Yes, he had betrayed me, yes, he made a very big mistake, but still I loved him. We were two tormented souls, barely holding on to that love we thought would last until eternity, but because Reiner took over our lives it had changed everything. If I had stayed in Diani, none of this would have happened. However, here we were in this moment sobbing, feeling sorry for ourselves, lost in the turmoil of our tainted love.

Truly this special love affair for now had altered, but was the magic gone? From this agonising unbearable situation, we would need to pick up the pieces and begin a new era. This would be the most daunting task of all for me. Although I wanted Dylan, I knew nothing would ever be the same again.

"I can't forgive you that easily, how can I? Trusting you meant that I loved you, and without trust there is nothing, but I will give you another chance Dylan because you are young and vulnerable. I should have stayed with you, but then I trusted you completely. You let me down but yourself too, or perhaps, you gave no thought to that did you? I do love you Dylan, I cannot say anymore, and you must give me time. Please don't think our relationship will continue as before. But I will try my best to carry on. I know you are very ashamed of your behaviour, so let us put on a brave face and see how we go, all right?" I whispered.

"Thank you, Jan, I promise you I will make it up to you, I know what I did was wrong, it was terrible for you. Let's get married and start over again, eh? We could have a nice wedding and put this entire nightmare behind us, what do you say?" he pleaded.

"Getting married will not change what's happened, you cannot undo what you have already done. I did want to marry you, but that was before all of this. Take one day at a time. Okay?"

We both knew the following days would be very uncomfortable, but our love was strong, and the bond had not been totally severed. If we supported each other now, there was a good possibility we would get through this nightmare and become stronger from it.

LATE IN THE AFTERNOON I CALLED AMIN

I decided to call Amin, unfortunately he was on government business, but I left a message all the same. It was almost seven in the evening when the response came through from Amin. We chatted very briefly, and he invited us to dinner the next evening at the Four Aces Casino. Dylan was feeling much better he was careful to pay me a lot of attention all day.

Arriving at the casino we were greeted by the tall good-looking doorman, and then subsequently ushered to the appropriate table. Amin was dashing around the gaming floor from one table to another; his silver hair flopped over his face as he hurried along. A very attractive man, light tan silky skin with very sensual full lips and hazel soulful eyes that lit up and sparkled behind his silver rimmed glasses.

Amin my guardian angel.

> *"You will love this man, he is so kind, I wish we knew him before all these problems started."*
>
> *"He looks very nice, not what I imagined at all."*

Eventually a cheerful Amin approached the table where we anxiously waited.

> *"Hello, you must be the boyfriend Janette has told me so much about, I am Amin Walji, everybody calls me Amin, because first I am your friend then an MP, never forget that"* he spoke softly.
>
> *"Drinks and proper Indian food will be coming shortly. Janette has disclosed to me, this incredible story of which you and Reiner Moser are the main players… correct? Now then, I have made some enquiries myself and this is what you must do. Do not talk to anyone about Andreas Koeltz, the government are not impressed with his disappearance, they are humiliated. If someone knew where he could be found, you would go to prison for sure. Now you tell me what happened from start to finish,"* he said firmly.

A gesture of patting my hand felt reassuring. I listened intently to the saga as it gradually unravelled. Amin maintained a serious expression, frowning and occasionally taking a deep sigh. He was used to hearing strange and unusual stories as a member of parliament. But somehow this situation went far beyond the norm. Amin took the compassionate decision to help us, rather than venerate and glorify himself. With all the information now available to him he could easily choose to expose us, he didn't.

The meal arrived, it was a superb mixture of Indian dishes all hot and spicy followed with fresh fruit in a sweet thick sauce.

Amin took an instant liking to Dylan and the three of us were very relaxed. Our new friend constantly smiling and reassured us not to worry. Dylan told the Andreas story in detail; many secrets were revealed to me also. The Jessie episode was aired at my request.

Amin would know exactly where he stood. No one could come to him and add to this account, and he appreciated we trusted him. Amin had previously heard from me everything about how we arrived in Kenya, now this, the last piece of the puzzle.

AMIN MY WONDERFUL SAVIOUR

Looking into my eyes he spoke very calmly and sincerely.

> *'This is what we shall do. You have told me of a possibility of a manager's job in Namanga with your two German friends. We shall do this. You contact Nazir the owner, because this man's cousin or half-brother, is buying one of my video shops. Nazir is part Arabic, Asian with some connections with Masai on his grandmother's side. He will be a very shifty fellow, not easy to do business with. However, you call him, go down to Namanga and see if you can do something with the place, maybe we could try to buy it later. It is better all four of you go Janette, but I can offer you a job here as catering manager today. That does not help Dylan, I am unable to offer you both a place in this casino, but later, I will have the perfect job for you. You have told me these*

Germans have also been conned by Reiner. He told you to throw them out of Chiromo, but you are helping them instead. Decide to leave Chiromo and stay in Esperia Hotel, tell no one that you are going there. The four of you can wait there, until I can sort out a deal with Nazir, then hopefully you can all go and stay at Namanga Safari Lodge. Away from the problems and especially Reiner. Later I can place you and your boyfriend together where I can keep a closer eye on you. Don't think about the money Reiner has taken from you. I know it must be very worrying for you Janette. But forget it for the moment and plan accordingly, step-by-step, I will guide you. I need to get you all away from Nairobi until the heats off and the dust has settled. You will be fine this I can promise."

We finished our drinks and said goodnight to our wonderful friend. At last, there was hope by telling our story to Amin it somehow had a therapeutic effect on me, I began to unwind and relax again. Dylan appeared happier as the burden he carried was now shared with a loyal friend.

Amin was my guardian angel, and no matter what happened, I would someday repay him. He owned three casinos, one in Diani Beach, Kisumu and this big new one in the heart of Nairobi. Video stores and more. How would I return the favour? Or maybe it wasn't expected of me anyway. This gentle humble man eased his way into my heart, where love and respect would blossom.

Back to Chiromo for more madness.

REINER ARRIVES THE NEXT DAY

Reiner arrived in the morning he seemed very aggressive and demanded to see us in his office.

His thunderous voice yelling abuse at everyone.

He bellowed and marched up and down like a caged lion in the gardens, scaring the resident cats.

"Where were you both?" he yelled at us with a seething glare.

"We were invited for dinner, and I left word with Inga and Klaus."

Reiner hollered at me to throw Inga and Klaus out of Chiromo onto the streets.

"That's a joke surely? You owe them over two million shillings, and you want me to throw them out. Who will put us on the street Reiner when our time is up?"

I yelled at him as he paraded up and down kicking things and sticking out his chest with the odd twitch of his arms.

"If and when Chiromo is finished, you can always work in another hotel for me can't you?"

"What exactly do you mean Reiner?"

"If I should lose the court case with the landlord of this hotel, I couldn't stay here very long and would need another hotel, I have my eye on one and you both can come with me," he grinned sarcastically.

"Reiner you conned us of all our money. You kept Dylan guarding a wanted villain Andreas Koeltz, and you have been very well rewarded, yet nothing for Dylan? Meanwhile in Diani our workshop was ruined, the staff took all the tools and woodworking equipment. Because you had Dylan preoccupied at the hotel with a whore and as bodyguard to Andreas, the rent for African Oasis wasn't paid. Now, the workshop is in debt, and I have given you in good faith my capital as a loan, or investment, for a partnership in your run-down hotel. The rent at the apartment has not been paid either and Crismani has confiscated

all my personal belongings. You have presented us with the bill for the car hire, which you arranged for Dylan to guard Andreas. I have not received a salary; the hotel owes me money for stock I have purchased and bills I have settled. Please return the loan. I didn't want to fall out with you Reiner, but because of your recent behaviour and everything that has been revealed, you are now an enemy."

"Janette I will return your money as promised, but the money from Andreas was to pay off the judge, the lawyer Kurgat and a string of other hangers on. For myself, I have gained nothing yet, as you know he disappeared from the safe house. But I will flush him out, and when I do, he will be a very sorry man for crossing me. He owes me ten million shillings, which was the agreement. I intend to give money to Dylan for his part in the work and pay you back Janette. I will return your money with interest also. Have you two had an argument or something?

"Dylan, you look very sheepish my friend?"

Dylan remarked very confidently that there were no secrets between us.

"So, you must have talked about the Ukunda girl you have been fucking, have you told Janette how you wanted her to accompany you to the hotel? And how she shared your room for three nights? Did you also mention that you spent money on her in the casinos in Diani and in Mombasa too? Janette, he has been fucking her for months, doesn't that bother you at all? Dylan you are an idiot a fool, just look at yourself. Take a good look at your woman, she is beautiful, intelligent. You make me sick because you don't deserve a real woman. You should have stayed with the slut, you chose for company when your wife, yes, I say wife waited here day after day for nothing. It was not all my fault, but it is true, I did

keep her here for as long as I could. I am in love with her, you know it, and she knows it. I have tried everything to seduce her, but I became an animal. Dylan, my friend you do not deserve such a rare gift as her. You are too young and stupid to appreciate her true worth, her value, she is priceless, and you are just a stupid idiot, foolish gypsy boy. Ein Idiot jungen nichts mehr, als dass!" he shouted.

Dylan burst into tears.

"Yes, I have been a bastard; I know there is no excuse. I went out had too much to drink and she came on to me. I didn't want anything to happen, but like you say Reiner the animal in me escaped. But you set me up at the hotel by forcing me to fetch Jessie, for Andreas, you already knew I had fucked her, Matua told you. You knew before she arrived. What are you trying to do to us Reiner we thought you were our friend, when all the time you were using us, you're a bastard."

Dylan slumped onto the chair and cried like a baby. Reiner looked on cold and expressionless then patted him on the head.

THE SAFE IN THE WALL

Reiner opened the safe and placed a bag of cash inside then handed me the key just as he had done before.

"Why don't you send him back to his mother and you stay here with me, it would be the best idea yet."

He walked out in a huff. I tried to console Dylan but most of what Reiner had said was true. He had jeopardised a beautiful relationship for a slut. Dylan had caused his own suffering; it was just so sad that it destroyed a piece of me too. Maybe one day, I might recover but for now we had an uphill climb ahead of us. It was senseless to say, if only this had not happened, it was too late. Now if we were to survive the coming weeks, we had to put it behind us and not let the past stand in the way. We had only the present moment and survival was overriding everything, staying alive would be the paramount and principal factor.

My only thoughts were surviving in Africa.

THE NEXT DAY CONTACTING NAZIR NAMANGA

The following day I reminded Inga about the safari lodge in Namanga, she phoned Nazir again. Inga and Klaus had wanted a partnership with Nazir two years previously, but it never got off the ground. Now Nazir wanted to take on managers or partners, so he could concentrate on his ostrich farm and other investments. He wasn't available for a week, but very interested and keen to meet with Amin Walji. Nazir was also a Muslim; he would be extremely honoured to eat at the casino next week.

Namanga, a small dusty village on the border of Tanzania, but it was said the safari lodge had great potential, in the right hands. Nazir's next-door neighbour was John Kean MP a close friend to Amin. John an elder African statesman was a well-respected gentleman in government circles. A giant of a man casting shadows over everyone in his company, he spoke with a powerful demanding and thunderous voice.

REINER RETREATED TO THE COAST

Before he departed for Diani, another meeting with us, and Dylan wouldn't let me out of his sight. He shadowed my every move. Once again, Reiner told us to evict his old German buddies Inga and Klaus. Under no circumstances would he be prepared to allow them to stay any longer, they were an annoyance, an irritation to him they must go now.

> *"Reiner please return my money before you leave, I know you have plenty of cash."*

I had seen the stack of money in the briefcase that day with Mungai.

> *"Is that why you showed me the graveyard? You have destroyed our business by keeping us away from it; you used my good credit for your contract with Teresa."*

> *"Listen, I will return your money when I can, now it isn't possible and if you open your mouth about Andreas Koeltz, or the cash in my office, I promise you both, I will have you shot. Janette, you must be very careful who you speak to about me or my business, if I should hear anything you will be very sorry, do I make myself clear?"* he growled.

> *"Reiner don't talk to Jan like that, this is our business as well, you involved us both in this fucking shit and because it's all back firing on you, we are of no more use to you."* Dylan shouted.

> *"I'm not arguing with you boy, tonight we go to the Mayfair Hotel, I have to meet Kurgat the lawyer and German journalists from Focus magazine, be there at nine!"* he demanded.

We were very confused he told us he was leaving for the coast, yet he wanted us to be at the Mayfair Hotel in the evening. Another plan to get himself out of the shit!

I shared with Inga and Klaus what was unfolding.

THE MAYFAIR HOTEL

Two German journalists from Focus Magazine were drinking at the bar with Reiner and Kurgat. We approached them cautiously and ordered drinks. The conversation was in German occasionally a little English, when referring to Andreas and a bodyguard. They mentioned an article that would appear the following day, in the Daily Nation a local newspaper.

They all appeared very satisfied and pleased with the meeting; we were baffled by the request for our presence. The conversation was primarily in German. But Reiner's devious and nefarious nature was at work and obviously there was a method in his madness. However, another late night was not on the cards for us. Dylan and I made our excuses and made a keen exit.

BACK AT CHIROMO AFTER MAYFAIR HOTEL

Inga waited at the hotel entrance to greet us, eager to know what transpired. I explained it was a complete waste of time because they spoke German.

"You should have been there Inga," I told her.

"Who was there Janette?"

"Just two reporters from Focus and Kurgat."

"Reiner, Reiner what are you up to," she laughed.

The next day splashed all over the Daily Nation newspaper was a photo of Andreas framed in a wanted notice. We were told the police were looking for him and decided to place a *wanted notice* with no reward. Reiner had left for the coast, now everyone that came to the hotel wanted to talk about the article. Some friends and regulars remarked.

"This looks like a Reiner job, if it is, he has bitten off more than he can chew."

Two scruffy undercover cops arrived in hot pursuit of the elusive Reiner, I informed them he was away for a few days down the coast, they told me quite matter of fact.

> *"If you are involved in this scandal, make yourself scarce lady."*

This only echoed Amin's concern that the government did not intend to turn a blind eye to this front-page story. That evening, I called Amin to update him, he calmly replied.

> *"Don't worry I am here if you need me, here is my home number just in case of an emergency."*

Several unknown faces coming and going, looking rather suspicious and asking the staff questions. Two men from Interpol also paid a brief visit, wanting information about Reiner and his associates. I called Inga to handle the two odd Interpol men who seemed obviously out of place in Chiromo.

Inga explained Reiner's absence to them, he was away for a few days, and she had no idea where he went. They mingled with other Germans for a short time leaving an odd atmosphere lingering in the air. Everyone was on edge and wanting to know what the hell was going on. The following day I received several phone calls from Reiner's friends and associates, inquiring to his whereabouts, asking several questions about the Koeltz story. Morris the old man who sat on a small wooden stool every day and night, guarding the entrance, was behaving very peculiar. A strange small dishevelled African, with white hair, rotten teeth, and very bad breath.

He stared continuously at me with his small spooky eyes; I felt very uncomfortable when he came close. I never understood why his name didn't appear on the salary list. I called him to the reception area.

"Morris, you seem very unsettled these days are you feeling alright," I asked him.

"Oh, dear mummy I fear the worst is going to happen to you and Mr. Reiner, I am his spy, I listen to everything, and I see everybody coming and going," he jabbered.

He was previously a prison officer where Reiner served his time for the bank fraud. Apparently, Morris was well rewarded for smuggling in drink, cigarettes, and arranging regular female company for Reiner's pleasure. For his loyalty to Reiner, he was removed from the prison service, to become a bodyguard and spy at Chiromo. Inga had mentioned that Morris had poisoned Reiner's late business partner and arranged a mysterious car crash that killed another person, Reiner needed disposing of. I took these rumours very seriously as anything was possible in Kenya.

I had recently experienced the way things operate at the hands of Reiner. Perhaps, I was a lucky one, and if Morris had been given the job to dispose of me, I would not be having this conversation. Morris was ordered to keep a watchful eye on me. I invited him in my office for a cold drink and cigarette, at first reluctant but agreed. He had something to show me in private. From his dirty brown and black torn jacket his grubby leathery hands produced a newspaper cutting; he placed it on the desk and searched his pockets for more of the same.

"Mummy have you seen this? Look closely at the article."

It stated quite clearly the following message:

ALL THOSE INVOLVED IN ASSISTING THE ESCAPE AND AIDING THE RELEASE ON BAIL OF THE WANTED GERMAN ANDREAS KOELTZ SHALL BE

BROUGHT TO JUSTICE AND MADE TO FACE THE CONSEQUENCES OF THIER ILLEGAL ACTIONS
[or similar wording]

I could not believe my eyes.

"What exactly does it mean Morris?" I enquired.

"It means that Reiner, Kurgat, Matua, the Judge and other court officials and any other person involved with this case will be severely dealt with," he said anxiously.

"But mummy this is very embarrassing for the government, when the German was held on bail, by means of bribery to the judge, then he disappears, and Interpol turn up to extradite him. I fear for Mr. Dylan he was a bodyguard and you mummy are Reiner's partner in Chiromo that makes you a part of the equation does it not?"

There was wisdom in what he said and for the first time since the start of this saga, I began to feel the pressure mounting up and extremely anxious for all of us.

"You know mummy Mr. Reiner may not have any problems, he has people in the right places, but you and Mr. Dylan it is different. If someone wanted you removed, you will be gone. You have heard of the English lady Julie Ward?" he said with a cold look in his eyes.

"Yes, I know the story she was murdered in the Masai Mara."

"You will also end up in the bush if you are not careful," he calmly informed me.

"Is that so Morris, is that what happens to people that are an embarrassment or in the way?"

"Yes, that is how it is in Kenya, but Reiner was well protected in government, he would get away with murder," he smirked.

I discussed the strange encounter with Morris to Inga, she suggested we pack our things very discreetly.

"Janette, you contact Amin and inform him about Interpol, the newspaper and Morris, tell him we are not safe," Inga whispered.

"Reiner will come looking for us Inga," I said.

"Yes, we will have Interpol, the secret police and the bloody der Pate (Godfather) too!" Inga feared.

"What about money Inga what shall we do?" I asked her.

"How much is in the safe Janette?" she asked.

"I am not sure, I will look, but Inga I can't touch that money, it belongs to the hotel, for God's sake that's stealing!"

"No, no listen carefully. Reiner owes you a great deal of money; he hasn't paid you a salary since you arrived. He has ruined your business in Diani and Dylan guarding Andreas. Janette what is in the safe is nothing compared to the money he owes you," she said convincingly.

DYLAN ARRIVED

"That's right Jan, listen to Inga she is telling the truth. I know you still care about that bastard, but I don't, he is rotten to the core. I am telling you Jan, he will have me arrested then if you don't do what he wants you're well and truly fucked, am I right Inga. So, fuck the Moser Mafia and fuck them all!!"

> *"I'm so sorry for you both because you trusted and loved him just as we did, and he conned us all for everything. You have each other and you can forget about what went on with that black bitch you will come out on top. Believe me we must stick together, and then he cannot harm us. He has threatened Klaus and I so many times and my son, but we are German. It is different for you however, he really is in love with Janette and if he cannot have her no one else will, not even you Dylan."*

He had cheated so many people, how I got caught in the trap too would puzzle me. I thought myself smart, yet I was so gullible, and I was only one of many of his victim's. What other experiences lay ahead for me; I really was taking a big gamble sharing all my innermost secrets with Amin. Somehow deep in my heart, I felt I could trust him, why should he put himself out for me, he would have nothing to gain we were flat broke now. Maybe he felt sorry for me, he was a mystery, and I was drawn to him. He was a very peaceful and serene man, rather mystical and spiritual, whatever the attraction I needed him now. We packed our clothes and bagged up everything securely ready to depart the next day. Not uttering a single word to a soul.

THE LAST SUPPER

Klaus and Inga cooked a wonderful meal, and we opened two bottles of sparkling wine. This was to be the last supper and we would make merry while we could. Meanwhile Reiner had not been seen on the coast nor in Nairobi, had he gone underground and hiding? That evening plenty of the local Germans passed through Chiromo with stories to tell about the Andreas Koeltz affair, others just looking for the illusive Reiner.

One of the German visitors was my friend Hacky, a cameraman for German television. Almost always drunk, but a nice fellow when sober. I had a big soft spot for Hacky. He was filming in Rwanda and witnessed many atrocities, those terrible experiences impacted his life, he had a nervous breakdown. Hacky shared stories about what he saw and filmed, I wished he hadn't. He was devastated when his wife changed her mind about coming to Kenya, at the last minute decided to remain in Germany with their son. Hacky was a broken man.

My watch was smashed from the Reiner saga in the bush, so Hacky kindly replaced it with one from his collection of Swatch watches. Then one chilly Nairobi night after going out for a drink with him and friends, he gave me his brown leather safari waistcoat, he had just bought back from Ethiopia.

"Janette, keep warm, here this is for you."

Later Wolfgang sauntered in rather drunk and invited us to stay at his Kindani Safari Lodge for a few days. He had no knowledge of our impending departure from the infamous Chiromo.

"Wolfgang, I have your home number, so I will contact you," said Inga smiling.

Another mysterious unapproachable German criminal came in; he worked for a giant pharmaceutical company up country. He obtained the latest drugs for HIV sufferers and sold them on the black market. Reiner purchased them for Udo. Inga and Klaus were positive the briefcase stuffed with stolen money; this unusual German took out of the country for Reiner. I discovered that both men were *German Mafia,* with many shady deals going on. Most of the customers that frequented Chiromo did so for unconventional purposes, rather than merely socialising or staying a night.

The bar filled quickly with the regular hideously dressed prostitutes. Always making a grand entrance and causing a commotion. A small group of Asian men I often sat with greeted us and later sent over drinks for everyone.

Gurdial, he had become a good and loyal friend to me. He summoned me over to the bar and offered me a glass of whiskey. He began to ask questions about Reiner. None of the group liked Reiner and they were aware he was in some serious trouble. News travels very fast in Nairobi. Gurdial casually passed me a note with a telephone number of his government contact, if I was interested in selling the wanted German story.

"What are you talking about Gurdial," I said.

"Come with me Janette."

He took my hand and squeezed it gently, we walked out to the garden, near the pool.

"First, I will remove my turban and show you my hair, you asked me about it. This is a sacred act to show I am trusting you, and you need to trust me too, love you, Janette."

He casually and seductively removed his turban and began unwinding a thin black ribbon that held his hair up. He beamed and smiled in a very sexy fashion. Then he said.

"I want you to see me as a Sikh."

Then he hastily removed his colourful shirt. He had an ornate silver dagger tucked into his trousers belt. Gurdial pulled at the black ribbon and his thick shiny black hair cascaded down his back to his thighs. I gasped in wonder at his delightful godly presence and thought, yes, I could easily fall for you my beautiful friend. He hugged me and quickly put his hair up. Replaced his shirt amazingly fast, tidying himself taking a deep breath.

> *"Oh, Janette if I wasn't married, I would want you as my lover, and you have Dylan he has hair like mine although not so long, but he is just a boy and shook his head. You need a man."*

We composed ourselves and he continued telling me there were several people who wanted to put Reiner away, but no one could do it. He was too protected by the corrupt government. However, if I would sign an affidavit to the full German story, his government contact would pay me one million shillings, but I would have to leave Kenya immediately. I was very intrigued by this conversation and asked him where he got the information from. He refused to divulge his sources but said it was straight from top government, and I believed him.

What he said made sense; he seemed to be very well informed. His lawyer was a prominent Asian who wanted to see the notorious Reiner locked away. Twice in the high courts he had lost his case against Reiner, but now with the Andreas affair, he hoped this might be the one to send him away for the rest of his days. Gurdial was a very interesting Sikh, a good man with a great sense of humour; I was very fond of him. It was common knowledge he was fascinated with me. He was an excellent storyteller in the true fashion of the art; therefore, it came as no surprise to me the Asian community were informed by Gurdial that he was having a wild affair with me.

At first, I became angry, but in retrospect he was harmless, I don't think his friends believed him anyway.

> *"Janette, you know this Reiner fellow is a bastard, we hate him very much, but we all stick together he can't touch us. He owes*

plenty of money to many people he has several enemies. If you have any information on this Andreas story, sell it and get out of Kenya. He can be an evil bastard, just because you are a woman, it means nothing to him. In fact, because he can't have you for himself, it's now very dangerous for you. I swear to you Janette, the plain-clothes police will come, maybe not this week, or next month but they will arrive. There are numerous undercover creeps who work swiftly to eliminate any form of annoyance, or embarrassment to the government. But there are good men in there too; I can introduce you to these people if you want to make some money. If not, get away from Chiromo and keep your mouth shut and Dylan's too. Get far away from Nairobi until it all dies down a bit, okay."

He spoke with great concern, in a very serious tone. Then he gave a gentle kiss on the lips and winked at me.

"Love you."

Gurdial was totally unaware of our plans to flee, and I couldn't tell him. I was being well cared for by Amin another dear friend who we would see the next day.

It was very late when we all ventured off to our rooms to spend the last night under the Chiromo roof. Although I was pleased to be leaving, I felt very sad that it all ended this way. One moment we were all the very best of friends and then it became just like a horror movie. The drama began to unfold rapidly, and I was stuck in the middle of it all. Now with so many warnings from different sources our escape was perfectly planned. I knew I would never see Gurdial again.

THE LAST DAY IN CHIROMO

The sun was shining through the open window as the resident cats sauntered across the garden, morning had arrived. I got up early and finished the hotel paperwork. Then Mungai appeared, I called him to my office. I asked him to witness the safe being opened and to counter sign a document to state the contents therein. After counting the cash together, I asked him to sign a note for the purpose of my removing the cash. It was because of outstanding money owed to me. The debt would far exceed the amount I was withholding. The note stated quite clearly, I intended to hold the cash until Reiner decided to honour my loan/partnership, salary, and debts to me. Mungai agreed it was all above board and correct to take this action. He was only too happy to help as he photocopied the note and promised to hand it over to Reiner when he returned.

"Are you leaving us Janette?" he asked.

"No Mungai, I am going for a couple of weeks to a friend in Diani, to think about what I intend to do."

"I don't blame you if you go, I wish I had the courage to leave, but I am a coward. Reiner would never let me go; I know far too much."

He looked a very frightened man, with a nervous disposition, and drank too much. I could see sadness in his face, haunted by apprehension, fear in his eyes. This would be a new chapter for all of us, with much uncertainty. At least Amin was there for me, but who would help poor Mungai? My heart went out to this frail nervous soul. He knew too much, he had seen it all, over many years. The sad thing was, even his wife helped in her own small way with forged documents, she worked as a clerk for the government. Neither of them got paid for their devious deeds. It was surely a terrible place Chiromo.

Mafia HQ?

LEAVING THE HOTEL

It was time to go, the taxi arrived, and we must be gone before the spies arrived. We paid the driver, *pesa kidogo* to keep quiet and not to tell anyone where he dropped us. We transferred to another taxi and headed to Esperia Hotel, a quaint family run two-star hotel, clean and very basic. The building was old, with odd additions to it and poorly designed. Two very friendly smiling faces greeted us at the reception.

> *"Jinsi wewe kuja kwa njia hiilt,* how are you, come this way."

There was an odd aroma, like mothballs and lavender floor polish, but at least it was clean and hot water would be a bonus. Dylan and I found a large bright airy room to stay in. We unpacked and made our room as homely as possible with a photograph here and there and some flowers from reception. Meanwhile Inga rushed from room to room searching for her space to hide. Klaus struggled with their endless boxes and cases constantly tripping over his big ugly brown shoes. So much luggage it looked as if they had moved house, it was all they owned. They too had lost everything on the Kenya adventure. The silence in our room was broken with a loud bell ringing; this signified the telephone receiver should be lifted.

> *"Mummy the honourable Amin Walji is on the line for you."*

> *"Thank you,"* I answered excitedly.

> *"Hello, is that Janette, is everything alright, have you left Chiromo for good?"*

> *"Hi Amin, yes, the four of us are settled in and we will not be returning."*

"Okay do this please, I would like you all to come tonight to the casino for dinner, but I cannot join you until later, will you do that?"

"Yes, thank you."

I was excited; Dylan opened the door holding two cold cokes and some sandwiches.

"Guess who just phoned me here?"

"They are all talking about it at the reception."

The girls were giggling and saying Mr Walji has just phoned here for mummy Janette. Dylan informed Inga we were eating at the casino; she was jumping up and down clapping her hands like a child going on an outing.

Inga was very childlike, and I found that very endearing.

AT THE CASINO WITH INGA AND KLAUS

At the casino, a wonderful welcome with star treatment as Amin's special guests with staff smiling and waving as we sat at the given table. Everything was on the house, an excellent Asian chicken dish with special fried rice and vegetables and drinks all round. It was a long night waiting for Amin, at twelve thirty he walked in smiling and heading towards our table.

"Good evening would you like a drink? Make yourselves at home please, Janette come with me for a moment."

We walked to the other side of the casino and talked about what had happened. I left nothing to the imagination giving every detail of each conversation that had taken place. Listening with great interest he took my hand and whispered softly.

"Don't worry please, I will look after you, but you must trust me, and do what I say."

He stirred my emotions and tears streamed down my cheeks. Amid all the chaos and mayhem for just a short while, I was in a semi hypnotic state as Amin's velvet voice soothed away my anxiety.

RETURN TO ESPERIA

It was very late we said goodbye to everyone. Amin had arranged for a driver and silver Mercedes to take us back to Esperia. We quietly return to our rooms. The next morning, after a hearty breakfast a stroll around the hotel grounds we played a card game called rummy. The sun shone brightly overhead; we were reasonably relaxed as we sipped our cold drinks. No phone call from Amin and no news of Reiner that day.

The following week remained silent, without any news whatsoever we had a chance to unwind and chill out. I knew Amin was a very busy man and we needed to sit quietly and wait. Then, as we sat in the reception area, I received a call from Amin, he said we were to visit Namanga at the beginning of the next week, Tuesday sounded most likely.

WOLFGANG APPEARS

We were very excited about getting away from the noise of Nairobi and chatting about the trip when our friend Wolfgang made a casual entrance. Wolfgang was married, he owned a travel agency and the Kindani Safari Camp in the Meru National Park.

"Wolfgang, Wolfgang kommen hier schnell," yelled Klaus.

"Oh, hi there you guys, so this is your secret hiding place ha! ha! Reiner would never think to look here for you, well done," he laughed.

Dylan stood up and started dancing like Michael Jackson.

"I'll have another beer on that, well he isn't going to find us here."

"He robbed greater people. He is a pig. He has conned people in the government," said Wolfgang.

Wolfgang was a most extraordinary man and very personable. Quite a handsome tan face, yet interestingly familiar. Straight blonde hair swept to one side, and ice blue eyes, typically Germanic. With a wonderful command of the English language and a quaint accent with a lisp, Wolfgang would hold my attention for hours. From Cologne originally, married to an attractive frau working for the German embassy. Wolfgang did very little work, an idle man. He smiled like a Cheshire cat with two deep lines both sides of his face and laughed at practically any situation. Almost always drinking alcohol, no matter what time of day, he was great fun to be with. A German with a splendid sense of humour, I so enjoyed his company.

"Okay guys, it's like this, sometimes I call here for a beer or two before going on to Chiromo, so you have bloody well caught me red handed ha, ha! So now, I am at your disposal why don't we piss off to Kindani for three days and enjoy a safari ride eh! What do you say Janette, Inga?"

"Great idea Wolfgang, fantastic, out of Nairobi for a few days just in case Reiner turns up."

"Well, it is my thinking that its Reiner's first time a rejection from a woman, ha-ha, he is very angry."

"Ya, this is very true, he is in love with Janette," laughed Inga.

"You have done something that no-one else has had the courage to do and for that you must pay the penalty. Still, you have done this thing and for that I must salute you, because people here do not say no to the Moser."

He chatted in German with Inga.

"Reiner gets what he wants, and if he cannot he eliminates, so that no-one else can have," remarked Inga.

"Ya this is correct. I am an officer and captain of submarine corps, and you deserve the medal for bravery Janette ha! ha! So, we are playing the hiding and seeking game, is this what you call it in English. He's going around telling people you were infatuated with him; we all know that Reiner was in love with you Janette. How come you're not afraid of this big bully that gets people killed."

"Well, I am not afraid of him, and I can change state and surround myself with a bubble of energy that protects me, its energy and magic."

"Jesus Christ. I wish I could do that," laughed Wolfgang.

TRIP TO KINDANI WITH WOLFGANG

MERU NATIONAL PARK

We all swiftly packed a few things, shorts, T-shirts, a pair of safari boots and jacket. Leaving behind all the cosmetics and female fancy items. Kindani was a long journey up country into the Meru National Park. Inga and Klaus had been there several times, but this was a new adventure for Dylan and me. It was much needed for us all to escape from this crazy experience for a few days. In Meru we would have no luxuries such as electricity, television, or telephone, only the open plains, rugged mountain range and wild animals roaming free. I called Amin to let him know what we were doing, he said.

> *"Great, you must go and relax before the trip to Namanga, and everything gets busy."*

We clambered into the dark green Mercedes jeep and set off on our safari in a very joyous mood. Keeping a sharp eye out for the infamous Reiner to appear, as we weaved our way through the traffic in the very busy city. Looking behind us but we didn't know who we were looking for, he had spies everywhere.

As we travelled outward from the hub of Nairobi the traffic sounds where just a distant drone. Out into the savannah. The roads were good for the first couple of hours, then bumpy, narrower, and dustier as we approached Meru district. It was still another two-hour jarring dusty drive through the bush.

As we neared the park, the heat of the day became almost unbearable, as the fine red almost talcum powder dust blew in the jeep, sticking to our sweaty faces and bodies. We tried travelling with the windows closed but it was insufferable.

> *"Time for a beer kubwa sana, biridi mingy sana," (very cold and very large), g*asped Wolfgang, whilst rubbing his dirty hand over his parched lips.

> *"Yes, please I'm so thirsty, it's so hot up here, I thought Mombasa was hot, but this is bloody awful, phew!"* Dylan remarked as he tried to get out of the jeep.

We were all stuck to our seats and our clothes were wringing wet with sweat and brown dirt. My clean white T-shirt now red and transparent, I was braless, so Dylan passed me a denim shirt to slip over my noticeable breasts. We stopped for thirty minutes rest, cold beer, and a sandwich, at an open café in a tourist lodge surrounded by lush green plants and trees. We freshened up and walked about for a while. A most delightful oasis, a glorious place in the middle of no-man's-land. It was wonderful to sit in the shade and relish the much-needed cold beer.

"Not long to go now, get back into ze jeep," laughed Wolfgang.

My back and bottom were aching and so sore, yet people pay good money to go on safari, what a punishment I thought. In the National Park the roads were horrendous, bumps and big potholes everywhere. As we ventured on deeper into the bush the dust and dirt got darker in colour, almost burnt orange.

"The only thing likely to kill you here is a Rhino, not a Reiner," said Wolfgang and laughed.

Many local villagers would take this winding road to the nearest market. As the local woman struggled with babies strapped on their backs, with colourful clothes tied around them they carried huge parcels on their heads. The men nonchalant, strolling along empty handed. It never ceased to amaze me how these fragile woman and girls could carry such large amounts on their heads. When our jeep passed each family group, they would immediately be engulfed by the thick trail of dust we left behind. We could barely see them through the thick haze.

"Only another hour or so and we will be at Kindani, I managed to get a radio message through so the fires will be lit, and the water shall be ready for the finest shower you will ever have in your life," Wolfgang delighted in telling us.

Another hour I thought, will this journey ever end?

> *"Oh, you two guys will love this place; you have never been to a safari camp before, well, this is an experience you will always remember,"* said Wolfgang.

At last, we approached a high mesh wire gate, Dylan jumped out and opened it, *we* would soon see the camp said Inga as she began getting excited. Most of the journey Klaus had spent snoozing and snoring, while Inga gave us an in-depth report of the whole Meru district. Inga had many safaris under her belt, not just here, but over twenty years of safari holidays and expeditions. We were in good hands; our German friends would see that we had a memorable experience.

IN THE COMPOUND OF KINDANI CAMP

As we entered the compound the staff came rushing toward the jeep to help carry the luggage and greeted us with, *karibu sana,* very welcome. Even though it was dusk by now, with the open fire casting shadows over the camp, it was breath taking and magical. On the right-hand side of the compound, a large open eating area, covered with an enormous makuti roof supported by huge timber beams, tall and narrow natural tree trunks. A long hand carved solid wood table and beautiful brown leather safari chairs. Brightly lit gleaming iridescent storm lights hanging from trees and timber poles casting strange shadows on the fast-moving river below. It was a perfect setting to relax and enjoy the food being prepared for us, especially after such a journey as this.

There were six beautiful round houses typically whitewashed, with very high makuti roofs. Each house was a large circular room, containing two substantial heavy carved single beds. Each bed draped in the familiar mosquito net, a white porcelain sink in one corner, two small wood framed windows. Outside the front split wooden door, were two dirt tracks. One leading to a spotlessly clean toilet, with an old-fashioned blue and white jug and bowl. At the end of the other track a tall round roofless construction, inside a tall shower pipe with an enormous rose spray outlet, a wooden seat and two large taps. Gazing up at the dark night sky with stars sparkling like diamonds as the intermittent cry of the wild far out in the bush, creating a mystifying experience.

Wolfgang remarked that the water was boiling hot due to a simple invention of his. He was a German Navy officer for many years, mostly on submarines, and very creative.

"My ingenious ideas come very easily to me."

Smiling and pointing to the river as he explained the hot water system. Pipes ran from the river up to the campsite and passed through huge old oil drums constantly heated, by a raging log fire. Thus, causing pressure and hot water, he explained. There was much more detail to the shower invention, but I got lost in the technicalities and the broken English.

Wolfgang a very intelligent interesting man who spoke many languages and lived in Japan for a few years he shared many fascinating stories about his life. A very beautiful small Somali girl who was serving the dinner turned out to be Wolfgang's mistress. She was a little shy and very young. She chatted to Inga in a strange mixed tongue, about how Wolfgang kindly paid lots of money to have her *vagina* unstitched. Inga, engrossed in the story, filled in the spaces she didn't understand, with Swahili and her own native German. Apparently, Somali Muslim girls are literally *stitched up,* so they remain virgins, until they marry. Wolfgang was so appalled by this story; he most admirably had her vagina freed in Nairobi. Only to recapture for himself later, but this was very noble of him she thought.

After a few merry German biertrinken *beer drinking* songs, plenty of delicious food Dylan and I took the dusty track to our cosy round house. Those merry Germans who remained behind, would barely interrupt the hush and silence of the night, as they preoccupied themselves with campfire stories. Dylan and I fell into a deep and glorious sleep, exhausted from the arduous journey, which had led us to this blissful, heavenly place. No one would ever stumble on this secluded hideaway in the bush, only the local tribesmen and Wolfgang. If by any remote chance a stranger did approach this faraway isolated sanctuary, we would know immediately. This place, this beautiful safari camp a haven set in a vastness most precarious, dangerous, and unpredictable.

EARLY MORNING IN KINDANI

At first light we were ready to explore the campsite. As the door opened to greet the early morning a wonderful cool breeze of fresh air filled our lungs. We were being welcomed to Meru National Park. An amber radiance glowing on the horizon, as the sun began to ascend the deep turquoise skyline, would be just one of the unforgettable moments of Kenya. Birds singing and chirping in the tall trees and flying high as they hovered above us, in contrast to the rushing sound of the river cascading over the huge rocks and boulders. This would be the only noise echoing and breaking the silent dawn.

We observed the glowing orange celestial orb rising against the clear blue cloudless sky, the most magnificent vista, a vision to behold. And oh, how fortunate were we to witness this wonderful day in Kindani.

The staff hurried around the open-air kitchen as we prepared the long breakfast table. Fresh exotic fruits, African dishes placed next to German food, as tea and coffee were poured, and chilled bottles of water at hand. After a hearty feast we decided to tour the local area and village with Wolfgang as the eager guide. The morning was mostly taken up by driving around in the jeep. It was agreed by all that we should walk to the marketplace, to stretch our stiff backs and aching legs.

We approached a very strange little village nothing like I had seen before, with only one available drinking place. It was a corrugated tin hut covered with brightly coloured murals, with part mud walls on both sides. A rickety wooden door leading through to the bar and yard, where scrawny white almost featherless and frightened chickens waited to be slaughtered.

A small and dirty broken bench with a matching table that wobbled and creaked. No drinking glasses, only bottles of beer or soft drinks. But at a price you could persuade the owner to sell some spirits if he felt so inclined. The heat of the day became overwhelming, so we made haste to Kindani, to cool off under the shade of the makuti roof and a few cold beers to quench our thirst. We rested in the cool breeze next to the rambling river and played a game of cards. It was great fun and nonsense; Wolfgang constantly tried his best to cheat, as sharp-eyed Dylan noticed every sneaky move. After a siesta, dusk was approaching and the heat of the day passing. We washed our tired bodies under the lustrous African sky, in our steamy hot showers, with only the call of wild animals echoing in the distance.

> *"Wolfgang wonderful, marvellous, wunderbare,"* shouted and overly excited Klaus.

Another very eventful entertaining night, when the local tribe joined us, after we had eaten an enormous feast. The main topic of conversation for some unknown reason was sex, as a giggling Wolfgang began the conversation.

"Let's get talking about stitching up vaginas!"

This led to the hasty retreat of the lovely Somali mistress and a deathly silence from the locals. The Germans in fits of laughter and giggles from Dylan and me. Encouraged on by Wolfgang, the locals told their story about condoms, which were too expensive, and they needed to reuse them repeatedly. Wolfgang wanted to know how they managed to reuse a condom and burst out in fits of hysterical laughter. They demonstrated to him in a very matter of fact way, how to roll it up after it was washed out. Wolfgang decided to experiment with a condom on a broom handle. This demonstration caused uproar and pandemonium as these naive innocent people looked on in amazement.

"Hakuna, hakuna wakuu, no, no chief, you roll it up this way," a young man wearing a torn faded green shirt and baggy brown shorts shouted.

"Give it to me bwana looky, looky like this," insisted an older man.

The wives were sitting firmly on their hands with heads bowed and staring at the floor in silent embarrassment. After a few glasses of the local hooch, these timid people began to communicate more freely. In Swahili explaining what they could or could not do sexually to their wives. With great roars of laughter from us, the mzungus, white people, they seemed so surprised to learn how much they were missing out on.

Klaus would burst out laughing slobbering.

> *"You are not allowed to do what? oh deary me, I don't believe it, look my friend you must try this first, and you can this or that too. It is all very lovely."*

Dylan asked if they were allowed to have oral sex?

> *"What is this mummy?"*

They enquired looking at me, and I was asked to explain? I did enlighten them and with loud screams and roars from some of them.

> *"No this is very horrible, you cannot do this, how you can be kissing these smelly things it is wrong?"*

We laughed so much at the innocence of these simple people. I could understand the point they were making, but of course, they are less hygienic than us. I guess to them it would sound disgusting. Washing themselves would not be high on the list of things to do daily; eating and drinking would take priority.

The once shy women now relaxing at this *mad hatter's tea party,* joined in with the sex stories fun. They revealed many tales and told us that women of one tribe are not allowed to touch the husband's penis, it was forbidden. If that wasn't hilarious enough, they told us that the women of another tribe in the north, must sit on the husband's penis when he died and have sex. This story was followed with a detailed account of young girl's circumcision. By now I had enough sex stories, laughter, and drink.

SANCTUARY IN MY ROOM

I took refuge in my room and read a little by candlelight until Dylan came in; the topic of conversation influenced him; he was eager to undress. He paraded around the room showing off his manhood and telling me just how horny he felt. Making love with Dylan was always special, but the Jessie story would linger in the inner most depths of my mind. No matter how I tried to push her out of my thoughts, she stayed that night and many more to haunt me.

Dylan kissed my face and neck and ran his hands over my body as he whispered softly.

"I love you Jan."

I cried and he did too. We loved each other passionately, however we both recognised that something had changed in our relationship.

THE NEXT DAY IN KINDANI

Another glorious morning, as the faint aroma of the late-night campfires lingered in the air, and Wolfgang hurried along the dirt track from his room shouting!

"Hurry up let's have breakfast and hit the road you guys; we are going on safari deep into the National Park. I want you to meet the park warden."

After a hearty breakfast we all piled into the dirty green jeep, for another interesting day out. We would travel through the park where the wild animals roamed free and let all our worries disappear. Deeper into the National Park we travelled leisurely passing giraffe, zebra, impala, gazelle, and many other small animals, stopping at the river to watch the hippos playing in the muddy water. Many other animals were spotted in the bush on our way to the warden's house.

"There it is, now we can have a cold beer and meet the warden."

In the distance we could vaguely see something; it was a bit hazy like a mirage, but noticeably large with something dark and shadowy moving around it.

As we approached the track leading to where the warden lived, a big, whitewashed lodge could be seen. There, in the middle of the bush, encircled by a large group of enormous baboons and other smaller monkeys, the wardens home.

> *"Oh my God Janette, look, look baboons I love them!"* shouted Inga, she was very childish but fun too.

I was very apprehensive and dubious of baboon behaviour; I let the others go first. The warden appeared from his house waving and laughing.

> *"Come it's okay they will not harm you, come tafadhali, please mummy."*

I made my way to the wooden porch to meet him. He was a very pleasant older man with greying hair and missing teeth, with a cheerful disposition. We sat outside on the veranda soaking up the picturesque scenery; the maid arrived with a tray filled with ice-cold beers and biscuits.

> *"Oh, just what we need lovely thank you,"* mumbled Klaus.

The topic of conversation was baboons for quite a while, then other monkey behaviour. The warden shared stories of his work in the park with other animals and declared his favourite species to be birds. It was terribly difficult to understand him; he had a peculiar lisp when he spoke. A weird and wonderful way he mispronounced words through the gap in his teeth. However, Klaus understood what he was saying, but then Klaus also spoke an odd language of his own, in broken English, German and Swahili. Somehow, they had rapport with each other, going into great details that only they understood.

We said our goodbye to the kind warden and made headway to the other side of the park to visit an old village chief, that Wolfgang had become very fond of.

Arriving at the village we were greeted by children pulling and pushing us around and tugging at our clothes. Mzungu, they shouted and clambering over each other, to touch my long blond hair, they giggled and found it all quite amusing. I was a spectacle for them, a rare site to see a white woman with long fair hair, and if they could touch me that would make a great topic of conversation for weeks. Grubby little hands pawing at my arms and legs, as the older children grouped around Dylan to get a closer look. Their cute faces lighting up with delight, at this tall handsome mzungu, with hair like a woman. The older girls were fascinated by Dylan, with eyes only for him. Inga and Klaus walked amongst the people smiling and *jumbo sana mazuri sana.*

The chief of the village, small scraggy elderly man gradually made his way from his little shabby house. Several seniors, one by one following in procession with a trail of laughing children running up to meet us.

"Karibu sana, Karibu habari gani?"

"Welcome, very welcome how are you?" the old man mumbled.

He spoke in a strange Swahili dialect and with most of his teeth missing it was barely understandable. Fortunately, Wolfgang could make more sense of it than the rest of us. So, without prompting, he would interpret the old chief's messages.

It was traditional to bring a gift when calling to the village chief, the most welcomed gift would be a large bottle of vodka. We were summoned to stand in a circle as the old man sipped the vodka from the bottle, holding the spirit in his mouth for a moment. With his eyes closed he began spitting it through his gummy mouth and spraying us one by one. It was a local tradition said Wolfgang, but I knew different, it was plain and simple to me; it was an act of magic, the start of a ritual. When the ritual was complete, we were asked to sit down on the ground and handed a chunk of dry bread to break and pass on to the next person.

Is this not the bread and wine Jesus' story I thought to myself?

I found it impossible to eat after viewing the scabby, filthy hands of the chiefs second in command, who grasped and fondled the bread first.

With much reassuring from the rest of the group and a piercing glare from the old chief, I swallowed the softer innermost part of the bread. Thus, avoiding the crust that had been previously mauled. After an hour of negotiating Wolfgang was handed ten fresh eggs and some strange looking ugly vegetables, as the chief stumbled back to his hut carrying more booze.

It was time to head back to camp, it was almost dusk, the sun was setting rapidly. An amber hue appearing across the vast sky as we ventured along the winding roads back to Kindani. Then not too far ahead the sight of the warm glowing storm lamps and the blazing open fire sending flames over six feet high, with hundreds of red sparks falling like rain overhead. It was a very welcoming and magical sight. The wonderful aroma of African food drifting gently in the evening breeze, a delightful welcome home, after a long hot day in the park.

Before leaving for the trip that morning, we tied three bottles of sparkling wine to a rope and dangled them in the icy flowing river. The water gushed over the clanking bottles and created a better cooling system than the old gas fridge, already packed to the brim with food. This would be our last supper at Kindani; we intended to have a party with the staff. Whoever else appeared, would be most welcome, but there would be no more sex talk or condom demonstrations.

Another walk along the dusty track to the wonderful open shower room and the familiar faint echoing sounds in the distance. It would be the last time to experience the hot steamy water cascading over my body, as I gazed up into the African night. An awesome heavenly vista, the full moon and enormous beam of silver light, in the vastness of space.

The evening progressed into a great feast. The food superb and the company delightful, as we sipped cold sparkling wine reminiscing on our remarkable time together in Kindani. A few local people arrived singing and dancing, especially enjoying the German bierkeller songs, as we all made merry. We had the pleasure of another older chief from a nearby tribe, who drank all the remaining beer and polished off half a bottle of vodka, to Wolfgang's dismay!

As the campfire died down to a warm red smouldering glow and the flickering candles vanished one by one, the clock struck 2am, it was time for Dylan and me to retreat for the last time. It was truly a brilliant day, and excellent last supper. Laughing, singing, and falling all along the dirt track, holding each other up, eventually we reached the welcoming beds, neatly covered with white sheets and huge fluffy pillows. We both fell asleep without removing our clothes. In the morning, we both complained of chronic hangovers, showered, and changed. A heavy rainstorm during the early morning hours, but we were totally oblivious to its presence. The cool fresh damp air hit us; it was very humid. The others already up enjoying a hearty breakfast.

The long dry grass and abundance of flowers now lovingly nourished by the rain. However, the dirt track was now a slippery mess of reddish muddy sludge.

> *"Good morning you guys, hope you had a good night's sleep ha-ha!"* laughed Wolfgang.

Klaus and Inga oblivious to the world around them tucking into the mountains of food and washing it down with several mugs of hot sweet coffee.

LEAVING KINDANI

It was time to leave the tranquillity and stillness of this magical place, our haven of joy, and return to the hectic chaos of Nairobi and the dread of Reiner Moser.

We loaded up the jeep and said farewell to the staff and waved goodbye to the locals, who were preparing to fish along the river.

> *"Kwaheri Kindani, goodbye Kindani."*

We all shouted out together, as we slowly made our way towards the big compound gates and back to another reality outside of the camp.

The return journey would prove quite dangerous and hazardous. The heavy rainfall on the dirt roads now very slippery, the surface at least three inches of reddish sludge with dense thick mud beneath. As we slid from side-to-side Wolfgang remarked it would take four hours to the main road and not the usual two. We slid around inside the jeep and glided across the road. Each side of the road had deep gullies, fatal to slide into, we would never get out. So, we moved very cautiously, gliding on top of the muddy road, like a performance on ice. When we reached the main road, we stopped by a tree to wash off the pounds of red clay, which stuck to the wheels and mudguards. Then we headed straight for the local watering hole. We rested for half an hour after a couple of much needed cold beers and a snack. We hit the road again leading us back to the madness in Nairobi and Reiner reality, but now a more pleasant journey on solid ground.

The trip seemed endless, especially after the long slow dicey first four hours on the slippery Kindani mud road.

ESPERIA HOTEL

Arriving at Esperia totally exhausted and extremely hungry. We ordered a large portion of chicken curry and several cold beers. After chatting about the camp experience, we were ready for a good night's sleep. I would never see Kindani again, nor would I find such a comfortable bed or marvellous shower experience. Wolfgang slumped on a chair in the dining room; he was too exhausted to move. In the morning, we met up in the reception area for breakfast. Still heavy-eyed and disorientated, Wolfgang explained he snored so loud he woke himself up. He was still drunk and thought he was in Kindani, until the resident ginger cat licked his face and he fell off the chair!

"Oh, fuck where am I?"

Dylan phoned Amin and filled in details of our wonderful adventurous safari to Kindani.

It was Tuesday morning, and a message was sent for us to travel to Namanga and meet with Nazir. Wolfgang offered us his jeep, his wife was away for a break, and he would use her car. After a wash down and removal of the thick red mud the jeep was ready for another adventure. We were now embarking on a journey which would lead us in the opposite direction. I mentioned to Wolfgang, it was such a wonderful experience, and I will always remember his kindness, laughter, and sheer crazy German entertainment.

"Safe safari to Namanga and watch out for the mad dog Reiner Moser!" Wolfgang grinned.

PART 5

NAMANGA

NAMANGA SAFARI LODGE STORY

Our journey to Namanga took us through lush green hillsides and rolling valleys, rugged mountainous landscape, and shadowy outlines of Kilimanjaro. Another incredible safari, but this journey would not compare to Meru National Park and Kindani Safari Camp.

By taking the Mombasa Road for an hour, we would then be turning inland, heading towards Tanzania. It was a nice straight road, compared to up and down hills in Meru. We were heading through Masai country, but we also experienced other tribes along route, as we passed through the small villages. The scenery along the way was breathtakingly stunning. Mountains barely visible as a hazy mist lay across the peaks, lush hills, and valleys, deep green and gold. Trees breaking up the vast flat plains of rugged land, where only Masai ventured.

It was a privileged sight to witness such noble tribesmen adorned with colourful elaborate beaded jewellery. Beautiful tall people elegantly draped with red or purple clothing, holding either a spear, or stick. These fine-looking, exquisite warriors that once roamed the open Mara plains, now stood side by side to modern man. Africa's past and present together in harmony. Kenya's finest, elite warriors, who for centuries wandered freely with their cattle, these people direct descendants of an ancient noble people. Strangely aloof, but with great dignity, the Masai stand alone, set apart unlike any other. Now succumb to Kenya's modernisation.

A peculiar giraffe like walk, that is noticeably different from all other tribes. With huge holes in their ear lobes filled with wood or stone, dozens of gloriously coloured beads around their necks and intricately designed belts. Large spread flat feet, stomping the dusty roads and long thin arms, they glide along in unison.

We were totally enthralled and temporarily shifted in a time warp. Only the roar of the heavy lorries that frequented this main route to the border would break the spell. Thundering along the hot dusty road carrying goods to and from Nairobi, I thought how different, yet strangely compatible the old and modern world.

Nearing our destination the scenery became more rugged and rocky, yet amazingly striking. We could almost see the magnificence of Kilimanjaro Mountain in the distance, yet somewhat obscured by white fluffy clouds. Not yet clearly visible, but a truly incredible vista. It was approximately three to four hours' drive depending on the weather, potholes, broken down lorries and the wild animals.

NOAH'S ARK EXPERIENCE

The road was quite good for Kenya, and slowly approaching a large sign that warned of animals crossing. We could see in the distance a substantial hand painted signboard displaying several strange creatures rather like cartoon figures, in bright colours.

Namanga Safari Lodge - Stop and see the Animals.

Painted on a pale blue background, zebras, camels, ostrich, baboons, and various birds. It looked ghastly and reminded me of a local school project. Turning right into Namanga a short bumpy road would lead us passed a few corrugated tin kiosks, selling soaps, sweets, and cigarettes. Another signpost beautifully painted pointing to John Kean's Namanga River Lodge with lush green gardens that surrounded several delightful little whitewashed cottages, however, this was not the lodge we were to stay at.

> *"Here we are at last, well Janette, I hope you like this place because Klaus and I love it here."*
>
> *"Look over there Dylan can you see the camels, oh! look there is more geese and turkeys Klaus,"* Inga said very excitedly.
>
> Like a child she bounced up and down on the seat, as we slowly moved along the bumpy driveway.
>
> *"Inga, Inga Nazir has a baby baboon now and the parrot is still here, hello Kazuku,"* Klaus babbled in English.

At the end of the drive, I could see a broken-down ruin. It reminded me of an old saloon bar, in a spaghetti western, surrounded by a strange variety of odd broken tables and chairs, packed together on the porch. One building with crumbling faded pale blue walls, large cracks and masonry missing, with iron barred windows. A grotesque building like a prison, rather than a tourist safari lodge. Dylan and I glanced at each other in disbelief, if this is the outside what will the rest of the lodge look like?

INSIDE THE COMPOUND

We were previously informed, it was a little run down, and only needed some cosmetic work. But this was clearly a complete renovation job. However, not to get too down hearted, we shared the same view with Inga, agreeing that it could be a lovely place. Some available cash and a lot of hard work might bring it back to life.

Beyond the main building stood several uncompleted structural projects, one with no roof, doors, or windows. Heaps of rubble strewn everywhere with huge rocks and gravel piled up against the walls of the unfinished buildings. Shabby old dirty tables and odd chairs in the middle of the patio garden. Peculiar metal bus shelters to shade the tables from the midday sun. Nothing matched; it looked ridiculous and very ugly.

To the right a strange type of barbeque fire, built from stone and brick. A large extended area with a kiosk under a makuti roof, with more rickety seating surrounding it. The gardens needed attending to, although some areas had flowers and shrubs neatly trimmed.

Running around in circles, annoying the few customers sitting outside, a fully grown male ostrich called Charlie. Pecking at anything in his path, and flapping his enormous wings causing havoc, as he dashed from one corner to another, like a giant headless chicken! Standing peacefully unnoticed at the gate, Charlie's girlfriend, much smaller in stature waiting patiently for him to stop the nonsensical behaviour. She appeared to be unimpressed by his ritualistic dramatic performance, preferring to remain obscure until he had tired himself out. Several squawking pigeons' flying overhead, feathers falling and zooming into action in search of scraps of food and landing on the customer's table.

The noise and flurry caused a battle scene, as the turkeys fought with the hungry pigeons. However calmly standing by were four magnificent creatures, Spanish fighting birds, with a glorious array of brightly coloured feathers. The turkeys were just ugly turkeys.

It was absolute bedlam for about ten minutes, as each species desperately fought for territory. Feathers flying, screeching, and screaming as they entertained the staff. Three scruffy mongrel bush dogs unexpectedly appeared from the gardens, barking and snarling. Consequently, chased the flock away, which left the original culprit Charlie quietly unconcerned and casually standing in the shade. Charlie sauntered off towards his patient girlfriend, and from under a large plant over a dozen baby ostriches came scuttling around the corner and disappeared through a hedge.

A massive, felled tree bordered by decaying branches and a six-month-old baby baboon called Suzy, partly restricted by a long chain around her right foot. She ran up and down the felled tree, yelling and screeching, displaying acrobatic skills and seeking attention.

Unexpectedly she leapt into the air landing on Dylan's shoulder, she began to groom his long wavy hair. Keeping everyone else at bay, with sudden outbursts of high-pitched screaming and flashing her enormous sharp teeth. We casually stepped back to watch her groom, Dylan. After a few minutes she calmed down and leaped back onto the tree showing off her acrobatic ability and then snarled aggressively, as she threw twigs at us.

LODGE INSPECTION

We headed towards a long narrow shabby timber building, with a corrugated tin roof covered in green slimy moss. This was the actual lodge with several rooms for guests. There were two unsafe wobbly wooden steps up to the veranda, with a few broken-down wooden bench seats. One small window covered with rusty metal mesh mosquito wire, a remnant from the past.

We made our way inside the building and entered a dark dingy room. The walls and ceiling were painted a pale cream colour, in need of redecoration. No mirrors, or pictures. Odd faded floral-patterned curtains, creating a stark contrast against the creamy walls. Two dirty mosquito nets barely hung from a poorly painted cardboard ceiling. On closer inspection they were completely covered in thick dust, several kinds of dead insects and full of holes. There were two old shabby single beds made of wood and metal. Filthy urine-stained mattresses, covered with thin worn grubby coloured sheets and pillows filled with old smelly lumpy foam and rags. The lighting was a dim light bulb, hanging from a threadbare wire above one of the beds.

Through a broken door held together with brown sticky tape a dirty shower and toilet. A very small window dressed in mosquito netting nailed to the wall and a small, cracked mirror dangling on a piece of string. No toilet seat and no cistern. A lead pipe sticking out of the wall with a few chipped or cracked discoloured white tiles. The shower was a pipe running up the wall with a rusty watering can rose and two odd, shaped taps at waist level, one blocked off; the other constantly dripping icy cold water onto the floor.

"Inga did you know it was this bad, it needs a renovation, not a facelift!" I grumbled.

This was the first guest room, was it going to be a typical example of the other rooms? To our horror it was the best room on offer. As we made our way from room to room it was obvious the building was becoming derelict, and in some parts a total ruin.

"Oh, Janette don't worry, we can do something together, eh Klaus? You tell her it will be alright."

"Ya, its vill be awright you see Janette," uttered Klaus.

Adjacent to the garden area, a gaggle of geese began attacking some white chickens and then spotted us. They scurried across the lawn sending flowers flying in the air and knocking over clay pots. They circled around screeching and flapping their wings, forcing us to retreat to one of the rooms for safety. We all laughed so much we fell onto the old wooden bed, which collapsed in a heap beneath our weight.

"Oh, Klaus help me up!" yelled Inga.

Dylan pulled me into his arms and kissed me.

"Well babe, it's better than Reiner killing us."

"You thought Chiromo was bad Janette, but that was heaven compared to this," laughed Inga.

"At least we are out of Nairobi, I think we could cope for a few months Inga."

For the first time in weeks, we laughed so much we forgot the Reiner danger that loomed behind us.

It was a deadbeat business with little trade or suitable accommodation, but if we had the financial support, it could be rather a quaint place. The Tanzanian border was a fifteen-minute walk from the lodge. Lorries and holidaymakers, people on safari would stop there. Amboseli Safari Park was on route and many people come for the wildlife, or to visit Kilimanjaro.

"Nazir never did anything with it as you can see, but now it's falling apart, so if we can raise the money for a partnership or buy him out, we will be alright. What do you say Janette?" asked Inga.

I agreed there was great potential, but first we need the meeting with Nazir and then inform Amin what terms Nazir is asking. Amin was the only one with money and he wanted us out of Nairobi quickly.

Someone shouted.

> *"Mzungu hapa hapa tafadali huraka sana!"* here, here white people please very quickly!

We hurried across the gardens now free of screaming geese, pigeon attacks and Charlie, as Nazir the owner strolled casually towards us.

> *"Jumbo sana sasa Inga and Klaus, hello what's happening?"* said Nazir.

> *"Habari mumbo vippi, Nazir, how are you what's the story then Nazir?"* shouted Klaus.

> *"Pleased to meet your two friends. Welcome to Namanga and my animal sanctuary. Please sit here; I will arrange food and cold beers. You must be thirsty after the long hot journey."*

NAZIR THE OWNER

Nazir in his early forties but much younger in appearance and especially attractive. He was rather short with an excellent physique. An interesting mix of Arab, Asian and Masai, he reminded me of a young Omar Sharif the movie star. Beautiful sparkling light brown hazel eyes with long thick black eyelashes, full lips, and magnificent perfect white teeth. Lovely thick dark auburn curly hair, that contrasted against his fresh clean white cotton shirt.

Nazir kept us entertained for over an hour or so, telling us funny stories about the guests at the lodge. Occasionally stopping to chew a local relaxing herb, a sort of grassy twig, and a constant supply of ice-cold coke at hand. Nazir offered some herbs to us, but we all refused, keeping to our cigarettes. He mentioned his wife Najma was in Tanzania visiting her sister, and then to Zanzibar to her aunties. She would be away for a couple of weeks. He said she was aware we were coming to join them at Namanga. After a meal of local chicken stew and bread we ate fruit and drank beer. Nazir explained we would run the lodge as managers for three months, with no interference from him or his wife. We would only pay rent to them, and the lodge would be our business. To include all guest rooms, bar, restaurant, and gardens. He said he had a figure in mind and would discuss it with Amin at the weekend, when he would journey to Nairobi. We mentioned there was no electricity.

> *"Yes, that's right but you will have the big generator and simply pay for the diesel, I will make sure that it runs perfectly for you, okay?"*

It all seemed satisfactory and with a few other questions regarding where the four of us would stay, and the stock in the small shop attached to the bar. He said he would make a list of everything, and we would pay for the stock as we sold it.

> *"Hakuna matata, no problem."*

THE RESTAURANT

It only remained to venture into the restaurant and kitchen to finish the tour of the lodge. The restaurant was reasonably tidy painted cream but very dirty. Nice pine tables and chairs, an old television and video player, a small serving hatch from the kitchen and another doorway leading off to the backyard. The shop was stacked to the ceiling with boxes, canned food, bottled drinks, and rubbish, all buried beneath layers of thick dust. The dust and cobwebs clung to a broken window patched up with cardboard and brown sticky tape. The only visible light via a small crack in the grimy window frame. Three enormous unsociable fluffy cats, lounging across the counter hissed and meowed as Nazir ordered them to move. The reluctant cats protested but eventually sauntered off disappearing in a thick haze of choking dust to the rear of the shop.

Knee deep in out-of-date biscuits, chocolates and tins of different vegetables, canned food. Several bottles of wine and spirit, lined up like soldiers on the shelves collecting dust, seemed to be the only stock of any value.

> *"My wife Najma never cleans the place, so she can see exactly where everything is, follow me through this door it's my living quarters, but naturally I will move out and take one of those rooms up there."*

He was pointing to a terrace of rundown rooms at the far end of the garden where more ugly turkeys roamed.

> *"It will not take long to clear our things out, but we have so much stuff it's a big problem, perhaps you might assist?"* grinned Nazir.

They lived in disgusting conditions with one small dark bedroom, the window boarded up. The room was extremely hot and stuffy due to the tin roof with a dreadful unpleasant aroma of damp clothes and stale food. A large bed-sitting room with a nice double pine bed and red cloth sofa, dining table and chairs. It was typically Asian, with several brightly coloured pictures and tourist ornaments on dusty shelves. Through a door to the kitchen, on the floor two pots on barbeque racks for cooking, vegetables stuffed in a sink, and cupboards bulging with packets of dry store. A large table covered with old books, videos, and piles of assorted magazines.

The back door led to a yard where they kept three bush dogs and several yapping puppies, adjacent to an overgrown garden with vegetables and herbs. Beyond the garden four other metal buildings containing squawking chickens, which they bred for the restaurant. A stinking accumulation of sludge and mud mixed with camel's dung. Nazir informed us that the camels were out walking, they will come back at dusk and bed down. The stench was atrocious; we could hardly breathe and began feeling nauseous, as the sun beat down on heaps of steamy manure, Dylan began to vomit and shake.

> *"You'll get used to it after a while, when all details are confirmed with Amin, you can do what you want here, you can clean up this area and move the camels somewhere else. Well anyway, you do what you like if the rent gets paid, I don't care. I want to concentrate on my ostrich farm."*

Returning to the restaurant area we stopped for a few minutes to catch our breath.

> *"Let's have a cold beer and cigarette before the kitchen tour?"* said Inga.

> *"What on earth will the kitchen look like Inga, this place is a pig sty,"* I gagged.

> *"Oh, Janette this is Africa, you will get used to it, believe me. You have been spoiled by the tourist areas like Diani Beach, this is the real Kenya. You will love it here."*

Inga gleefully informed me, heaving up her enormous bosoms grinning as she marched off to the kitchen. Klaus and Dylan were both giggling when they saw the expression on my face, as Charlie the ostrich casually sauntered out of the restaurant.

> *"My God! This is bloody Noah's Ark,"* I said in sheer disbelief.

Then the two huge colourful Spanish fighting birds came scurrying out with feathers flying everywhere, Klaus and Inga oblivious to them!

"How are we ever going to get these animals to keep out of the eating areas Nazir?"

"No worries, I will make a compound over there," smiled Nazir.

Somehow, I didn't believe him.

THE KITCHEN

A dark narrow corridor leading to the kitchen with boxes of food and rubbish scattered on the floor. What would greet us at the other end of this black tunnel? I couldn't help but be concerned for what lay ahead.

"Ah! Daylight," laughed Dylan.

We pushed our way through the half open door to the kitchen. A ghastly noxious stench of dung, urine and rotten food filled the steamy stagnant air. A barbecue charcoal fire blazed in one corner, heating three large aluminium pots of water. Two disgusting grubby sinks with dripping taps, and a constant leak from the waste pipe. One mucky soiled wooden table, stacked up with plates and dirty utensils hanging on string over the sinks. Greasy unwashed pots and pans piled high on the floor. A family of baby ostriches huddled up next to the charcoal fire, previously last seen hiding in the hedge.

Nazir informed us the baby ostriches must sleep in the kitchen at night, heat was crucial, and they might get stolen if left outside. A short bamboo pole placed between some old iron pots as a sleeping place for Kazuku, the unsightly squawking resident parrot. Suzy the boisterous baboon would also sleep on the floor in the kitchen chained to the sink.

"What on earth are these animals doing in the kitchen? We could get seriously ill with food poisoning from them. Look at the shit everywhere. It's bloody disgusting!" I mentioned.

"You don't understand, they must sleep in here at night it is safe and warm," said Nazir.

Horrified by Nazir's blasé comment I hastily left the stinking kitchen. As I stumbled along the dark passage tripping over the boxes gasping for air from the noxious kitchen experience, I finally reached the garden. A concerned member of the staff, ran over to assist me.

"Sorry mummy you look very sick can I get something for you."

The waiter enquired, whose name was Mohamed.

"Yes please," I gasped.

"A large vodka."

He laughed.

"You know mummy we Africans don't live like this, it's the dirty people, Asian Africans. We have complained so many times to Nazir about the animals in the kitchen, what kind of person keeps a baboon, ostriches, and a parrot in his kitchen? It is a restaurant mummy; oh, dear may Allah forgive him."

Suddenly, six or seven meowing kittens scurried out of the kitchen, through a small hole in the crumbling wall.

"Look you see mummy, cats, dogs, baboon, ostriches and that ugly parrot called Kazuku," laughed Mohamed.

"Please hurry with the vodka!" I gasped.

One by one the others emerged from the darkness of the passage, very pale and shaken from the entire experience.

> *"Are you having a whisky or something, Inga?"*

I suggested with a sarcastic tone and a wry smile.

> *"It was never ever like this before Janette, honestly, I don't know what Nazir has been up to since we last met, but the whole place is falling apart?"*

As the colour drained from her face, Inga gasped for oxygen and shook her head in sheer disbelief. There was only one rusty chest freezer, which doubled up as a fridge. Only the essential items were kept inside said Nazir, like beers and sodas, but not the food. Attached to the kitchen a small kiosk construction where a member of staff worked, taking orders for food and drink. Nothing was given out without a receipt, written down several times in different reference books, typically Asian book-keeping. We all laughed so much at the silly construction resembling a wooden 1930s telephone box. We couldn't believe this small black girl Carol, was in there day and night invoicing, booking in and out a few simple meals and drinks.

As the shock of the lodge subsided and thoughts of heading back to Esperia, we bid farewell to Nazir and his animals. Waving goodbye to Noah's Ark as we drove away in total dismay and fits of laughter.

BACK TO NAIROBI

The return journey was filled with laughter and disbelief at how people could possibly live in such horrendous conditions. We chatted about the animals roaming around freely and the outrageous kitchen scenario.

"What do we tell Amin? He wants us to work there, but we must tell him the truth about Noah's Ark."

Arriving back to Esperia we made straight for the bar, then with our cold beers in hand, we all disappeared to our rooms. Scrubbing ourselves clean of the Namanga experience and resting to reflect on the madness. Later I contacted Amin, he suggested we should rest for a few days, and he was very busy at work.

We reflected on the Noah's Ark story, as we played cards and drank beer on the patio, for three days.

VISITORS ARRIVE BEN AND JENNY PONT

"Hi you guys," Ben smiled.

A surprise visit from Jenny and Ben Pont they were meeting up with friends. They mentioned they were filming Michael Jackson's video *Earth Song* with a giant elephant made especially for the part. Michael Jackson was a bit unconventional, but he was nice enough for an oddball Jenny giggled. Ben promised to get a signed photograph for us and a copy of the video on completion. We shared our amusing story about the horror scenes at Namanga, with Ben laughing and suggesting he could make a good film from such madness.

"Are you really going to work at this Noah's Ark place?" asked Jenny.

"Unfortunately, we cannot return to Chiromo and Amin has work for us in the New Year. It is a job, and we all need to stick together as you must know, we have problems at Chiromo and with Reiner," I said.

"Reiner is a first-class bastard Janette, everyone knows that. Inga you should have warned them not to part with their money. This country is a very dangerous place for the naive, believe me even the best of us get conned. So don't think it is just you Janette, Inga and Klaus lost money too. Reiner makes promises he never keeps."

After a few beers and much laughter about the Noah's Ark visit, it was time for our friends to head back home.

WOLFGANG ARRIVES

The next morning after breakfast Wolfgang arrived to pick up his jeep and enquired about the trip.

"So, my friends how did the safari to Namanga go, hey?"

Wolfgang was falling about in hysterics after we revealed the story of our Noah's Ark experience.

"This bloody Noah's Ark place I must see for myself. Anyway, I thought you ought to know Reiner is in town and looking for you. He is fuming, fucking mad with Janette for taking the money from the safe and has told me, if I should by chance bump into you guys, that to say you are all 'dead meat' would be about right. Yes, guys he is one very uptight nasty Bavarian looking for revenge, he swears he will find you and have you killed. Well Janette and Dylan are on the hit list! As for you Inga and Klaus, he will sort you both out another day. No rush for them."

We reminisced about Kindani safari and laughed about Namanga; Wolfgang needed to leave but would return the following day to update us on anymore Reiner madness.

FOUR ACES AND AMIN

A few days passed and we were getting ready to meet Amin. At the casino we met a few government people milling around the tables. Amin was late as usual; we had our meal before his arrival. Dylan was standing at one of the blackjack tables with Inga, as Klaus chatted to the staff at the bar. I was sitting alone, and a tall African man approached me.

"May I?" he asked pointing to the seat next to me.

"Yes, please do."

"I have seen you in Chiromo many times. Reiner is a good friend of mine. If you ever talk about Reiner's business to anyone, then I will personally make sure you will end up buried in the bush, well you've been warned, goodnight."

I was stunned, I couldn't recall seeing him in Chiromo and the threat was very real. Although this man was mixing with the government group, he could have been anyone. I waved to Dylan to come over and told him what occurred, I looked for the stranger, but he had disappeared. Amin arrived and after twenty minutes came over to our table. We enlightened him with the Noah's Ark Namanga experience, and in-between the hilarity and laughter, he would say to us.

"It will be alright these people are not clean, and the animals, well Janette, you could eat them if you get hungry, ha-ha, at least it is out of Nairobi, and you are all together."

Amin mentioned a meeting must be arranged with Nazir as soon as possible and we departed the casino rather exhausted but feeling very hopeful.

ANDREAS KOELTZ ARTICLE OCTOBER 1ST

The following day in the Daily Nation newspaper a big article that said, Andreas Koeltz had come out of hiding fearing his life and felt safer in the hands of the police. He was taken to prison and would remain there until the courts decided on his future. At the same time Interpol were making an application for his extradition to Germany, to stand trial for fraud. We couldn't believe he had just given himself up. But after some discussion it was agreed, he made the right decision; at least his life was no longer in danger from the mad Moser. Dylan wanted to visit and support him, but everyone out voted him and we would keep quiet about the whole Andreas affair.

We heard on the grapevine that Reiner would keep his distance from us for now, but the message was to remember that he would wait for us when we appeared again; tell them when they do surface, I will be waiting. Although concerned by his death threats, our plan to go to Namanga remained our paramount concern. We didn't venture out in Nairobi, only taxied from Esperia to the Four Aces Casino. We stayed within the hotel grounds playing cards and reading, with exception of the safaris to Kindani and Namanga.

NAZIR AND AMIN MEETING CASINO

At last, the meeting was ready for all parties to attend and as usual we dined at the casinos expense. Most of the hour-long conversation between Nazir and Amin was spoken in their own language. So, we waited patiently as requested and the two men bartered the agreement. Finally, Amin spoke.

> *"You will go to Namanga this weekend and will be managers, you will have full control of all areas and you will pay Nazir his rent, every month for three months. You will take over the stock*

and pay him the same as he paid for it. The profits will be yours, and all the money you make from the rooms will be yours to purchase goods and pay salaries, the remaining profits are yours. This is for three months, on this agreement between Nazir and me and I have told him, if you cannot pay the rent from your profits, then I will pay it for you. This will help you to build up the business. Janette, you will report to me weekly by phone from Namanga and prepare all bookwork for me to review monthly. If all goes well then, we can discuss the purchase of the Safari Lodge for us."

Nazir mentioned that he would vacate the rooms he was in and move to a small house in the grounds; he would not interfere with the running of the lodge. It all sounded plausible and credible. They shook hands and with a very serious expression on his face Amin expressed to Nazir.

"You must honour our agreement, if you do not, I will be very angry, do you understand me?"

Nazir grinned and replied.

"Don't worry Amin, everything will work out for all of us."

Klaus and Inga were instructed to leave at the end of the week, and we would follow shortly thereafter. Although we had our work cut out, it all sounded optimistic. However, Nazir had forgotten to mention his wife Najma oblivious to this agreement between us.

WOLFGANG RETURNS TO ESPERIA

The following day at Esperia our old friend made a brief entrance. Wolfgang appeared very scruffy, dirty, and somewhat incoherent, with a copy of the Daily Nation newspaper under his arm. He told us he was arrested for a vehicle violation and endured the entire week in the same cell as Andreas.

"Hello guys how are you. Yes, you are wondering where Wolfgang has been for these days. Surprise, since I went to this safari to Kindani, I was arrested on a small charge; I have been on a different safari with a fellow German called Andreas Koeltz. Very interesting indeed to share a cell with a fellow German, and especially this guy. You can learn an awful lot when you live with someone, Ha! Ha! Reiner is waiting for him to be released. It's a fucking hell hole in there, my God let me get back to Kindani for heaven's sake, but at least I have some strength to get there. Poor Andreas is a very sick man, he may not make it Dylan," shaking his head.

"I need to go and see Andreas!" supposed Dylan.

"Vere are your brains – are you keeping ze brains in your arse, you are a fucking idiot? Do you not think you have caused sufficient problems as it is my boy? Apparently, Reiner has lost interest in you, but you must surface at some time or the other and he will be waiting that's what I hear around town. He is a fucking animal, so you must be very careful guys. Oh, and how is the Noah's Ark agreement coming on? You must be a glutton for punishment Janette, taking Inga and Klaus with you, please be careful, they spent too long hanging around the mad dog Moser. Anyway, good luck to you, I'm having a few beers at Chiromo."

AMIN CALLED

Amin phoned and requested that we go to the casino that evening. I explained Wolfgang was with Andreas in the local prison and everything seemed to be gathering momentum.

At the casino after eating, Amin arrived.

"I don't think you should wait, go as soon as possible. Don't all go together. Let the Germans go first, wait two days then go."

Great excitement as Inga and Klaus packed ready for the trip back to the madness of Noah's Ark. We questioned if they would even make the journey with all their belongings weighing the taxi down. Suitcases, boxes and the two fat Germans stuffed into the matatu, with huge bags piled high on the roof rack. They waved goodbye as the old rusty matatu taxi slowly manoeuvred its way from Esperia Hotel.

LAST NIGHT AT FOUR ACES CASINO

Dylan and I had one last evening with Amin before our departure to Noah's Ark. I was able to have a private moment with my dear friend.

"You can do this. I don't feel good in myself that this is where you must be for a time. You prove you can make something of this lodge, and I will make something better for you. I am only a phone call away. And every couple of weeks I want you to come back to Nairobi."

A couple of days passed by, and we prepared to leave Esperia. It was another long hot tiring journey back to Namanga, we were forced to stop twice with punctures. As the sun beat fiercely down on the metal roof of the taxi, it became unbearably hot like a mobile sauna. As we passed the villages on route, we saw several groups of young Masai men and boys called the Moran (warrior), who are sent out into the wilderness to defend themselves, as a rite of passage. It is an initiation from boy to man. Before Kenya's wildlife policy became law, the Moran would have to kill a lion before they were permitted to return to their village. Now the lion is protected, and this ancient ritual no longer exists.

Litibikwan Lekararo the askari at African Oasis had mentioned this experience to us.

ARRIVING AT NAMANGA

The cheerful taxi driver grinned as he wiped the dirt from his wet brow and muttered under his breath mzungu kwaheri, goodbye white man.

> *"Here bwana Namanga, oh you are to stay at that awful Safari Lodge, pole sana,* very sorry."

Running over to meet us Klaus puffing and panting waving a colourful handkerchief in the air, followed by some of the staff, turkeys and Charlie.

> *"So glad you are here Janette, oh deary me, we having many problems,"* Klaus blurted out dashing towards us in a panic.

> *"Karibu sana, willkommen zurück, very welcome,"* Inga shouted from her small dingy room.

The staff took our luggage and put in the room next to Inga and Klaus, we strolled a few steps behind feeling rather tired, confused, and disorientated.

A short overweight very angry Asian lady dressed in bright clothing, greeted us.

> *"What do you want here, this is my lodge!"*

She shouted in a high-pitched voice. That was the introduction to Najma, Nazir's crazy hysterical wife.

As we sat sipping a cold beer, listening to what had developed, Najma stood a few yards away glaring at me. Confused staff dashing from one place to another trying to appear busy, we could sense an awfully uncomfortable atmosphere. As for Nazir he was nowhere to be found and didn't show his face that day. The next morning eager to start work we made our way across the gardens to the restaurant, passing by the noisy turkeys and Charlie the ostrich on the way. We ordered breakfast, Nazir, and Najma where absent. After half an hour waiting to eat, it arrived on a dirty tin tray. Bread barely toasted, runny eggs, tea too milky and bruised or rotten fruit.

"This is a good start, Inga!" I said with a giggle.

We skipped the bland tea for orange juice instead.

Unexpectedly there was shouting and screaming coming from Nazir's rooms. Banging and pounding, more yelling continued for about twenty minutes. A thick cloud of dirt covered Charlie as Nazir's car sped up the driveway, followed by Najma running after him waving a stick.

The peace and tranquillity of the lodge would never return. Suzy the baboon went wild running up and down the tree screeching. The chickens and turkeys ran for cover, as the barking yapping dogs chased after the car and ran straight out of the gate. The staff looked petrified as they dashed about trying to find something to do. Najma strolled back slowly waving her fist in the air, seething, and disappeared in her rooms.

I called Mohammed over to explain what was occurring, but he was very reluctant to disclose details of the argument.

"Oh, mummy I cannot say what it is, but it is not good for all of us."

But he did say it was because Najma wasn't informed about us taking over the lodge, and she wanted us to leave right now!

Nazir had taken flight from his enraged wife, there would be no work done today. At lunchtime we were approached by

Mohamed holding a tray with an unsavoury meal of cold stew. It was formally placed on the table, with a bill for bed and breakfast and the meal we were about to eat. The situation was getting out of hand nothing was straightforward or going to plan. Nazir eventually returned and casually strolled over to us with an air of importance and a supercilious grin.

"What's going on Nazir?" asked Klaus.

"It will be alright I promise, it's just Najma doesn't like the idea of change, and everything is in her name."

"Oh, dear Nazir, you have not been very straight with us have you," Inga interrupted.

"She will get used to the idea of you here, but she refuses to move out of our rooms and will not allow you to have all the guest rooms either, Najma wants to keep four rooms on one side, and you can have the other ten," he said firmly.

"We must use two to sleep in, until you move out so that gives us only eight rooms, we cannot possibly make any money on just those rooms," argued Inga.

"She is refusing to leave our rooms also, so what do you want me to do?"

Nazir marched off in a huff waving his arms in the air.

"We must talk tonight before this situation gets worse," Inga demanded.

Later that evening Nazir arrived to tell us his wife had nothing more to say, and we could not begin our management position, until the first day of the month. It was the middle of October, we couldn't sit around waiting to start work, it was agreed in Nairobi we would begin today. Najma insisted she would charge us bed and breakfast and evening meal, obviously this was not going to work out. We had little money for food and drink, plus the return fare to Nairobi. We urgently needed to contact Amin.

GENERATOR BREAKS DOWN

It was a very stormy night and trying to make the call to Nairobi proved impossible. There was only one telephone available, and it was next door at John Kean's lodge. The four of us sat in Inga's little room, to plan our strategy. This situation was outrageous, we had no friends, and we were merely mzungu strangers, in an offbeat border town.

Najma refused to talk to us. Nazir was obviously in fear of his hysterical wife. There was no electricity power and we relied solely on the old worn-out generator. Curiously, one night it just stopped, there was complete darkness. Only the cry of the Noah's Ark animals and other wild beasts in the bush, broke the still of the night. Torches began to shine; several candles and storm lamps were lit, as people stumbled about the compound. We had our suspicions that Najma was behind the power cut, as another means to get rid of us. The generator would stay off for the next three days and nights. It began to feel a little spooky and eerie. No communication with Najma, but she peered out of her window occasionally. Nazir reassured us there was nothing to worry about, and he would destroy the bed and breakfast bills. After a fruitless long search for a spare part at the lodge, two mechanics arrived from the village to repair the generator. The defrosted food fed to the animals and Najma presented us with the bill for it. Nothing was as it should be, it was crazy behaviour. After several attempts to call Amin, we finally got through, but the line was very crackly, however. He understood our plight, but we couldn't understand his answers. Nevertheless, he advised me to return to Nairobi for the weekend, as Nazir had promised to attend another meeting.

HEADING BACK TO NAIROBI

Leaving the two Germans behind we squeezed into a matatu full of Tanzanians also heading for the capital. We purchased two seats each, for the extra room. The taxi moved away slowly with the weight of heavy bags piled on top of the roof rack, with chickens clucking in the back. Even though the windows were open, the awful odour of sweaty African bodies would make our journey unbearable. No matter which way the breeze blew, the stench was overbearing and constant.

We arrived safely and driven through the back streets of Nairobi, as one by one the Tanzanians were dropped off. We paid the driver extra money *pesa kidogo*, to take us to the front door of Esperia Hotel. The usual two sweet girls were cleaning the reception area and appeared very surprised yet pleased to see us back so soon.

> *"Mr Dylan what are you doing back here, we thought you were in Namanga?"*

> *"Jambo sana habari gani sasa?"*

We asked the girls how they were doing too.

> *"We are very sorry you cannot have the same room. An Asian rock band has taken the whole floor and rooms downstairs. Janette they are very loud, shouting and screaming all hours of the night. They start to practice with instruments, so loud we can't hear the phone when it rings, and the manager is not strong*

enough to tell them, they are booked here for three months. It is all paid for by an Indian boss."

Our room was much smaller than the one we stayed in before, but it didn't really matter we needed only two nights. We were requested to head for the casino in the morning and wait for Amin to arrive. We were having coffee in the casino when Amin came dashing up the stairs, he was wearing a cream-coloured shirt, with his chest slightly exposed, and a pair of badly fitting light blue trousers.

"Come you two let's go!"

We followed quickly down the stairs to his driver waiting in his white Mercedes car.

"Jump in then, hurry up I want to get something in town."

We began the conversation about Nazir and Najma in Namanga. Amin amused, nonetheless getting angry.

"These bloody Arabs you can never trust them, don't worry I will fix it for you, Nazir is a bloody fox."

As we drove into the city centre, we were amazed with Amin's easy-going nature, and how he constantly joked with us. An unpretentious MP, very down to earth, a very extraordinary man. Never boasting about his position, just simple and easy to be around.

Suddenly the car stopped at the traffic lights.

"Let's go," he said, grabbing his small brown cloth bag.

The three of us got out and left the car and driver at the roadside by the red lights. He briskly walked along the street, two steps ahead of us as people called out.

"Look that's Amin Walji!"

People waving to attract his attention. Pushing through the crowds he took my arm and led me to a very big supermarket store, with practically everything you could ever want yet totally disorganised and piled in massive heaps everywhere. The shop staff recognised Amin and made a fuss around him, yet he had no concern to the special attention he was getting. A rich casino owner and an MP, Amin was just taking his two friends out shopping.

From one place to another he pulled me around in circles, with Dylan following in line. As he stopped at each item, he would explain to me how to get the bargains. He was pricing everything for the safari lodge, new linen, crockery, and kitchen utensils. We looked at the latest charcoal and gas cookers, fridges, and freezers. After making notes of all the items and prices, he grabbed a bundle of leaflets and then dashed off to two other stores. Finally, an hour or so later we returned to the car, where several police officers were surrounding the driver.

"What's the matter?" Amin asked one policeman.

"Hakuna matata, no problem, Mr Walji, we are waiting for you to return."

Weaving our way through the crowded streets and back to Westland's area and stopping for a wonderful meal at an Indian restaurant. We were taken back to Esperia and Amin continued his journey back home to wash and change, for the busy night ahead. Later we were at the casino waiting for Amin. When he finally arrived it was getting late, about midnight. First, we discussed Andreas Koeltz and our friend Wolfgang's report of his condition in there.

"This is good news for us. Now they have him they will cool down a bit, but why was Reiner still at large? My God he is a sneaky fellow."

Back to the Namanga situation, he said it would be difficult to push Nazir anymore at this moment, as nothing was written down; it was only a verbal agreement. He would talk to his family about the possibility of buying the lodge, for us to run for him. At the same time, he would talk to John Kean about a possibility for Dylan and me to manage his lodge. Inga and Klaus would have to stay at Nazir's.

All in all, there were many options open to us. But first we must make a list of all the repairs needed and all the things we must replace. Meanwhile Nazir made excuses on the phone that he had to travel to Tanzania and couldn't possibly make the trip to Nairobi until next weekend. Amin decided that we should return and start working as agreed, he had talked to Nazir, and it was all approved to take over.

AMIN'S MISTRESS PLAN

Conversation with Amin.

> *"Why are you so kind to me Amin?"*
>
> *"It is not that I am kind to you, it is because you are in a hopeless situation, and I am merely holding your hand."* he whispered softly.
>
> *"Look my dear friend you have been conned and lost your business and capital, and that is happening to people every day here in Kenya. Some extremely clever people have been in this situation; so, don't blame yourself too much. Many good men have fallen victim to this. You are a very attractive, nice white lady, an easy target indeed. You are very vulnerable because your foolish boyfriend has let you down, very badly. He has got you both into this mess and the involvement with Koeltz. A boy trying to be a gangster, in a very dangerous place like Nairobi, he is simply asking for trouble. Now it is like this, when I first met you, I*

wanted very much to meet with you alone, come with me now, into my office we can chat privately."

In Amin's office he continued to talk.

"Janette let me be honest with you, I really wanted to get to know you more personally, however, you told me of your love for Dylan and that was good enough. I am married to a beautiful wife; I love her very much and you have met one of my sons. My other son is studying in England, he is a smart young man, and he will go far. My daughter is a strong woman too. But you know when Asian women get to a certain age, they no longer want to have sex, this is always the case. I hope, I am not embarrassing you. I have lost something in my marriage and at times I need the company of another woman. It is extremely difficult for me because I must be very discreet. We would have to meet in secret, and no one can know what is going on. Do you understand me? I find it very hard to trust a woman, sorry, but it's true. I trust you, and I am terribly fond of you. I would very much like to get to know you better. However, you have a young stupid boyfriend, who you love, and you have devoted yourself to him. Albeit foolishly, you gave up everything for him and he has repaid you with so much stress and pain. Not just the Reiner problems but he has cheated on you, with a black girl."

"Please Amin stop! I am hurting as it is. I am trying so hard to put on a brave face."

"Janette, I know these things and I don't want to send you to Namanga, a dusty broken-down Lodge, but there is nowhere I can put all of you together. You can stay here with me and manage the catering for me. I would be delighted, but I cannot place your boyfriend here. He must work you cannot keep him anymore. Let us do this, I know you will not be parted from him okay, you both return to Namanga and do your best there for the

three months. If you make money or not, what difference does it make, you are safe. Come up regularly with him, to see me, and let me know the progress. After the three months, I will place you and Dylan in my casino as managers at Kisumu. I cannot do it yet, as there are too many things involved and besides, I want to see how good you really are at the job, is that fair? When it is time for you to takeover Kisumu, we can discuss the issue about if you would care to be my mistress or not?"

"What, you want me to be your mistress?"

"Yes of course."

"You will have a nice house and a very good income too, but Dylan will have to work for his own keep, think about it, you have three months to decide. Anyway, surely, I'm not that bad, am I?" he chuckled.

"Amin, you are handsome, and I am very attracted to you. I can't think of anyone else I would be a mistress to, in fact I am honoured you asked."

"It's very difficult for me to be seen talking alone with you, there are too many eyes watching me. There are cousins, nephews, aunties, and my own son all watching us. So, it is good we only meet with Dylan around, isn't it? Let's go back into the casino now and you think about my offer, I will give you the kind of life you were used to, the one you walked away from, for your silly boyfriend. You can talk to your boyfriend about it if you want to, after all what can he say eh? He has had his fun; he cannot say anything really, can he? And at least you will have money in your pocket again; I will arrange a car and driver for you too."

OLD WISE MAN IN THE CASINO

Amin took my hand.

"Come on I want to take you to meet someone."

An elderly white haired Asian gentleman sitting alone.

"You sit here, and you wait with my friend Panjab [incorrect spelling and pronunciation], and you listen to him. He is a wise man. Have a drink with him. You know I must be busy in the office for a while and then I will come back to you."

We chatted for a while. He was very charming, educated with a fatherly manner about him.

"You know Amin is a very good and kind man If he can do anything for you, he will, and it will help you."

"Yes. I know that."

"Good, do you understand the depth of this issue that you're set up in?"

"I do, well I think I do," I said.

"I don't imagine you do, because you know that any moment something can happen, and you all can be removed, do you understand that?"

"Yes, I do understand," I said.

"But there is an opportunity for you, for just you and if I were a woman, I would take this golden moment. You know, you will have everything of which you have ever dreamed. You will move away from this nightmare. You will have a beautiful home and a bodyguard. A whole new life, but you must walk away from everything that you are right now. Everything that you know. Then all will become right for you. Otherwise, you are going to have the responsibility of these other people and who knows what

may happen if somebody says something about this story. There are options that are open to you – but not to everyone else, and you know the best choice for you, is that you are the personal special friend to Amin and let these others go."

I loved Amin, he was such a wonderful man. But I could not abandon Dylan, I promised his mother to look after him and he was my responsibility. I also felt accountable for Inga and Klaus. He took my hand, smiled.

"Thank you for your kindness," I said.

I walked over to the bar, Dylan mesmerised at the roulette table and mixing with the rich young Asians.

"Hi Jan, do you want a drink?"

It was Rod a Scotsman who I had previously met; he was living in Nairobi with his parents. I had Amin on my mind and a warm glow inside of me. But Rod broke the spell, to say.

"As you guys are leaving tomorrow, perhaps you would like to meet up for lunch at Gypsies?"

We would be leaving in the afternoon for Namanga.

"Yes, that would be great Rod."

GYPSIES BAR MEETING WITH ROD

We met Rod and chatted about how we started African Oasis and the Reiner scenario, when his friend Duncan joined our company. Duncan another Scotsman, a very handsome young man with long dark hair tied back, a goatee beard and moustache. His gorgeous hazel eyes and sexy deep voice would hold my attention.

"How are you my old friend," said Rod in his slight Scottish accent.

"Hi Rod, I'm fine who's these lovely looking people then," he asked.

"Oh, this is Janette and Dylan from Diani Beach."

"Pleased to meet you both, I am Duncan Scott, I've lived here since I was a kid, I am in my thirties now so what are you guys doing in Nairobi?" he enquired.

As the Reiner story was disclosed, he spoke out of the blue.

"Oh, dear not another Reiner swindle, he is famous in Kenya for his rip off tricks, well anyway, I'm sorry to hear that. I was swindled by him myself. It can happen to anyone, so don't feel too bad about it. You're just one of many."

Duncan was in the local rugby team and quite a sportsman too. He said he was dating a lovely English lady older than himself, then smiled at Dylan and winked. He was dating our friend Judy.

His mum lived in Diani, and he knew almost everyone there, it was uncanny. We talked, laughed, and drank beer until the taxi arrived, to take us back into the bush, where Inga and Klaus waited for news. Waving farewell to the two new friends, we both felt a little sad at having to return to Namanga and the problems at the lodge.

BACK TO NOAH'S ARK AT NAMANGA

Amin had paid the Esperia Hotel bill, paid the fare back and some cash to ease the pressure, until we could start to make some profit. Before he left that night, he promised me faithfully, he would never let me down and would be there day or night if needed.

Another long tiring journey back to Namanga, by now we knew every bump in the road and every village. We returned there with mixed feelings. I had Amin on my mind, he had stirred my feelings.

> *"Janette, Dylan you are back, we have missed you very much. Nazir and Najma have gone to Tanzania, and we begin work tomorrow. Mama Najma has spoken, but still very unhappy, how did you get on?"* Inga blurted out.
>
> *"Inga we are very tired; let's get changed and meet you outside in twenty minutes."*

In our room on the floor was a large puddle of murky water, due to a heavy rainfall the previous night. The cardboard ceiling had collapsed, with a huge gaping hole in it. A handful of enormous dead cockroach, massive black beetles and other insects washed down from the roof space, floated around in the pool of dirty water. A distinct foul smell of sewage filled the room. The rains had forced the waste pipe to collapse, sewage overflowed the drains, and the awful stench was sickening. We arranged for staff to clean up the mess and used another room to take a shower and change.

Welcome back to paradise in Namanga, we thought.

There was a strange tense atmosphere at the lodge. Inga and Klaus had taken hold of the situation, and everyone was on edge under the German command. Inga had the staff running around in circles like dogs chasing their tails. In our absence had the Germans taken over the lodge as a surprise?

> *"We are in control Janette."*

Inga shouted in a deep gruff authoritative voice. They had announced to Najma we were there to work, not hang around waiting. Whatever had occurred in our absence it worked. The orders were dished out, and all we could hear was.

"Yes, mummy Inga."

THE GERMAN HIGH COMMAND

I called to Inga to explain the meeting with Amin and what had developed. She was oblivious to the conversation with one eye on the staff and Klaus.

"Inga, we must tell you what Amin is going to do and what he wants before we start working."

"That can wait for later Janette, come, first let's scrub the filthy kitchen and rearrange it, the men can start on the gardens. We will need to disinfect the entire place from top to bottom, it's disgusting, unhygienic and hazardous. Avoiding food poisoning would be our main priority, not what Amin had to say, eh what?"

Inga started work in the kitchen, with staff helping her. I headed towards the sleeping cats in the overstocked dismal, filthy shop. My work was mountainous.

The overwhelming stench was everywhere outside; it was unbearable, with sludge and excrement floating around. In massive pools of muddy water from the downfall. It would prove quite a task for us. After stock taking and scrubbing out the shop, two thirds of the goods were either past their sale by date or eaten by mice. Finally, after dumping the rubbish the shop looked empty, but fresh and clean.

As the layers and layers of dust and grime were wiped away with hot soapy water, the little shop began to take shape, revealing beautiful wooden shelves and a nice glass counter. Daylight shone through the washed windows and the grubby nasty dingy room was now quite pleasant and acceptable.

Inga with her troops threw out anything that wasn't nailed to the ground and the heap of junk grew bigger and bigger. The small kitchen began to take shape, shelves were quickly fitted to hold the numerous scrubbed pots and pans, with a brand-new pine tabletop nailed over the germ infested old one. All boxes and packets were opened to see the contents, with the majority alive with insects, creepy crawlies everywhere. After a thorough scrubbing down with bleach and boiling water, the kitchen became reasonably acceptable.

All creatures' great and small were sent packing out to the backyard. Nazir had no say in the matter. By the end of the first day, we were totally exhausted. We had fixed the shop, kitchen, restaurant, repaired fences and cut down the overgrown shrubs. What a transformation, we were extremely pleased with our efforts. However, there was very little of our own food to eat, nevertheless we found tins of corned beef, several bags of tasty ripe tomatoes, and two enormous onions. Then the cook arrived with a big pot of boiled potatoes. It looked an odd combination, but it tasted delicious, especially when washed down with cold tusker beer. It was nearly midnight, and we were ready to hit the sack.

As I sat on the edge of the bed, I thought to myself, Amin and the old man are right I would have a better life. But that was just a passing moment.

Camels were bedding down for the night outside guest rooms and the dreadful reek of urine. The constant grunting sounds that bellowed through the stillness of the night. At daybreak, Suzy the screeching baboon and gaggling geese racing from one garden to the next, and the aggressive ugly turkeys fighting with the fancy chickens. Some of the bigger turkeys chased after customers; some leaving without paying and would be seen disappearing in a cloud of dust out the gate. The lodge was like an Alfred Hitchcock horror movie.

Dogs and cats in hot pursuit of chickens, thirty or more pigeons nesting in the veranda roof space, with their droppings and feathers landing on tables as the customers dined. A sudden whoosh as they vacated their home for the nearby trees each afternoon. With feathers flying everywhere, their scraps of food and bird shit dropping down on the passersby.

The constant shrill and cry of orphaned Suzy seeking attention, this place was like no other, it was indeed a circus. How could we upgrade the lodge and improve the trade with this menagerie, aside of all the building repairs. This was an impossible task. Amin meant well when he said he would see for himself, but in truth he had neither the time nor could he prioritise the trip.

NAJMA'S BORDER SHOP

During the day Najma would be in *no-man's land* at her own shop, in the area between Kenya and Tanzania. She made spare cash wheeling and dealing with the locals, each side of the border. She was Asian Tanzanian whose parents had been murdered, by their black servants some years previously. A ruthless trader, with an immensely loud voice, she would shout and yell at the nervous tradesmen until they gave in to her demands. Chasing them and waving a stick, promising them, they would never get business in Kenya again, if they refused to accept her price. Sometimes ushered away by her overweight young son. The son and a fat cousins' pastime was annoying other traders or eating the stock.

DYLAN MALARIA AND VIRUS

A couple of days passed by cleaning and sorting out the room. Dylan became very sick, vomiting in the toilet and sweating profusely, I called for Inga to look at him.

"Oh dear, you look awful it looks like malaria again, Klaus will fetch the doctor from the village."

"Oh no Inga I cannot take any more stress, and he can't have malaria again surely?"

"Yes, he can, because we have moved climate again and you both were in Nairobi for a couple of days back and forward in Kenya, this is not good for you, but don't worry."

It was only thirty minutes or so after Klaus returned with the local doctor, a tall attractive slim Asian in his thirties smiling and carrying a small black bag.

"Jambo sana," as he brushed the dust from his thin grey torn jacket.

"Oh, my goodness, the patient is looking very sick indeed, isn't he, and are you married?"

After a thorough examination he concluded malaria as the cause, but there was a possibility he might have typhoid, or another virus. He was very concerned about Dylan's health; he would get the blood tested quickly. Meanwhile I was to keep Dylan as cool as possible and make sure he drank plenty of bottled water. There was no mention of a fee, this kind man put the patient first.

Inga and Klaus carried on cleaning and tidying up the place as I played nurse once more. Dylan looked so ill; I wouldn't leave him for a moment. Within the hour the doctor returned with his little bag of tricks, he confirmed malaria at an advanced stage. But needed to wait for results on any other virus he may have. After an injection and more examining he said Dylan could only be treated for the malaria now. It was too dangerous to take any antibiotics with malaria drugs. He explained that it was only possible to treat the virus after the malaria was clear, but one way or the other, we would need to watch him carefully. If the fever got worse, then he must be taken into hospital at once. The problem for us was the only adequate hospital to be found, would be in Nairobi, three or four hours' drive away.

Severe sweating and constantly changing the soaking wet sheets, I was very concerned about his health. Although he drank plenty of water and fruit juice the copious sweating continued.

NAZIR RETURNS FROM TANZANIA

Nazir returned from his trip in Tanzania and immediately called in to see Dylan. We were informed that the generator needed repairing and this would take only a day or so. We were not to worry about the trade, as the customers would use torches, candles, and storm lights. As soon as Dylan felt better, we would all have a meeting to discuss exactly what we could do at the lodge and what restrictions Najma had hidden up her sleeve.

> *"You have made the place look wonderful in my absence; I have never seen it so good."*

The following two days were crucial for Dylan, the fever seemed to subside during the day, but at night he was burning up again. His face so pale, with dark circles around his eyes, he looked nothing like the man I fell in love with. As he rested peacefully, he was unaware of the developments happening at the lodge with Najma and Nazir. For Dylan, there was some stillness and calm. He needed to be quiet in the sick room, but for the rest of us, there was a spate of arguing shouting and fighting.

An extremely uncomfortable environment, Najma continued her constant visits to our kitchen. Annoying us by preparing her own meals and interfering with the running of the catering. Meanwhile Nazir's voice echoed day and night, as he bellowed out orders to our staff and confusing everyone who was the boss of the lodge. Nazir and Najma seemed to have ganged up on us and were constantly spying. We called the staff together and requested that the landlords resolve the problems they created.

STAFF MEETING WITH NAZIR AND NAJMA

It was total bedlam, everyone yelling and shouting at each other, when finally, they calmed down and grouped together, under the shade of a large tree.

> *'Enough of this bloody nonsense, let us keep calm, sit down all of you, that includes you Nazir and Mama Najma,"* Inga demanded.

As she waved her chubby arms around and pointed at the two Asians looking very surprised at her outburst, I thought there would be a riot.

> *'Let's get things clear, I do not intend to put up with this ridiculous situation anymore. I came here to do a job and you*

Nazir and your silly childish wife are causing all this uproar with the staff," Inga had grabbed their attention.

"We will give you full control, you are the managers now and we will keep out of all working areas and keep to our own accommodation," interrupted Nazir.

So now the staff need not listen to any orders from the two bullying Asians. Nazir mentioned the generator repair bill would be ours, which was contrary to the original agreement, made with Amin. Now we owed him for the previous repairs. He also added any plumbing bills relating to the lodge, including his accommodation. They suggested all these repairs would be our responsibility.

"You must be crazy, why are we paying for all the bloody broken pipes that have been like it for years?" Inga yelled.

Najma told us she would withdraw her linen from the rooms and instructed the chef to take out several items of equipment of hers from the kitchen. As the showdown went on, it became more apparent that although they accepted the fact, we would be here for three months, they intended to make it a living hell.

Nazir became verbally aggressive and abusive shouting like a sergeant major on parade and finally demanded we must pay for the gravel in his driveway, which he had delivered months before our arrival. Some of the younger girls started to giggle, as the two Asians displayed their influence and obstinate authority with ridiculous demands. With these new preposterous requirements, we decided to contact Amin.

BACK TO NAIROBI AND HOSPITAL

Slowly Dylan improved but lost so much weight I was extremely worried for him. He looked years older and so thin; it was obvious that he must have something else wrong with him apart from malaria. He had enough injections and pills by now, he ought to be perking up. After a quick chat with the doctor, we both agreed he must take the journey to Nairobi in the next day or so, he was wasting away. As calm eventually came to the lodge with Nazir and Najma keeping a good distance from us, Inga, Klaus, and I cracked open a bottle of whisky, with a chicken curry, I had prepared for us earlier. Dylan would attempt a plain omelette and vegetable soup followed by fresh orange juice; he managed very little of each.

Several failed attempts to contact Amin, but the line was down, due to storms. I gave up!

NO GENERATOR

The generator remained off although it had been repaired, it would not go back on until we paid Nazir for the repair. But he would turn it on at night for a couple of hours, for his Asian friends to watch videos and drink cold beer. The sound blasting from their room would drive away the few customers that remained.

Inga and I changed the menu and immediately after that, the inevitable visit, from the two spies peering through the recently cleaned window. Nazir had promised to herd up his animals and make his Noah's Ark in the far corner of the grounds, however another broken promise. Charlie the ostrich and his girlfriend continued to run havoc, scaring off the customers and a tourist buses, arriving in from Nairobi. They didn't stop for refreshments; the driver traumatised and off to Amboseli with the bus full of thirsty occupants, all horrified by the barrage of animals making horrendous noises and ambushing them.

We were about to depart for Nairobi, when a rusty old maroon car arrived at the lodge with a group of Asians; they were from Zanzibar and Najma's family. Apparently, Najma summoned them for moral support, in the never-ending battle of power. Stepping out of the car very gracefully her aunty dressed in grand colourful clothes. Her head covered with a huge creation of bright orange and green silky material. She seemed to glide very gracefully through the main entrance smiling and nodding and whispered to Inga.

> *"Don't worry my friend, if you cannot put up with Mama Najma anymore, you are welcome to work for us, in our hotel in Zanzibar."*

With a loud outburst of laughter Inga and Klaus followed the colourful party into the restaurant. She was aware of our insane circumstances and truly empathised with the intolerable situation.

> *"Thank you very much; we will keep that in mind."*

We said farewell to the staff as they huddled around the matatu. Najma's family waved from the veranda, as the staff shouted.

> *"Hurry up and come back bwana Dylan."*

We departed leaving the two Germans battling it out against the two crazy Asians and the colourful, flamboyant Zanzibar visitors.

ARRIVING BACK IN NAIROBI

Arriving in Nairobi we went directly to the best hospital in town. Dylan would be guaranteed to receive first class treatment, from a very modern medical centre. After much deliberation and hours of tests, it was concluded he had malaria. However, he had a virus like typhoid, a water bacteria germ, probably from the ice in his drinks, or bottled water that had been tampered with. Or the Noah's Ark flood experience?

After paying Dr Faya, he handed over boxes full of tablets that would alleviate the bacteria and restore Dylan's health. I was instructed to continue taking his temperature for the next ten days. He must rest, drink plenty of fluids and try to eat small meals. We got a taxi to our hotel with our spirits lifted a little. Esperia Hotel felt like home from home. After booking in and greeted by the friendly staff we took to our bed for the remainder of the day.

THE NATION NEWSPAPER

ANDREAS KOELTZ ARTICLE

The following morning in the Daily Nation newspaper it was stated that Andreas Koeltz had been seriously ill in prison. He desperately wanted to return home to Germany. Realising that he might die in prison or be killed if released! It was only a short appearance at court and the judge made the decision to deport him as requested by the German government. A photograph in the newspaper of Andreas handcuffed to a policeman outside the courts, was confirmation enough, that at least he was still alive. Dylan wanted to say goodbye to the man he guarded and befriended, but circumstances would not allow such a meeting. Andreas was extradited back to

Germany, unaware that Dylan did not receive any payment for being his bodyguard and loyal friend.

ANOTHER MEETING WITH AMIN

Another meeting with our friend Amin, I was so pleased to see him. He arrived at the casino looking ever more attractive, with his silver rimmed glasses, immaculate grey business suit.

> *"Sorry to hear you have been so ill Dylan, you do not look like the same person. Perhaps Kenya is not a good place for you, you seem to have created so many problems here for you both? Is that not, correct?"*

I explained the madness of Namanga to Amin, he would laugh, raise his eyebrows, and shake his head.

> *"Oh, dear this is not good, is it?"*

He agreed with us, that there was very little we could do at Namanga with Nazir; he was obviously not a man of his word. The crazy wife was the real problem.

> *"What can I do? We only have a gentleman's agreement a handshake we have nothing on paper. What can you do with a bad dog? Shoot the bastard, or keep out of its way? I just don't know with this fellow. However, you will remain there and do you're very best; we must stand true to our word and by doing so, we have nothing to fear."*

Evermore fascinated with Amin; I admired and respected him. His soft velvet voice, which seemed to soothe away my troubles. Although I had the occasion to daydream about him, I knew in my heart I would not be a lover, or mistress to Amin. Our relationship must remain pure, and it would always be nonphysical. An extraordinary bond grew between us and silently we knew that love, if we let it in, was only a whisper away. The chemistry between us was more powerful and apparent each time we met. Happy to confide and trust each other, my liaison with Amin was a secret affair of the mind, not the body. We shared a unique relationship with dignity and integrity. We would speak in confidence and exchange many secrets, in a very tender way.

Dylan left our company for a chat at the bar with Rod the Scotsman. Amin asked me if I had given thought to his previous mistress proposal.

> *"Give me time please, you are married, and I love Dylan, and yes, he is a very foolish boy."*

> *"If you can endure this Namanga saga, you could face almost anything after that, especially with the stress of Reiner's death squad, always at hand. I truly admire you. I love and trust you Janette, you are a marvellous woman, an amazing person."*

I was very touched by his kind words, therefore even more determined to prove my worth to him as a loyal friend.

I loved Amin.

HACKY ARRIVED AT ESPERIA HOTEL

The next morning, my friend Hacky arrived, Wolfgang told him about our *hiding and seeking story.*

> *"Hey, I am going to Russia in the New Year, I have some exciting work there for a television show. I will never forget you my lovely friend, come let us kiss goodbye, you need to be careful, you must take great care of her and not be so stupid Dylan."*

He kissed and hugged me; I never saw Hacky again.

I received a call from Amin to wish us well and not to worry, he would be coming to Namanga whenever he had the free time. Amin never had free time.

What would we have to face now?

MEETING FATHER PHILIP

As we approached the driveway of the lodge, an elderly Masai friend was standing on guard waving a stick.

"Mummy Karibu sana."

A white dirty jeep pulled over in front of us, the driver stepped out and greeted us. It was Father Philip, from the local Catholic Church, we had previously heard about him. His big smile, one gold tooth and beaming face was certainly a welcoming sight. Nevertheless, this priest was quite different, he had more in common with a Mexican bandit, rather than a servant of God. He greeted us both with open arms.

"Allo, ow, er yous my friends?"

A short well-built muscular man, in his late forties. He reminded me of a character in a spaghetti western, with tied back black curly hair, deep brown expressive eyes and a very distinct accent. A couple of noticeable deep scars on his brown rugged face; he looked more the villain than the priest. Dressed in brown leather cowboy boots and blue denims, with a red bandana around his neck, it seemed very weird and wonderful in contrast, a Mexican standing close to the old Masai.

"I'm Father Philip, you, English couple working for Nazir, he's my old buddy."

"I'm pleased to meet you Father Philip, I am Janette, and this is my partner, Dylan."

"I have been working away up country for a few weeks, I invite you both for a meal with me at the church. It doesn't matter what religion you are before you say anything to me about not being a Catholic or whatever, because God is not interested, and neither am I."

"Father that would be lovely thank you."

"So, tomorrow then, if you are feeling up to it, if not let me know and we can make it another night, but I can pick you up and take you, so don't worry about walking eh."

INVITED TO FATHER PHILIP'S CHURCH

We were very pleased to be invited to the church and spoke to Inga and Klaus about it when we arrived at the restaurant. They did not like the idea that we were invited without them. I noticed there had been several changes once again, but this time Inga had it in her mind that she was the boss.

"Look Janette we cannot have two female bosses, it will not work out, when you were away, I decided to take over, because I am older and wiser than you."

She told us we must work with them, or she would make our lives hell. This was a takeover and she sounded like Najma! I had little interest in who was going to be the boss, but I did not intend to be bullied by them. After all, she would not be here if not for my relationship with Amin, I had paid their way from the time of leaving Chiromo.

"Do not shout or bully me, it is not a good idea Inga, we have just returned and tired from the journey, we can discuss it later."

With a rather shocked look on her fat wrinkled face, she agreed that it was me, that saved us all from the hands of the notorious Reiner Moser.

> *"Janette these people must have one boss, they cannot cope with too many at a time, I am that much older than you, so it is better if I take control of the situation and you look after your boyfriend, okay?"*

It made sense what she said, for me to look after Dylan until he was stronger, however her idea of taking control was somewhat different to mine. She was a big-hearted woman and very experienced in catering, however, she was also a German frau with a short fuse. I didn't want to experience her temper when she did erupt. I had witnessed her violent outbursts at Chiromo, and I wasn't prepared to tolerate her madness.

Whilst away she had changed all the bookkeeping, and the new system was only suitable for a big hotel like Chiromo. Inga was certainly very apt with bookwork and figures; her technique worried me somewhat. It was too complicated for the African's, and I feared not seeing the cash box or books again. I knew I would struggle to find out exactly what was going on. She insisted on getting up early to open the restaurant and Klaus was elected to do the shopping. Dylan and I would have no control over the buying or selling.

> *"I am in charge and will look after everything and hold onto the daily takings,"* demanded Inga.

There wasn't an opportunity to talk about Father Philip's invitation or discuss the news from Nairobi.

VISITING FATHER PHILIP

The time was approaching for us to visit Father Philip and I left a message with the staff to inform Inga. We decided to walk there it wasn't too far away. We had previously seen the quaint little church, which was almost hidden from the main road and reached only by way of a dirt path full of potholes and heaps of debris.

It was clearly newly built and presented itself as quite attractive for a church in Namanga, and a newly built modest house giving ample room for the father and his older companion.

We drank chilled beers, smoked, and chatted for a couple of hours about our life in Kenya. Father Philip told stories of his life in Mexico, before receiving God's calling. He talked of other countries he had preached in over the years. He was a very casual man laughing and joking all the time and unlike any other Catholic priest I had met before. A modern man with interesting ideas, with a big heart, whose desire was to build small homes for the Masai people. He showed us his latest project of small houses, which would soon be built when funds became available from the church and invited Dylan to help on the project. We explained our disappointment with Nazir and how the whole situation was getting rapidly out of hand.

> *"Nazir is a well-known character, a small-time crook but harmless, although very stubborn and he lives in a fantasy world of his own. The wife is a different matter. She is a difficult one for sure."*

TANZANIA WITH FATHER PHILIP

> *"I will take you to my good friends place over the border in Tanzania."*

It was a ten-minute drive in his jeep over the border to a lovely open-air restaurant with a wonderful aroma of charcoal cooked chicken, wafting over the grounds. The most delightful and welcoming place I had seen in some time, with smiling staff and no shortage of cold beer. We tucked into wonderful succulent spicy chicken, which melted in the mouth, with rice and local vegetables. It was a wonderful night, as we all chatted and shared our experiences. Father Philip's past in Mexico he revealed was with some very shady people. We guessed he was once a criminal himself. I laughed and commented Mexican Mafia? Dylan shared stories of his gypsy life and trips to Romania, and I reminisced of Ireland. It was time for us to leave, we thanked him, and he dropped us off at the lodge.

> *"We must do this again, and Dylan think about the Masai housing project, it would be nice to have you help, goodnight."*

Inga appeared from the restaurant with folded arms and an annoyingly angry expression on her face.

> *"So, where have you been… to the church? Why has it taken you this long? Did you go anywhere else with the priest?"*

I explained we needed to pray with the Father, giggled and went to bed.

> *"Goodnight Inga, time for sleeping now, talk with you in the morning."*

LOCAL POLICE CHIEF ARRANGING A PARTY FOR THE VICE PRESIDENT OF KENYA

The next morning, we met with the Germans to tell them what Amin had to say, they seemed rather nonchalant about it. Not even enquiring how Dylan was feeling after the hospital visit. However, demanding to be given details on our outing with Father Philip, we remained silent about our secret meal out to Tanzania!

It was midday extremely hot, and shouting -

> *"Mummy Janette we have a special visitor come quickly, fetch Inga and the others, tafadhali, please."*

It was a sight to be remembered as the local police chief strutted towards us like an enormous white chicken waving a stick. Short and very stout, dressed up in colonial style from the movie Zulu. Wearing a hard top white safari hat, rather like a safety helmet, adorned with huge plumes of white feathers. His white uniform decorated with an abundance of rather fake looking strange medals.

A most curious and gruff officer reported that luncheon would be required for the Vice President of Kenya and approximately thirty officials, the following week.

The menu required was written on a piece of cardboard and handed to me with a cash deposit. I was informed that the Vice President would supply his own drinks, but we must supply free sodas to all the police and bodyguards. We would not be informed of the layout of the tables, until the last minute, because of the security required. He demanded that bodyguards would be nearby watching us prepare and cook the food, and that the staff were not permitted to speak to the Vice President Mr George Saitoti.

"Do you understand me? All sodas are free to the bodyguards and police, and you must make sure this lodge is safe and secure for Mr George."

I duly contacted Amin with this information, who promptly confirmed the intended visit and told us to do our very best to impress the honourable Vice President.

There was a shortage of crockery and cutlery, so we headed across the road to John Kean's lodge and asked them to help us out. They were very accommodating and gave us everything we needed to facilitate the expected party.

PREPARING THE LODGE AND GROUNDS

It was an exceptionally hot stuffy day, as the staff ran about the grounds picking up all the stones and dry wood, to make the entrance suitable for the governmental visit. Water was sprayed over the dusty driveway, as the four of us rushed around preparing the crockery and sorting out the provisions. Three official cars arrived early and policemen with guns began organising other officials requesting cold drinks and making their way to the kitchen. Several kilos of beef, that I had prepared the night before, now boiling gently on the charcoal grills. Dylan and I hurriedly chopped through kilos of carrots, potatoes, and onions to make the requested African stew. It was a very hectic morning.

Meanwhile, the two cooks prepared the favourite local salad known as Kachumbari, shredded white cabbage, onions, and carrots. A whole goat was being prepared and cut into large chunks, ready to grill, as soon as the party arrived. This type of grilled meat was known as nyama choma, an African style barbeque.

POLICE IN THE KITCHEN

Squashed up in the hot steamy kitchen we had great difficulty in moving around. Almost impossible to work around the grills, the massive bodyguards and police stood at any space available. It soon became impossible to work efficiently. The heat became unbearable in the tiny space, as the policemen watched over our every move, tasting everything, we prepared.

"Tafadhali hamisha, please move out the way, we cannot cook with so many of you in here," I shouted in frustration.

After making it obvious to them, four guards, two cooks, two kitchen helpers, Dylan and I couldn't move in such a small space. The guards eventually retreated and stood huddled in the doorway, with their guns in one hand and constantly eating the hot grilled goat meat.

"This meat is very good mummy, mzuri sana," they repeated.

"Yes, it's the Vice President's, we ordered it especially for his guests if you keep eating it there will be none for the boss, come on move away from the door please?"

PEOPLE ARRIVING

As the entourage began to arrive, Inga and Klaus were ordered to arrange the tables in an L shape in the gardens and bring cold drinks quickly.

"Haraka, haraka sana, mummy mzungu." Meanwhile in the kitchen it was increasingly becoming a nightmare to operate and function efficiently. One tall, huge police officer was demanding to taste the food, pushing through the staff. I was about to put some cooked meat in a dish, but he grabbed it.

"Tafadhali hamisha, please move, I must hurry this food is to be served in one hour, if you keep stopping me and if it is not ready, I shall blame you and tell Mr George."

They backed off into a corner with a handful of meat and salad. It was unbearable conditions to work in, scorching hot outside and three large open grills burning, two huge pots of stew boiling on another stove, and the guards pushing us around with their rifles. Dylan and I began to panic and loose our temper when yet more officials appeared at the doors and windows.

"What is wrong in here?" they shouted.

"How can we expect to work in these conditions, just look at us."

I pointed to our soaking wet clothes and sweat pouring down our faces.

"These men are blocking the breeze from the back door, and we can't breathe in here."

"You know we are close friends of Amin Walji he sent us here to work, he will not be happy that you are disrupting our efforts, to make this party successful."

Suddenly a familiar face appeared.

"Hello yes, I know these two people, move back, come on please let them do their work."

A gust of air came rushing through the door, as the overanxious guards retreated to the garden, leaving only one man to oversee the food was not tampered with.

"Thank God," we all yelled and hastily set to the finishing touches.

Nazir made an appearance dressed in a smart white outfit looking like a character from a film Casa Blanca. Constantly interfering with our methods of approach. He was evicted from the kitchen very promptly.

"Janette, Janette there's more than seventy people here already, what can we do?" shouted Inga in a panic.

"No problem, Inga we have prepared plenty of rice, ugali and vegetables, Nazir warned us there would be more than expected."

"Thank God, I imagined running out of food," she flustered.

Everyone was settled down ready to eat. The constant flow of food going through the hatch reminded me of a works canteen. We were running out of plates and utilised anything that was suitable, even pot lids.

VICE PRESIDENT ASKS FOR RECIPE

Overwhelmed by the tasty stew, I was required to reveal the recipe.

"Mr George wants to know the recipe for the stew, what is the secret of the wonderful flavour?"

"It's a secret; it's an old Irish recipe," I giggled.

The guards puzzled by my answer, dare I disobey the Vice President's request? Mr George waved and beckoned me to his table.

"Mzuri sana, very lovely, what is the secret?"

"I'm sorry sir but I can't reveal the secret of my stew, but I'm so happy you enjoyed it and wanted more."

Mr George chuckled.

Smiling to myself I left the party and returned to the stuffy kitchen. The secret was a few tins of baked beans, several caramelised fried onions, boiled onions, beef and beef stock with herbs and plenty of vegetables. African stew was a watery tasteless soup with little vegetables and very little meat.

It was a total success and the party of officials gradually departed thanking us for our effort. It was time for us to enjoy our much-needed meal, followed by a few chilled bottles of wine. As the staff cleared up the mess and the kitchen became recognisable again, the four of us took shelter under the trees, for a quiet snooze.

That evening a loud noise coming from Nazir's rooms. He turned the generator back on to watch videos with a few Asian guests. After a while it was very rowdy with shouting and yelling, as the kung fu movies continued late into the night. To my horror I discovered that Dylan was one of the noisy guests.

> *"Well, babe it was a great night my favourite martial arts movies and a few beers with the men."*
>
> *"Are you stupid or what? Nazir is charging me for the diesel for you all to watch his movies. You are the manager, where is the loyalty, Dylan?"*

Dylan apologised.

THE OLD MASAI MAN

Very often in the early hours of the morning, I would hear the jingle jangle of beads clanking together. It was an old Masai heading to the restaurant porch. He would sit on a broken wooden bench fiddling with his bracelets mesmerised by the African sunrise. However, this old man had seen so many over his lifetime. Oblivious to his surroundings entranced by the amber glowing horizon, as the sun appeared in full glory.

The old man had few teeth and a leathery face with deep set almost black eyes. Very tall and thin, his silky skin the colour of chocolate. Adorned with brightly coloured tiny glass beaded bangles and necklaces. A worn tatty red cloth loosely fell over his bony shoulder and wrapped around his small waist. Long skinny scarred legs with big wide bare feet. He was often seen in the gardens during the day as he glided across the grounds like a giraffe. His big flat feet leaving indentations on the freshly watered grass.

Red ochre clay daubed on his head and the few remaining braids of hair.

"Mummy tea, tafadali, please, mummy."

He would say and grin showing an almost toothless smile. He would sip his tea from a large blue chipped mug and then ask for another, more sweetly mummy meaning more sugar. Like a gentle giant, a silent man with a great presence. His ancient heritage all too obvious as he sat fixated and gazing at the sky, oblivious to the world around him.

Often, I chatted to him in my poor Swahili and English, and he would say, *hadithi zaidi,* more story mummy. One day as he stared into space he began to cry, the tears streamed down his dusty face. He abruptly stood up and banged his spear a few times on the hard dry ground and spoke.

"Mummy, Masai."

As he pointed out into the wilderness, I called to Mohamed the waiter and asked him what he wanted. After a few moments the old man who I named Papa, gently placed his grubby hand on my head, nodded then slowly strolled away, and waving as he left the compound. Mohamed told me that we were to go to his village the following day, to visit his people.

Mohamed and I ambled along for about an hour before the first vision of the old man's village was apparent. We could see a circle of strange looking mud and straw houses, surrounded by small shrubs and wispy trees. Several goats and chickens roaming around.

"Here we are mummy this is the village."

A lorry driver was shouting and some commotion when chickens ran around in circles, then darted across the busy road causing the lorry to swerve. Clouds of dirt rising upwards choking everyone as a few goats scurried around the brush. Mohamed and I were greeted by some of the villagers all dressed in the same manner as the old man. They began leaping up and down and shouting in Masai. The old man who I called Papa, came towards us, and waved his stick in the air then nodded. He directed us to a little house where a small fire was burning with a large black pot heating up some liquid. Mohamed and I were given a drink from the pot, it was dreadful, but we managed to swallow it. A younger man invited us to walk with him around the village. After the stroll we returned to Papa, who handed me a beautiful, beaded belt, and a grassy substance to chew on. I passed on the herb but lit up a cigarette to join them in the welcome ritual.

The villagers sang and danced by leaping up and down to great heights, waving their hands in the air. It was time to go back to the animal madness at the lodge.

I walked away feeling very privileged by the whole experience, Mohamed had seen it all before.

PARTY OVER THE ROAD

It was an average day, with nothing too out of the ordinary happening until a young couple sauntered in the restaurant and asked to see the managers.

Dylan popped up from behind the counter and said,

"Habari hakuna matata, hello what's up?"

The young girl smiled and asked if we would like to come to a small party across the road with her family and friends. One of their friends was a regular at the bar and we had a few drinks with him. The girl said the party would start when it got dark and go on until dawn.

"Thanks, yes, we will be there later," grinned Dylan.

As we showered and changed, we could hear the pounding music echoing across the road in the still dark night. The aroma of food, nyama choma cooking on the open fire, wafting across into the lodge.

Dylan and I scurried over the road to the small brightly painted house lit up like a Christmas tree and disco style music thumping, next to small children sleeping on mats on the floor.

"Hi there what's the party for."

I asked one of the men at the doorway.

"It's to celebrate the life of one of the children recently killed on the road, by a speeding lorry."

I was quite shocked that this festive mood was for a child killed on the road, but I also understood the local ways. The funeral was held days before. Staff at the lodge mentioned some kids were playing nearby that got injured, by a hasty lorry driver.

I wondered if it was the same lorry driver at the Masai village that alarmed the chickens and goats.

The mood changed when several people came to the house crying and singing gospel songs. After an hour or so they moved on to a local bar. A young man dressed in a purple shirt put a UB40 CD on and we danced to the hit record, Red, Red Wine. It was a great evening with several people coming and going all night. Plenty of good food and drink. It was time to go back to the lodge, we were tired but enjoyed the party. They thanked us for coming and laughed at us.

"Mzungus not like Africans, dancing night and day ha-ha!"

NAZIR AND NAJMA OFF TO MOMBASA

A week or so after the government party more problems and confrontations as Nazir and Najma continued to spy and interfere. However, an opportunity to relax and reassess the situation presented itself when they attended a funeral in Mombasa. For three days the generator sat still, noiseless. Yet, running the lodge in the absence of Nazir and Najma was relatively stress-free. However, a tragedy struck the lodge on the second night of their departure; someone had broken into the grounds. The askari guard was sleeping on duty having had too much booze, and Charlie the ostrich was killed.

I wept and asked them to show me his body so I could say farewell. I couldn't understand why they giggled and found my request so amusing? Perhaps they didn't pray for animals as we do. As I approached the scene of the crime, Charlie was nowhere to be found. I noticed to my shock and horror, spread along the fence Charlie had been butchered. Nothing of the Charlie I once knew, just huge chunks of meat, a heap of feathers and his inners boiling in an enormous pot. I was distraught and very bewildered by the bloody scene.

"What have you done, poor Charlie, this is monstrous," I yelled at them.

"Oh mummy, we have to cut up quickly and cook him, it is too hot and no fridge working, we must not waste good meat, such as this," laughed Carol, the young girl from the restaurant 1930s telephone kiosk.

"Yes, I guess you're right, it's just I expected to see him as a dead ostrich, not cut up into joints of meat, and so quickly too, Oh, dear this is really sad."

Nevertheless, I stood silently in prayer for Charlie.

How would we explain this to Nazir when he returned? He is going to be furious and blame us for Charlie's slaughter? Yet more excuses to get us off his land.

Meanwhile a small party of Muslim Asians had booked two tables in the restaurant for a hot chicken curry meal for late afternoon. Mohamed the only Muslim with halal experience at the lodge, would kill and prepare the chickens. However, he was away for the day and couldn't be found. After chasing the poultry around the garden Dylan finally captured one clucking bird, and rushed into the kitchen where Inga and I were mixing the spices for the curry sauce.

"Inga what are we going to do, we cannot halal this bird it's a Muslim ritual," I asked her.

Grabbing the frantic chicken from Dylan, with wings flapping and feathers flying, she slapped it down hard on the table!

"Halal, I vill show you halal, schnell und einfach, quick and easy!!"

Inga grabbed a small machete and quickly chopped off its head. After we gutted and plucked the lifeless bird, Inga abruptly burst into fits of laughter.

> *"Oh, dear Janette, ha-ha, Allah does not care about cutting the throat of a chicken, Jesus Christ just curry it and I will boil the rice!!"*

The party of Muslims thoroughly enjoyed the meal and relished the hot curried chicken none the wiser.

We kept the halal event a secret.

NAZIR RETURNED

Nazir returned he was livid and immediately put the blame of Charlie's sad ending onto us. Followed by a ferocious warning that we might end up dead too.

> *"You might end up on the fence in pieces like Charlie,"* he snarled.

> *"I am not afraid of you Nazir; you may not wake up in the morning to be able to do it. You must sleep my friend. Don't forget that."*

CHRISTMAS WAS ARRIVING

It was almost Christmas and for the first time the lodge was reasonably busy. Staff rushed around repairing leaking pipes and broken furniture. The tension between Inga, Klaus and I had increased so much we hardly ever spoke. After the chicken curry halal event with the machete, Inga became evermore power crazy. She would parade around the grounds, with her enormous heaving bosoms bouncing around like footballs in her T-shirt, yelling at everybody in her path. Even Nazir had fallen out with the German duo. The atmosphere became very intense and uncomfortable, life was difficult enough for us, but Inga made it insufferable.

A mild dose of malaria hit me again.

I was almost asleep after a long restless night of fever with mild recurring malaria and noises from the animals outside, when Dylan popped in to check on me.

> *"Hi, honey I'm going to the border of Tanzania to get you a Christmas present,"* he gasped and dashed back out the door.

Our room was very small with crumbling walls, a dark and dingy space with a tiny shower area and a broken toilet. I had to fill a bucket of water to flush the toilet after use, and the toilet leaked from a deep crack that constantly seeped. It was very unhygienic, but Nazir refused to repair anything. Nearby the camels would bed down for the night even though we had moved them several times, they preferred sleeping outside my bedroom window. The stench of urine and excrement became so noxious at times, I could hardly breathe. Moving us to this room was Nazir's way of hinting what little value we were to him and part of the bigger plan to get rid of us.

Each night as dusk approached the camels would saunter along the Nairobi Tanzania Road, heading back to bed down for the night. They would make terrible grunting sounds as they shuffled around, constantly banging their huge bodies against the wall of my bedroom. Sleep was not an option for Dylan and me at the best of times. During the long hot lazy days, the camels would stroll off into the wilderness and now and again Nazir would change the straw bedding.

There was a knock on the door.

"Hello mummy, do you want orange juice and some food?"

It was Mohamed the waiter.

"Come in Mohamed," I called back to him.

As Mohamed entered the room, he was followed by an out of breath Dylan, puffing and panting carrying a parcel under his arm.

"Thanks for the food and drink just put it down Mohamed."

"Hi babe I went to a few shops over the border and found a lovely top for you, here you are it's your Christmas present, have it now."

Dylan sat on the bed so excited and opened the parcel to reveal a beautiful light pink embroidered jacket. I was very touched by his kind gesture and the long trek to the border to buy it for me.

He kissed me on the cheek and smiled.

"I love you Jan let's try and have a nice Christmas together in Noah's Ark ha-ha."

A few days passed, I was much better and desperate to get out of the room. It was Christmas Eve, Inga and Klaus stayed hidden in their rooms stocked up with plenty of booze and food. Nazir, Najma, and the staff were all away for the festive season. There was an eerie silence, with the occasional bellowing or screeching from Suzy and grunting from the camels. The ugly turkeys and geese went walk about all day. A few goats sauntered in the compound but were quickly forced to retreat by the yapping dogs.

CHRISTMAS EVE STORY

We were sitting in the restaurant having a cold beer when two young men suddenly appeared at the doorway.

"Hello, are you open for business?"

A short thin fair-haired man, in denim jeans and a camouflage jacket asked.

"Yes, we are open, your names aren't Mary and Joseph," Dylan joked.

"That's quite funny, no we are two English blokes, ha-ha," he answered.

So, it was Christmas Eve and two English men called Bob and Steve arrived at the door with a large pot of Foie Gras (goose pate) cracker biscuits, sweets, and cake. Dylan and I went to the kitchen storeroom and rustled up some delicious curry pasties made by one of the young girls. We managed to put together a plate of cold cooked chicken with vegetables, different sauces, toast, and biscuits. There was one bottle of sparkling wine in the cooler, left when we took over the lodge. In the shop plenty of whisky, beers, and several bottles of red wine. The four of us sat together having a wonderful Christmas Eve meal and laughing about the bizarre circumstances that we all found ourselves in. Dylan sang a few Christmas songs; Michael Jackson dancing and we told jokes until the early hours of the morning.

"Is it time for Santa Claus to come," slurred Bob.

He tripped over a chair and fell to the floor laughing.

We were all rather pissed and giggling at nonsense as we stumbled to our rooms to sleep.

The sound of turkeys gaggling and pigeons squawking awakened us to Christmas day, it was late morning. The two men were still in their room in bed as we crept outside to sing, we wish you a Merry Christmas.

"What the fucks going on, where the fuck are we?"

Dylan and I smiled at each other and said, just another day in paradise. Bob and Steve eventually ventured out into the daylight and stumbled around the grounds to discover a real-life nativity event unfolding. They were shocked to encounter camels, geese, chickens, and turkeys sauntering around. We introduced them to Suzy the baboon and the late ostrich Charlies girlfriend, who we named Rose and her babies now quite big scurrying about the grounds in hot pursuit of the cats. The Englishmen felt quite at home in the madness, and decided to stay another night at Noah's Ark. They laughed so much at the menagerie of animals and thought it would make a great story to share when back home in the UK. I assured them I would write an account of it one day. I said it must have been quite a shock to get pissed Christmas Eve and wake up to the Noah's Ark story in Africa. We waved farewell to our two random visitors as they headed to the Tanzanian border in search of another interesting adventure.

It was a very out of the ordinary Christmas experience to say the least.

AT WAR WITH INGA

I would arrange for a task to be done, and Klaus or Inga would give a different order, causing animosity and confusion between the staff. Inga would intimidate everyone, and she became very demanding. Klaus was leaning towards supporting us at times, even though he was just her slobbering lap dog.

"Klaus, Klaus schnell! I want you now. This instant!"

Inga would holler commands, as her thunderous voice echoed in the grounds. The animals ran for cover, hiding in bushes the moment they caught sight of her. Or heard her feet thud along the dirt path, carrying a large bottle of whisky to gulp down in the sanctuary of her little room. Eventually I called Amin, to say that it was getting out of hand and the Germans were trying to take over the lodge once again.

> *"Be patient, please Janette don't let them boss you around, you are very strong, and I am here for you,"* Amin replied.

It was difficult to comprehend; we were such good friends at one time. The last of my capital was for us all when we went into hiding at Esperia Hotel. Now so much hate, resentment and aggression came from Inga, as if we were the enemy and not Reiner.

Inga continued her Gestapo style attitude towards everyone, no-one escaped her madness, like a woman possessed with a demon. At least it appeared that way.

She started the day by choosing me as her target and began bullying others, then Klaus joined in yelling at staff. Dylan couldn't take any more of her offensive outrageous behaviour. Normally he was easy-going and relaxed, however on this day he just exploded at Inga.

This is when World War 3 began at the lodge.

> *"How dare you speak to Jan like that she saved your bloody necks, you fucking German bastards. She gave you half of her money and got you a job here, you ungrateful ugly fat slobs."*

In desperation he pounced forward at Klaus and threatened to flatten him, if he didn't shut his crazy wife up.

"You pair of thieving bastards; you're fiddling the money for yourselves. You have taken over everything just so you can control the cash. Where's the books and receipts for everything, I want to see them. Get them you are fucking greedy bastards."

THE GERMANS LEAVING A SINKING SHIP

After much quarrelling they agreed to show us all the paperwork and casually mentioned they would be arranging to leave for Germany shortly. We discovered Klaus was staying illegally in the country and his permit had run out, almost six months ago. Also, Inga had only a temporary one, which was unsuitable for her to work at the lodge. Nazir heard the shouting and called Dylan into his rooms to inform him he was in possession of their passports. They had recently paid him to help them get out of Kenya. He was trying to arrange an *exit* document at the border but couldn't pay the bribe; Inga had not given him sufficient money.

This infuriated Dylan, realising the money was our profits, Dylan and I had received nothing from the business to date. After inspecting the books, I could clearly see there was money missing and Inga was the culprit. She had stolen from the cash box and once again we had worked for nothing. We confronted them both about taking our funds to pay for the exit permits. Another explosive hour of yelling and shouting with the two fat Germans. Abruptly departed with food and drink and to their room, to hide until morning.

Finally, they made an appearance at noon, rather dishevelled and sheepish.

"You can run this lodge Janette, soon we are leaving for Nairobi, and then to Germany. Klaus has money from a Will, his mother died. We shall go and collect what is ours."

I wasn't entirely sure about them returning to Germany I did wonder if they were heading off to Zanzibar, to work for the flamboyant colourful aunty.

THE ACCOUNTANT ARRIVES

Within a few days a short, lean, and stern looking man with silver hair and very white teeth, carrying a black briefcase arrived.

> *"I am the accountant, I'm here to look over the books for my friend Nazir."*

After a few hours had passed he said there was several mistakes in the bookwork and vehemently insisted Inga settled the accounts, before departing the lodge. However, there was another twist in the bookkeeping story. Nazir expected me to settle the finances for all the stock in the shop and pay all other outstanding rent. Aside of several bottles of whisky the two Germans guzzled.

> *"Before the Germans go Janette you and Dylan will settle all the outstanding debts to the accountant. Including the bed and breakfast money you all refused to pay my wife. There is a bill for the generator, stock, and a few other things we need to discuss."*

This situation was getting impossible; Inga had control of all the money and books. After the accountant's inspection it became clear, if not obvious, she had no money to show for the time we had worked there. They also took the emergency money Amin had given to me.

I was flabbergasted; this was another nightmare scenario, which I needed to get Dylan and I out of.

As Inga and Klaus said farewell to the staff and departed Namanga a great sadness swept over me. They were my good friends but because of control and greed, we would lose our companions. Dylan and I were left behind in far more debt, than when we arrived, with little money we were forced to work for nothing until the account was satisfied. We thought to ask Father Philip for help, and then thought not to, after all, we got ourselves into this mess and we would need to get out of it too.

TANZANIA TRIP

WANTING TO LEAVE NAMANGA

I phoned Amin to update him on the latest development stressing that we could no longer tolerate the situation and I was not in the best of health. He agreed it was now time to leave Namanga and return to Nairobi. The three months stay was indeed an experience; we had discovered so much and witnessed some very strange and bizarre events. Before leaving for Nairobi, we would have a short break in Tanzania. We would use half the little cash we had left.

A two-day trip to Arusha would be another episode in this great Kenyan adventure. Our German friends had abandoned us, leaving us to the Asian vultures.

We boarded the matatu heading for Arusha and stopped at the border. As we queued for the passports to be stamped a strange feeling came over me. What if they refused us entry? Supposing Nazir had someone in the customs stop us from getting out of Kenya? My mind raced with scenarios leading to us ending up here having to work as slaves for him. Anything was possible in Kenya I thought. Oh, my God Amin help us get away from the insane place, Noah's Ark, and the lunatics.

We were given entry to Tanzania by a very smart and handsome border officer. As the matatu bumped along through the hilly landscape, thoughts of Namanga quickly faded. We would enjoy our two days break no matter what. Surprisingly, Tanzania a more scenic country than Kenya, with grassy fields and beautiful little white houses dotted around the vast lush green countryside.

The dust churned up by the heavy flow of lorries along the busy road, made it impossible to see the town of Arusha. A constant flow of traffic that seemed never ending thundering down the Namanga road. Finally reaching the small cheap hotel where we wanted to stay the night. An old-fashioned 2star accommodation, with the strong pungent aroma of camphor and damp clothes. It was packed with lorry drivers; yet was surprisingly clean and tidy. After a light meal of vegetable soup and bread we took a stroll around the town, dodging the cars as they sped up and down the road, hooting. The town itself was neatly laid out in rows of small shops with McDonalds next to a Pizza restaurant, as the prominent buildings. Quite hilly but very wide roads with narrow lanes leading off to the open marketplaces, where all the real business was conducted. After an hour or so, I was too tired to walk anymore, and we made our way back to the hotel.

Our room was very basic, clean, and painted cream. I was a little nervous in the unfamiliar hotel surroundings and we had to walk some distance along a dark corridor to find the bathrooms. A broken toilet, small dirty mirror, and no hot water for a bath or shower. Two metal framed single beds with dirty mosquito nets as dust fell all over us. Coughing and sneezing we made a quick escape to the dark corridor. We had great difficulty in opening the windows as we desperately tried to rid the room of the dust, but the noise from the heavy traffic was unbearable. We shut the windows and remained in a hazy mist for some time. Neither of us slept that night. There was so much noise in the hotel and the matatus and cars honking all night. In the morning, we washed in cold water. The food looked unappealing, we decided on a stale cheese sandwich with a large glass of orange juice and resolved not to stay another night. Forgetting there was a nice Mc Donalds and a Pizza place, we took the first available matatu back to Kenya.

RETURN FROM TANZANIA

That evening we met Nazir and found the courage to tell him we were leaving. He laughed and jabbered in mixed languages, then spit his grassy chewing herb on the ground and turned away walking towards the restaurant.

It was time to go.

Najma refused to let us have any of our belongings.

> *"You will leave behind all your things, until you have settled with us. That includes the Germans money too."*

She spat at us, as she shouted in Swahili waving her fist and frothing at the mouth. The next day an unpleasant atmosphere loomed as we became apprehensive leaving the lodge for Nairobi, with one set of clothes. Everything else we owned was locked away with Nazir holding the key. Grinning with an air of arrogance.

> *"See you soon my friends."*

OFF TO NAIROBI

Once again, we would travel to Nairobi, but this time knowing our future was safe and secure if we made it there in one piece. As we neared the city, we both sighed with relief that the internment at the lodge was truly over. Amin greeted us with open arms and smiling.

"Welcome home," and kissed me on the cheek.

He handed us a bunch of keys.

"You must eat and rest a little before going to the house, there is plenty to drink so take your time."

We were to stay at one of Amin's houses, the casino staff were extremely happy to hear we were going to be managers of the Flamingo Casino in Kisumu. As we relaxed with Amin, and chatted about the latest events from Namanga, I could feel the stress leaving my body. I explained Nazir refused to give us our belongings until the accounts were settled.

"It will all be sorted out, even if you have to go to Kisumu, without your things, you are going at the end of this week I promise you that."

During the delicious meal, Amin talked about our new job and how happy he was to see us again. Often touching my hand, smiling, and gazing into my eyes.

"I have missed you Janette, now that you are employed with my company, I will be able to see you, whenever it is possible, no one will think anything of it."

Amin phoned Nazir several times but failed to get any response and finally he wrote a beautiful letter that he insisted we hand deliver which read: -

"Janette and Dylan are now employed by my company and will shortly be able to repay any outstanding debt to you. I sincerely urge you to hand over their belongings immediately. If for any reason this letter does not satisfy your needs, do not hesitate to contact me at my office or home number."

I could not believe that he wanted us to go back to Namanga again and with this letter. But it made sense; we had to collect a lot of boxes and bags of clothes.

DUNCAN TO THE RESCUE

Our friend Duncan Scott called in the casino and kindly offered to take us to Namanga. Amin had no available cars we could use. We were very apprehensive about going back there but with the letter for Nazir, we felt sure there could be no more problems. Another tiresome journey back to Noah's Ark and the two crazy Asians I thought. I was tired of this Namanga story. Dylan and I weary from all the stress and illnesses, and Duncan the knight in shining armour, to the rescue. Our final journey to Namanga but what awaited us there? We arrived in good time and parked the jeep facing the gate for a quick escape. Nazir greeted us with a wry sarcastic tone. After reading the letter twice aloud he laughed.

"Take only your clothes and nothing else."

He refused to let me have my electric typewriter, and all other personal items until Najma was satisfied there was no more money owing by the Germans or us. It was very tense and volatile situation. Without any arguing we hurriedly packed our bags with Nazir watching over us. A large box filled with private documents and photographs; Nazir took to his rooms. Just as we were about to leave, the staff rushed over to ask about their salary.

"I gave the money to Nazir before leaving," I told them.

"But he will not pay us what are we to do mummy?"

I advised them to go back over to the restaurant and see Nazir, because he had all the money. After a few moments we noticed that several other African people were gathering around the restaurant, friends and family, now there was a boisterous crowd. Duncan suggested we make a hasty retreat to Nairobi as the staff might turn on us, not knowing exactly what Nazir had told them, we should hurry and go. We gathered our bags and moved quickly to the jeep with Duncan as the getaway man. As we jumped in, he spun the wheels causing a dust cloud and put his foot to the pedal. We could hear yelling and shouting and through the haze see the staff and noisy crowd heading rapidly towards us.

"Quickly Duncan for Christ's sake get us out of here, it's a fucking mob coming for us," Dylan cried out.

Duncan grew up in Kenya and told us as we sped down the driveway that there might be trouble ahead. Perhaps a lorry will be across the road, or a dead animal; they could try anything to stop us. We held our breath and prayed that we could get far enough away without hitting a pothole, or some old clapped-out vehicle. Even a herd of giraffe or zebras would slow us down. We drove in haste, not looking back. We were all bloody terrified. Non-stop all the way back to Nairobi, with the windows open, choking dust blowing in and very little water between us. We were in real danger and fled for our lives.

"Fucking hell, that was too scary, what a bloody close shave that was," huffed Duncan.

We were so grateful to Duncan for helping us escape the madness at Namanga. A cold beer at Gypsies would quench our thirst, and share the story with the ex-pats. We met with Amin later. He laughed at the madness, but realised the danger was a grave issue that we had escaped from.

> *"You have your clothes at least, now I will invite Nazir to the Casino for dinner. I will promise to help him in any possible way with his projects in Namanga. I can help the locals with a school and a clinic, these things I can do as an MP he will accept and be happy to think he has a good friend in Government. That's how they think. These small, minded idiot people."*

I was so pleased I didn't need to see Noah's Ark again, however, sad that my friends Inga and Klaus turned into an unrecognisable couple, with only their own agenda to stay alive. I had supported them in Chiromo and helped them escape, yet they turned on me in the end. Just another day in Kenya I thought.

PART 6

KISUMU

FLAMINGO CASINO STORY

Amin made a point of constantly fussing over me, as Dylan waited around the blackjack tables.

> *"Will you be my mistress? I can visit you in Kisumu whenever I wish to. Also, you can visit Nairobi for a couple of days, no one need ever know that we are seeing each other. When you go to Kisumu you will stay at my brother's house. He has two stepchildren that need guidance and help. I want you to keep an eye on them for me, can you do that?"*

We stayed in Nairobi at one of Amin's four bed roomed houses for a week, and during that time two Romanian croupiers arrived. They were young couple, and with a good command of English. We saw little of them because they slept during the day. Both highly regarded as croupiers and I wanted them to travel to Kisumu with us, however Amin needed them at the Four Aces. As we prepared to leave Nairobi our feelings of apprehension grew ever stronger. Kisumu was a long journey up country on the Ugandan border. The climate there would be extremely hot and humid, and the scenery extraordinary. Lake Victoria washed the dry shores of Kisumu so we could expect a cool breeze, unlike Noah's Ark and the stench of manure.

ARRIVING IN KISUMU

Arriving after a tiresome six and a half hours drive, we stepped out of the matatu exhausted at the Flamingo Casino, centrally in the town. This would be our next assignment for however long Amin decided. We met a short slender built African man wearing a brown jacket two sizes too big outside the Flamingo Casino. He welcomed us and took us onward to Amin's brother's house. Travelling along a wide rough road for a mile or so and arriving at our new home.

It was a very dark and eerie night, only a glimpse of a new moon appearing in the vastness of space. A chubby-faced jovial housekeeper directed us to a small gloomy bedroom. She said it was Monty's room but now we could have it. The house itself was appealing, but in dire need of repairs and cluttered with strange objects from the seventies. Two hissing scrawny black and white cats and two small raucous mongrel dogs, chasing each other in and out of the rooms.

The following morning, we met the two stepchildren.

> *"This is Baby, she's supposed to be at school, and this is Monty her brother he's' your driver until Amin arranges a car for you,"* stuttered one of the house maids.

Baby was stunning, appearing older than the age of fourteen, when suddenly she removed her dress paraded her half naked body in front of Dylan. She was glancing at him in a very seductive manner. Dylan smiled back at her flaunting her beautiful young body. I felt a sense of impending doom as she posed in provocative positions as if modelling showing off her lovely figure. Monty on the other hand seemed aloof and antisocial. He was indifferent and unresponsive, ignoring our presence.

We were aware their mother had died of Aids six months earlier, because Amin's brother worked in Nairobi the two teenagers required guidance. Nonetheless, I could not imagine Baby would behave like a young harlot. As we left the house, a cheerful elderly man in the garden peering through broken sunglasses, greeted us.

> *"Karibu sana."*

"Asante Ninafurahi kukutana nawe, thank you nice to meet you," I answered.

The following day on the way to the town, I noticed so many banks and financial houses. Interesting small shopping parades, wide roads, and nice open spaces to explore, a well-planned and pleasant town. But that would be another day, for now it was work.

ARRIVING AT THE FLAMINGO CASINO

The Flamingo Casino was once a popular cinema in its day, with wide stone steps leading to two enormous glass doors. Inside an impressive and grand entrance of wooden stairs that led to a significant foyer, festooned with stuffed trophies. An impressive yet taunting full-size taxidermy lion greeted us at the top of the stairs. Although the lion was ornamental, stuffed, and harmless it bore a snarling glare that was quite unnerving. Peering down and looking out of place, more appreciated in a local museum or better alive in the bush, mounted on a wooden frame a gazelle, and buffalo head draped in huge cobwebs. An odd combination of weird and wonderful relics mixed in with Africa's great wildlife, stuffed and lifeless. Additionally, bright-coloured knick-knacks, dating from around the 1970s, randomly placed around the area.

Dreadfully faded wild animal pictures covered in dust precariously hanging on string and inappropriate inexpensive lighting, casting strange shadows across the lifeless animals. However, the recognisable roulette wheel spinning and ball clattering quickly reminded us we were in a casino and not a museum. A short fat lady appeared and escorted us to a large black wrought iron gate, where we entered the gloomy restaurant disco area. An odd mixture of hideous colours painted on the walls with a dark blue ceiling, the atmosphere was terribly dismal. The entire ceiling covered with low-priced faded light shades, different shapes and sizes huddled together like bats. A cluttered creepy shadowy space overhead.

Faded red velvet curtains torn and tatty, barely hanging on the rusty brass hooks, various shades of vinyl floor tiles cracked and split, others curling up at the edges like a dry stale sandwich. A choice of different tables and chairs covered with an assortment of worn creased tablecloths, nothing matched.

Waiters in jogging pants or shabby trousers with various shades of white or grey shirts, with dickey bows or ties. Wandering around in scruffy trainers or unpolished worn-out shoes and others in flip flops. What a dreadful sight, it was truly appalling.

Namanga safari lodge on the edge of an offbeat border town was excusable, however the Flamingo Casino had seen better days.

> *"Oh my God Dylan is this for real?"*
>
> *"Do not worry Jan, you knew it was going to need redecorating. Amin told you to make a list and get a professional person in to estimate the cost, it will be all right."*
>
> *"Dylan this place needs complete refurbishing, not a new carpet and paint the walls as Amin suggested. I honestly thought it needed a face lift, look at this place its disgustingly filthy and falling apart."*

Amin wanted me to examine the financial books, he was certain there would be problems with the accounts.

Remembering Amin-

"Your job will be to watch over the children and let me know what is going on at the casino, make notes of everything, you can sack unnecessary staff too."

MANAGER SHAMSHAE MEETING

A nice looking, cheerful Asian man who appeared in his late thirties, walked briskly towards us with his right hand out, ready to shake mine.

"Mzuri, mzuri, lovely, lovely, asante, thank you for coming all this way to help us, we are very grateful to you, welcome. Oh, I am Shamshae the general manager."

"Hello, I am Janette, and this is Dylan, Amin has sent us to manage the place."

"Oh, I understood that you are here to help me, not to be managers, we have Walter manager of the casino. I oversee everything, perhaps your job is to manage the restaurant and bar? Never mind, you are here now. So, first, you must be hungry, then I will show you around. It is so lovely to have new people here, thank you again for coming. Come let me introduce you to the head waiter."

A tall thin middle-aged African man appeared out of the drab corridor. Fumbling awkwardly to adjust his black and grey tie, with his collar curled up, wearing scrunched up black trousers held up with a colourful strap and dirty scuffed white trainers. As he sauntered towards us, it was noticeably obvious his shirt was too small and badly creased.

"Welcome to our restaurant and especially welcome to Kisumu," he smiled and scurried off into the darkness.

"Oh God, Dylan, is this for real, Namanga was bad enough, but this is shocking, apart from the staff just look around you?"

"Don't worry Jan, you knew it needed redecorating and rearranging."

Hideous orange vintage lamps scattered about, and haphazard cubicles made from random timber, a peculiar contrast against the dull flock maroon wallpaper, peeling away from the damp walls. A curious timber construction, like a hut, with steps leading up to it, apparently the main bar! Totally obscured by years of layered grime and cobwebs. Several empty packets of cigarettes and other random rubbish, thrown on the brown varnished roof.

"I cannot believe no-one has removed the rubbish from that strange bar Shamshae, surely it's the first thing you see when you enter the restaurant?"

"Oh, deary me you are right to say that, but you know we have just got used to the place. We need fresh eyes to tell us what to do."

"I'm just stuck for words, this place is disgusting, filthy and a complete mess and you tell me it needs fresh eyes to see it?"

"Well, we have lost interest and it's as simple as that. You will bring light to this place Janette, and everything will have new life again, eh?"

The bizarre hut bar was too low and the man behind it too tall, it looked ridiculous. The barman wore what appeared to be a pair of cut down black Wellington boots and sporting a hotel porters red jacket rather tight and too short! The counter suitable for dwarfs and surrounded by a selection of wobbly bar stools.

THE RESTAURANT

Shamshae excited and enthusiastic to show us the restaurant.

"Look at this pleasant restaurant mummy, it can look very, very nice. You are coming in here when it's a little bit shabby and empty now. When it's full of people it is very lovely."

Plastic vases filled with nasty synthetic flowers. Table numbers written on pieces of cardboard and others made of white plastic. It was a terribly unappealing and unsightly restaurant.

"Janette, Dylan please sit and enjoy our food," grinned Shamshae.

A small poorly dressed but smiling waiter arrived with a tray filled with Chinese dishes, and plenty of red wine to wash it down. The cuisine was surprisingly delicious, the wine excellent. After eating we were directed along a dimly lit narrow passage, comparable to a tunnel, with a heavy black and red door leading to the casino.

"This is the casino mummy; I hope you like it?"

A dimly lit claustrophobic room, with a red patterned threadbare carpet. Strategically placed some creepy pictures of animals, covering large holes or cracks in the walls. Odd broken lampshades and several menacing curios. A bizarre array of cheap broken souvenirs originating from China, India, and other faraway places. Four gaming tables, two blackjack and two roulette surrounded by plastic chairs of various shapes, colour and size. One large round but dull mirror hanging on a rusty hook, in a dark obscure damp corner. Dylan and I gazed around and stared at each other bursting into fits of laughter, with members of the staff watching our unexpected reaction. They looked puzzled, intrigued by our behaviour, but joined in with spontaneous laughter regardless. Their big white dazzling teeth lit up the dullness of the place. Stifling stale air overpowered the room, to the burring sound of the roulette wheel spinning. Not my idea of a casino. It was a fanciful and dreadful dungeon.

MEETING WALTER CASINO MANAGER

Later that day Shamshae introduced us to a very attractive man in his early forties, with an excellent command of the English language, his name was Walter. A pompous African, rather extraordinarily well dressed, in this dreadfully dull casino.

> *"I am the casino manager, my name is Walter, and you will answer to me,"* he sarcastically quipped.

> *"No Walter, I answer only to Amin, not to you, or Shamshae. Do I make myself clear?"*

Walter stepped back in surprise almost falling off balance and hollered back at me.

> *"Oh, we shall see about that madam!"*

Intensely glaring at me, snarling Swahili and with a supercilious grin, made a quick exit through the heavy wooden door. Walter a rather pretentious, narcissistic character.

STAFF INSPECTION

We returned to the restaurant with Shamshae.

> *"Here are most of the staff. Well, some are away now. Come and have a look mummy."*

As the staff lined up for inspection I was greeted.

> *"Karibu sana welcome mummy."*

Some of the men I had met earlier all wearing old shabby, scruffy trousers, too long or too short and worn-out shoes, with or without laces.

> *"You have no shoes? And you are wearing jogging trousers?"* I asked a young shy waiter.
>
> *"Yes, mummy it's my brothers turn to wear the black shoes today, we share them."*

He pointed out his older brother further up the line wearing the shared unpolished black shoes.

THE KITCHEN

I was shocked and surprised; it was excellent a very professional galley kitchen. Then I noticed broken fridges and freezers. On closer inspection the kitchen was grimy, yet plenty of staff sitting around chatting and doing little work. Someone chopping up food and eating it, as the chef relaxed reading a newspaper, with his feet up on the cooker.

No interest and no action with the staff sitting quite still like statues.

Good quality professional kitchen equipment, however, everything was coated in grease or blackened from the cookers. We marched out with mixed feelings and entered a pleasant bright, nevertheless dusty office.

> *"This is the best office, but you can't have this one, this belongs to the accountant."*

Further along the passage Shamshae's office in total disarray, and a smaller cluttered room for me. Walter's office rather modest although tidy.

Still fatigued after the arduous journey, we made our way back to the street where Monty drove us back to the house, in an old grey car.

AT THE HOUSE

A very miserable long faced elderly man in the garden, peering through a pair of wired cracked sunglasses, greeted us as the dogs ran circles around him barking and jumping up and down. From the outside a rather charming house painted pale blue and white, with two large, shuttered windows and climbing plants. Some pretty trees and shrubs lined the pathway to the front door. A quaint colonial feel with a white trellis porch covered with plants. Although the house was pleasant, it needed updating, as did the Flamingo Casino, Noah's Ark and Chiromo Garden Hotel.

After a few days settling in the house and getting down to the mundane daily work, reorganising staff routines and several meetings, things started to fall into place.

THE KITCHEN CLEAN UP

I thought we ought to clean and sanitise the kitchen first.

> *"Empty all the cupboards and clear the shelves. Everything must be scrubbed clean and hygienic, ok?"*

No one wanted to move off their seats, so I yelled at them, if they didn't do it everyone would be fired, and I would get new staff who would take my orders.

> *"We are helping you, come on now let's all get to work,"* Dylan yelled.

Although they loathed doing it, eventually one by one they got stuck in.

> *"If you make a really good job of it, you can all have a soft drink and a meal with me later."*

As the cleaning progressed the pest control man arrived to rid the place of vermin. We all stepped out into the restaurant as an army of giant cockroaches scurried across the floor and disappeared down a huge crack in the wall. Later I decided to change the menu; it was all Chinese or Indian food. Sunday lunch would be special, we could attract a good business clientele. I seemingly impressed the kitchen staff with different concepts for recipes and donning the chef's outfit to cook. As the new dishes appeared one by one, the illusive customers slowly returned, day-by-day the run-down neglected club was transformed.

> *"Roast lamb with vegetables, Yorkshire pudding and herb roasted potatoes that's what we are doing this Sunday, I will cook it. Everyone will have lunch with me and then if we think it's good, next week we start to cook it for the restaurant."*

The experiment was a big success; the staff loved my cooking, and so started a new phase in the Flamingo restaurant. Very quickly the word spread that a new mzungu manager was working at the casino and delicious new meals on the menu, the place spruced up and a great atmosphere. The British Sunday roast dinner was such a success we needed to turn people away, due to insufficient food.

THE DISCO

The next challenge was the disco area where Monty played at being a DJ, he was not, and it was dreadful. Music blasting out at any given hour during the day and night with just his friends dancing around on the multi coloured vinyl tiles. Monty and Baby arriving very impromptu without warning, behaving appallingly, and helping themselves to food and drink without asking permission.

> *"We don't need to ask you for anything, this is our families club, and you are just an employee don't forget that, oh and our aunty works in the casino too."*

Later I discovered aunty was Walter's unsociable croupier girlfriend, and the people I thought most likely to be on the fiddle.

STOCK CHECK IN STOREROOM

One day I decided to do a full stock check and lined everything up on the worktop. In came a small unfriendly African lady with a large blue plastic shopping bag. She began filling her bag with packets of rice, flour, sugar, and canned food.

> *"Hey, excuse me what are you doing? Who are you? You can't just come into my kitchen and take food. You are stealing it, and I am the manager here, stop!"*
>
> *"This is for Baby's aunty, Rafiki, friend"* she demanded.
>
> *"No, no Baby's aunty will have to come and see me if she wants anything, she works for the casino, she has no right to have food. She doesn't work in the restaurant, what is this about. Do not call me Rafiki I am not your friend I am the Manager, call me mummy?"*

From a distance I could hear thud, thud, of heavy shoes promptly marching towards the storeroom.

"Come on hurry up, we must leave now, get the stuff, hurry, hurry, haraka sana mamma."

"Stop right there and put that food down," I demanded.

"You come in here, you mzungu, telling us what we can have or can't have. This used to be my sisters place, and I am entitled to take whatever I want."

Yes, the sister had died and that's the reason I was put there to manage it and be responsible for the wilful children.

"You will not take anything from here or the casino without a receipt and it must be for a good reason, not just for you to gobble up."

They left furiously empty handed. Within ten minutes Walter the casino manager appeared shaking his finger with a sinister glare, extremely angry and foaming at the mouth.

"What is going on, she is going to leave the casino because of this!" he yelled at me.

"Walter you are the manager of the casino, go away and manage that and tell your girlfriend I am on to her fiddling and whatever else Monty and Baby have been up to. No wonder the place is running at a loss."

Walter and his overweight croupier girlfriend didn't take kindly to being corrected and me observing their every move. They both tried every conceivable means of distraction to confuse me. I had good work experience in a casino many years previously, at the Silhouette Club in Southampton and knew what to look out for. Both Walter and his girlfriend became very resentful and indignant. I investigated everything they did. It became obvious they had many swindles and ways to glean money from the casino. But that was before I came on the scene.

REPORTING TO AMIN

"Keep an eye on Walter and his girlfriend and get me a list of all the alterations required."

I approached a local builder to inspect the whole place; he was very charming and helpful. We discovered an old door jammed up for years, wrenched it open, and discovered an enormous balcony.

"So, it must have been a theatre at one time, look what you could create up here. It's got so much potential."

I created a long list of essential work required, it was much more than the Namanga renovation and not simply a quick paint and repair job. I decided to call Amin and discuss everything concerning the casino's maintenances and situation on the accounts.

STAFF TRAINING

One waiter had great difficulty walking in his hideous shoes that looked like big flippers, he wobbled about like a penguin. Others tripping over their own feet. I explained the necessity to arrive at work smart and clean.

Two hours of staff training, I explained that I intended to observe them serving the diners, and I would pretend to be a customer.

"Hello mummy."

"No don't call me mummy. I'm a customer, you don't know who I am."

"Yes mummy," the waiter answered.

"You don't know who I am. I'm just a customer and I'm going to sit at the table behind the menu."

"Eer, hmmm, Eer. Have you chosen what you want mummy?" he asked.

"I'm not mummy; I'm just a customer."

"Oh yes mummy that's right."

I couldn't get them to understand I was pretending to be a customer and therefore not mummy. I stacked up a tray with plates, cups and glasses as a demonstration and walked around the restaurant. I had worked as a stewardette in the British Merchant Navy for a few years, so thought I would teach them how to balance trays, and approach diners.

"This is what I had to do with the tray on a ship. The ship is moving up and down like this."

"Oh, are we on the ship mummy?" he said.

They all began swaying back and forth in their seats, as if onboard the vessel. It was hilarious.

"No, I'm moving like this because I'm on a ship that's where I was taught to do this. It's moving on the water, but this floor here is not on water is it, do you understand?"

"Oh yes mummy you're on a ship with a big tray."

"I am going to serve you now watch carefully as I do it without dropping things."

When I finished the demonstration, they clapped and cheered, I wanted to inspire them.

"Now you're going to learn how to do it,"

I grinned.

"Oh no mummy we're not going on a ship, we are staying here."

They didn't understand the purpose of the exercise. They couldn't coordinate and balance a tray, I simply wanted to show them it's easy in a restaurant, but very difficult on a ship. It was fun trying to teach a little silver service to these innocent young men, dressed in hideous clothes and random shoes.

THE KITCHEN STAFF TRAINING

In the kitchen I would tell someone to just watch a pot of water boil for potatoes to go in.

"When the pot boils, you shout out to mummy. I'll come to you."

I'm waiting for the call, but it was taking too long to boil. They were standing there just watching it, with sweat pouring off them.

"It's very hot mummy watching it."

"Yes, because you are standing over steam."

"Yes, mummy I am watching water like you said."

"But you're supposed to call me, and say come on mummy it has boiled, then you will put potatoes in the water," I giggled.

"Oh no mummy you do it, I can't do it that's not my job."

"What is your job?" I asked.

"My job is putting plates down on tables."

"Ok, well let's just change your job for now, you try this it's very easy you just pick up potatoes and put them in the pot, chef come over here, will you please tell him he can put the potatoes into the water."

"He won't do it mummy, his job is putting plates on the table, he cannot do anything else than that," laughed the chef.

If the person allocated to wash dishes was not there for the day, it would pile up unless the chef did it.

> *"Ok, tomorrow everyone must wear the same colour clothes, white shirt and black trousers, do you understand that?"* I asked.

> *"Oh no mummy black trousers not possible for me, brother is wearing them tomorrow."*

Just another day in Kenya, I thought.

CASINO TRAINING

Walter was entitled to have one free drink on a chitty, but he used it repeatedly. Therefore, he had free drinks all night, I sorted out a book with numbered pages that he needed to sign and kept it to avoid any possible tampering.

> *"Here it is for your free drink. When you have shown that to the barman you bring it back to me, otherwise tomorrow you don't get a drink unless you return it."*

> *"I am going to phone Amin because I have never been treated like this in my life. I must sign for my own drinks, and I am manager of the casino,"* he ranted.

> *"The trouble is Walter, you've been drinking the bottles, and you are only entitled to have a glass not a bottle."*

Next it was the manager Shamshae to deal with. He was an alcoholic, I could hear the bottles clank, in his shopping bag, but they came from the storeroom. He was a nice man, I felt sorry for him. Dylan and I were invited a few times to his charming house for a meal. His wife and children were delightful.

CONVERSATION WITH AMIN

I mentioned to Amin that there were too many managers at the Flamingo Casino.

> *"I cannot remove just one person and put you in charge, it doesn't work like that. What you must do is to stir up all the problems and let them know you will tell me,"* Amin laughed.

> *"Last time I nearly got killed by Nazir and his staff at Namanga,"* I said.

He chuckled.

> *"Maybe you will come back to Nairobi to be with me here after all. I think that you might soon. But you see it is very easy for me to go up there, I have a very good excuse to go up to Kisumu and spend some time with my lovely manageress."*

Amin was so charming, and I loved him.

THE BOOKKEEPER

I needed to gain the confidence of the bookkeeper, to handover the accounts for inspection.

> *"Oh, you can't have the books, I am the accountant and responsible for them."*

> *"But I must see them, I am the manageress."*

> *"Oh no you have to see Shamshae,"* she smirked.

> *"I don't have to see anybody. I will call Amin right now from this office!"*

> *"Oh no, no mummy here they are."*

> *"We are going to sit together and look at them, come here sit with me."*

"No, no, I don't want anything to do with it, I can't mummy. I'll leave, I'll leave!" she flustered.

She quickly dashed out and headed towards Shamshae's office. Everyone was aware of the deceitful system set up by Walter, and because he was an authoritarian character, they were too afraid to speak out. I was probing around in their storerooms and scrutinising the accounts, revealing his devious behaviour. One swindle after the other, as I continued to dig deeper into Walter's nefarious actions. Constantly searching for incriminating evidence and determined to expose the culprit.

DISCOVERING THE PROBLEMS

As the weeks passed by, and gruelling hours sifting through the numerous books it was noticeable to me what was occurring. Hours of observing Walter and girlfriend fiddling money out of the casino and night club. I was satisfied that I had sufficient incriminating evidence for Amin. Oblivious to Walter creaming off the profits, aunty stealing the food and Shamshae drinking the rest.

After several phone calls to Amin, we confirmed a date to return to the Four Aces with our information and records, he asked for evidence, and proof positive. It was quite a task searching and discovering what was going on and having to cope with Baby and Monty constantly breezing in and out of the club. They were undesirable young people; they took whatever they wanted and simply ignored me.

Baby would rub herself up against Dylan and snigger, I began to feel threatened by her actions, reminding me of the Jessie affair in Diani Beach. At the house she would constantly change into slinky clothes to provoke Dylan to glance at her. Parading around like a stripper, laughing as she sauntered from room to room. It was extremely uncomfortable for me, for Dylan it was sheer sexual entertainment. Baby had a much older boyfriend in his thirties who called at the house now and then. On one occasion he was waiting outside for her and became impatient.

"Hurry up Baby why are you taking so long?"

"Wait, wait I am busy doing magic on the mzungus, they will soon leave us alone."

"Do not try magic on me Baby, you have no idea who I am, or what I am capable of doing!"

"I'm doing black magic on you mzungu."

She was a very tenacious and disruptive girl.

RAMADAM

January 22nd ending February 20th.

It was almost the end of Ramadan and very stressful in the house, everyone on edge. Monty continued to blast his music as loud as possible, to prevent us from getting any rest whenever we could snatch a few hours from the heavy workload. Arguments triggered off very easily because I was unable to communicate with Baby or Monty. Dylan and I began to loathe these two unmanageable selfish kids.

Walter and aunty had a showdown in my office, when I exposed their scams and arrogant attitude towards me. Walter retaliated with threats to murder me and dispose of my body or black magic to make sure I leave Kenya. I had no fear of the threats, but it was disturbing all the same, knowing what these people were capable of doing. I had experienced the juju magic at African Oasis and the Reiner *grave and bush* madness, but this was different. Day by day the pressure grew on me, as I uncovered more deception to report to Amin. The quiet accountant who assisted in uncovering the fiddling of cash, began to shy away from me. Whenever I approached her, she would merely walk away.

We never spoke again.

All other members of staff who assisted in the undercover search for the fiddles, suddenly took sick leave, or never communicated again. I heard that one croupier had a mysterious accident, I could only guess that Walter and his girlfriend had a hand in it.

Walter, the aunty and the two children were taking the money, food, drinks and whatever they wanted. No longer surprised that Walter could afford such quality clothing, on such a small salary. Between them they had it pretty much sewn up, the casino simply served them, not Amin.

Amin phoned requesting we leave for Nairobi as soon as the feast of Ramadan was over. It would be a matter of days before heading back to the capital, excited and very eager to see Amin again.

AMIN IS SICK

It was the day before the planned Nairobi trip when Amin's son Babu called my office to say.

"Dad is really sick in hospital."

Babu advised us to wait a couple of days until he was sure his dad was feeling better.

"What's wrong with him Babu?"

"We don't know Janette, but it seems after the Ramadan feast, he immediately became very sick."

"Oh no, I'm so sorry to hear that, please don't hesitate to call me with any news."

"Okay, I'm sure dad will be fine in a few days," Babu replied.

After two long days waiting for an update, Babu called to inform us Amin was improving, and not to worry.

"Dads doing fine and expected to be home at the weekend," he revealed.

I called a staff meeting to explain the situation about Amin's hospitalisation and imminent return to his home. Everyone seemed cheerful with the update, apart from Walter and aunty. They appeared quite blasé and unconcerned about the whole affair. I spoke to Baby and Monty about their uncle's health; they gave the same disinterested reaction as Walter!

I phoned Babu several times during the next two days for an update, but intuitively sensed something was amiss. Nevertheless, Babu mentioned he was on a kidney dialysis machine, which had apparently broken down and was subsequently moved to another hospital. The dialysis machine wasn't operating at the second hospital either. I thought this was very suspicious! Whilst in the club checking on the staff, I noticed Amin's bodyguard slumped in a chair drinking a coke.

"Why is he here? Why isn't he with Amin?" I asked Walter.

"You ask too many questions madam!" he retorted.

Who was looking after Amin now? Did he have a bodyguard there? I was genuinely concerned for my dear friend's safety. I sought to approach the bodyguard however he quickly proceeded to the exit glancing at Walter. I tried calling Babu early that evening, there was no response, I knew something wasn't right.

STRANGE ATMOSPHERE

That night there was a very strange atmosphere. It was rather creepy and unsettling. Walter sat in my office looking very uneasy and turning a pale coffee colour, normally dark chocolate complexion. Shamshae appeared with his usual supply of pilfered booze and suggested we all sit in the office and have a few drinks to ease the tension. We were all anxiously waiting for some news! Suddenly the phone rang with a message from Babu that Amin was well and over the worst, out of danger and not to worry anymore.

I was so excited and couldn't wait to tell the staff.

But immediately after the good news and raising our filled glasses to Amin's recovery, an awful lingering sound bellowed through the restaurant and disco. Everyone looked frightened as doors banged, and a thumping sound on the ceiling rattled the building. A gust of wind sending shivers up my spine whistled through the office.

Walter looked almost white, shaking, and grabbed onto Dylan's arm. Shamshae shocked and fixed to the floor with fright, some staff running out the front door screaming in Swahili. Walter yelled out in panic, his thick lips quivering and his big eyes bulging out of his head.

> *"What the bloody hell was that?"*
>
> *"It's the cry of the Banshee,"* I giggled.
>
> *"What's the Banshee?"* he could barely speak, almost choking, just a mumble.

"A spirit guide to take our spirit home, she comes to us all Walter. I have heard this sound before, when an aunty died in Ireland."

Although I was teasing Walter with the Banshee story a deep sense of loss overwhelmed me, I felt terribly cold and shivered. Suddenly the phone began to ring, yet no one wanted to answer it. Eventually I picked up the receiver, there was an inaudible sound and heavy breathing, almost gasping, followed by an outburst of sobbing.

"It's dad Janette! he's dead, he's' gone, he was alright and now he's gone," sobbed Babu.

"Oh no! God no! I don't believe it, I'm so sorry Babu!"

I was in shock and could barely utter a word, so Dylan spoke to Babu for a few moments. Shamshae burst into tears and gulped the remainder of the brandy, Walter turned around in a circle like a dog chasing its tail, in total shock and disbelief. Dylan slumped to the floor where I sat and wept like a baby in my arms. Trying to cope with the news of Amin's death after hearing he was okay was an absolute nightmare. It was impossible to understand that only a short time ago, we were told he was over the worst, then the bombshell he was dead. How could it be so? We stayed in the casino until almost dawn, Walter albeit drunk, gave us a lift in his car near to the house.

DAYBREAK ARRIVED

As the sorrowful night of darkness gave way to the amber radiance glowing against the deep blue skyline, dawn was breaking. Far beyond the sleepy town of Kisumu a shadowy outline appeared, in the distance as the rugged mountain range began to emerge. An eerie stillness, as the morning light revealed the sun rising from the deep dark vastness of space. Dylan and I stood silently, awestruck. Some time passed by. Oblivious to the world around us, faintly recognising the sweet sound of the morning call, as the birds began to stir. We slowly moved step by step towards the house. The sunlight engulfed the entire sky, turning various shades of amber and red, an awesome phenomenon. I whispered a prayer for my dear friend Amin and cried silently into my cupped hands.

We entered the house as the dogs barked and jumped over the furniture. Baby and Monty appeared from the dark dingy bedrooms half asleep and sat in the front room with us. I didn't hesitate to break the dreadful news about Amin's passing. They were both silent, then ran off in different directions, doors slamming behind them. Dylan and I made coffee and sat in the garden to soak up the early morning sun and reflect upon the dreadful news. Within an hour of our arrival, we received a call from Nairobi.

> *"Whatever happens don't let the children travel alone to Nairobi, you must bring them Janette, please take charge of them… thank you,"* requested Amin's brother.

It did not make sense of what had happened that night, Amin was fine, then he died? Contemplating the idea he was killed, poisoned crossed my mind several times.

Walter and the girlfriend swindle about to be exposed any day, could Walter have been instrumental in this bizarre scenario? Or Nazir had he gone back on his word?

I remembered Amin saying to me.

> *"The government will not be happy if I win my seat in the next election. They don't want good MPs who help the community, they want corrupt ones."*

Was it a political assassination? Or was it an act of God?

A few hours passed by, there would be no sleep. We showered and returned to the club. We met the staff waiting outside, weeping, and wailing. Others crouching down on the pathway or steps, huddled in groups and strange mutterings with muffled cries.

It was a very sorrowful event.

"The club is closed until further notice." I declared.

"Mummy this is horrible news what shall we do?"

"It is terrible, a very sad day for everyone, please you must go home."

We chatted to Shamshae, it was agreed that Dylan and I would travel back to Nairobi with him and the children for the funeral. Walter would make his own arrangements. We returned to the house and explained the Walji family wanted the children in my care. They neither listened nor answered but stormed off in the old grey car to the casino. For the rest of that day Dylan and I cuddled up on the bed and cried, occasionally drifting off into a very uneasy sleep.

THE FOLLOWING DAY

Walter had left town with Baby and Monty, travelling to Nairobi, yet he was aware the family wanted them arriving with Shamshae and me. Amin previously mentioned Baby and Monty were not welcome by some of the Walji family. There was animosity towards them because of their disruptive behaviour.

This journey would be the unhappiest trip to Nairobi, life without Amin would be unbearable for me, I couldn't imagine living in Kenya without him. He was always there for me. Only a whisper away he would say.

I loved him. I believe I was falling in love with him.

He was the very best of men.

NAIROBI TRIP AMIN'S FUNERAL

It was a sweltering day as the old, battered taxi bumped its way homeward bound to Nairobi and the Four Aces Casino. A solemn greeting by the staff who directed us to one of Amin's cars, with a security guard to go with us. Approaching Westland's area crowds of grieving people surrounding Amin's house. People adored him, constituents gathered amongst the crowds with security men. Closer to the house Amin's beautiful wife gracefully waving a white handkerchief turned her head to acknowledge the silver Mercedes pull into the driveway. Four security guards slowly approached the car, dragging their feet across the grass.

"Hello welcome, please follow me mummy."

It was indeed the most heartrending moment for us. I grasped Dylan's hand as we neared the house. Amin's wife held out her hand to greet us, with our heads bowed in respect and tears welling in our eyes. She placed her soft hand in mine and whispered.

"Thank you for being here today for Amin."

She could sense my grief, and just patted me gently on the shoulder. Confused guests milled around the gardens and in the house. The sound of sorrow echoed throughout the rooms as people wandered around aimlessly in a daze. An hour quickly passed by, then we were all summoned onto the front lawn and directed to the car we would travel in. Silver and white Mercedes cars were waiting on the driveway. Slowly we pulled away from Amin's impressive home onto the road that would take us to the mosque. The journey was short but intense!

An enormous, magnificent mosque filled with the people who loved and cared for Amin. He was being honoured and I felt deeply moved and immensely proud to be present at this outpouring of grief. He was highly respected by his community. It was a strange poignant moment realising that we all shared a collective understanding. Muslims, Christians, Hindus, Sikhs, and other religions gathered under one roof, experiencing the same emotions. Love and sorrow.

Everyone's shoes piled up at the entrance and people queuing to enter the grand mosque. Two sad security men appeared and escorted us to the correct seating area.

As the heady fragrant aroma wafted through the building filling the air with a thick smoky haze of incense, it was overwhelming. The atmosphere was sombre, heavy, and pungent, with a lack of oxygen and truly little air to breathe. Echoing throughout the mosque the sudden deafening weeping and howling rising from those attending to Amin's body, which rested surrounded with an abundance of beautiful, colourful flowers.

From the utter solemnity of silence to a loudening crescendo of voices singing for this kind gentleman loved by so many. The wailing and singing became louder, as the people shuffled slowly towards his body laid out silently on the floor. One by one the mourners shuffled along, people from all social classes coming together in a pitiful procession, to say a last farewell to a dear friend. It seemed endless as each person said goodbye and returned to their seat, or simply sat on the floor crying.

In an orderly fashion everyone sat silently for ten minutes or so, in anticipation for the grand entrance of the President. Finally, President Daniel arap Moi and his entourage appeared out of the heavy overpowering misty haze of incense burning. Ignoring protocol by wearing his shoes, he promptly shuffled over to Amin's body, closely followed by his fellow MPs, secret police, and bodyguards.

He paused for just a moment, nodded, and then disappeared behind a curtain; we did not see him again. After his departure we all began singing and chanting that echoed eerily throughout the mosque. After the prayers were quietly narrated, we were to leave and wait outside.

All the men of the family gathered to go with Amin to his last resting place. In true Muslim tradition, this was not a place for women. The men removed Amin as the women chanted. Upon their return we regrouped, and the cavalcade of cars set forth to return to the house of Amin's widow. Soft drinks served with small dishes of delicious food, as an eerie silence broken only by the occasional sobbing echoed throughout the house. Amongst the crowds we noticed Baby, Monty and Walter chatting with members of the Four Aces casino. Then it was time to leave. Amin's houses were all occupied by his family and close friends, nevertheless we needed to find a hotel.

REINER AT THE IMPALA HOTEL

We intended to stay at the Esperia Hotel as per norm, unfortunately there were no available rooms due to the funeral. Nonetheless, I knew the old African man who owned the Impala Hotel, so we headed there. The reception lady was very understanding and offered a room at a small discount.

"Very sad Mr. Walji mummy, he was a very good man."

In a contemplative state and utterly overwhelmed by the day's events, we laid on our beds exhausted. Sleep avoided us and when dawn broke, we were eager to sit outside on the verandah for breakfast. Still in a pensive mood and weary from the whole episode, we sipped freshly made orange juice, with toast and eggs.

Our sad faces puffed up from sobbing and bloodshot eyes, we could barely recognise ourselves.

It was only a matter of time when the usual hub-hub Nairobi commotion began from the busy traffic on the crowded streets. The constant foggy haze of dust and vehicle exhaust fumes, as the morning rush hour began. Tradesmen were arriving at the hotel with pushcarts filled with fresh fruit and vegetables. Trucks, vans, bicycles, and boxes dumped outside the hotel, causing havoc in the driveway. Hotel guests desperately trying to leave, shouting, and yelling at each other. Beeping car horns and arms waving from open windows, no one could move in or out. Surprisingly, I recognised a familiar face amongst the chaos, ready to explode in frustration at any moment due to the pandemonium.

"Move your fucking self you idiot, get out of the fucking way, move, move, haraka sana," yelled the overweight impatient German.

"Shit its fucking Reiner Moser," yelled Dylan.

We could not believe our eyes as he bellowed more abuse at the poor tradesman trying to sell his vegetables to the cook. Potatoes and carrots rolled around the driveway, followed by two small children who appeared from nowhere scavenging as much as they could carry. Abruptly Reiner's car surged forward with his arm waving in the air and his other hand on the hooter. Then he glanced over to our table and burst into a loud roar of hearty laughter. I cannot believe it, he shouted at the top of his voice.

"Well, well it can't be, I must be seeing things, ya, I am having too much vodka and beer last night, ha-ha!"

Unexpectedly he fell out of the car, rolled on the ground in the dirt, and stumbled towards Dylan and me, shocked and engrossed in his behaviour.

Without warning Dylan jumped up.

"Oh, well I guess you have found us Reiner; we can't run so what's next?"

"What do you mean what is next you fool, how the bloody hell are you my old friend. So, you must be here for the funeral as you are such good friends with the Walji family eh, ha-ha."

Grinning sarcastically and ignoring me, he slumped his huge body down onto a bench and lit a cigarette.

"Sorry to hear about Walji he was an ok guy, anyway, it's good to see you Dylan, but not so good to see you, Janette," he snarled.

Reiner spat on the floor just missing the resident scruffy black cat, as she scampered past the big Bavarian.

I could not believe my eyes, Reiner Moser the last person we needed on the day after the funeral. He chatted to Dylan for a time, and they were laughing as if nothing ever happened. Then unexpectedly he stood up, stuck out his enormous chest and belly and shuffled towards me smiling.

> *"Well, Janette I can't say we will ever be good friends again, but we will not be enemies either, let's bury the hatchet with poor Walji, ok?"* he grinned.

I reluctantly agreed, but I knew there had to be peace for now. Reiner would think the truce would leave us vulnerable and off guard, but he was wrong. I could not trust him, remembering the terrible frightening experiences he had put me through before. After an hour of listening to his stories Reiner told us things were bad for him. He explained that after we departed Chiromo everything went wrong for him. We chuckled at the way things had turned out for all of us. But at least we were alive to talk about it, and that was more than we could say for our friend Amin. We raised our glasses of orange juice and Reiner his cold beer to say farewell to Amin. However, keeping silent about our intentions to return to Kisumu.

As for Reiner Moser, we said farewell, and never saw him again after that curious meeting at the Impala Hotel.

I considered the old African owner of Impala might have contacted Reiner to inform of our stay there. Although the old man was kind to me once, I discovered I could trust only one man, and now he was gone.

JOURNEY BACK TO KISUMU

We headed back to Kisumu; it was a silent and contemplative journey. When we arrived back, the house was quiet, no staff or animals there, the place was abandoned, we had much needed time alone.

Over the next two days we simply rested, anticipating any unexpected events that could unfold.

Babu, Amin's son phoned and expressed his desire to have the casino remain closed, until further notice. We arranged for a car to take us to the to the Flamingo casino to witness the staff sitting outside or pacing up and down. It was a tragedy that Amin died, and pitiful souls wanting to know about their jobs. The casino was their meeting place, they all socialised there when not working. With Amin no longer here, their wages would be frozen for a while. I was reminded of our lucky escape from the unfortunate staff at Namanga Noah's Ark. I prayed we wouldn't face a similar scenario with this awful situation unfolding.

Shamshae hit the bottle and remained at home. Baby and Monty lingered with family in Nairobi. Walter returned alone and hid himself away.

A week after returning to Kisumu I became very ill with a day in hospital having tests. It was concluded I had malaria again. I was so depressed due to Amin's death, I imagined I was going to die too. Then one day whilst resting on the bed, I thought I'm not dying in this awful house, or in Kenya. Dylan was dashing around looking after me, as I lay helplessly weak in bed for over a week. I realised that Kisumu was not where I wanted to be anymore, I was grieving for Amin, I had no appetite.

PHONE CALL TO DYLAN'S MOTHER

One afternoon I decided to call Dylan's mother and ask her for help with air fares to get us out of Kenya. When she answered the phone, I immediately sensed she had no time for me, however she would speak to Dylan.

She offered to help him but refused to assist me.

> *"I told you not to go out there, now you have trouble and want my help. Typical,"* she grunted.

Dylan was very upset by his mother's insensitive attitude but agreed that he would pay her back the money.

Baby and Monty did not return from Nairobi.

A maid arrived with the two fat scruffy cats and two ugly mongrel dogs. The peace in the house departed with the dishevelled maid as she grinned and waved farewell. Chaos and madness had returned.

Amin's brother phoned to say that we should travel back up to Nairobi; he wanted to look at the casino report I had prepared for Amin. However, I was too ill to do anything, and would remain at the house until stronger. Later in the week arrangements were made by Babu to return to the Four Aces Casino for a meeting.

We hadn't set foot in the Flamingo Casino since our return and neither of us had any desire to go back and continue working there. Devoid of my one true friend, and the peace with Reiner held no value to me. He was an irrational man who manipulated vulnerable people. He had killed before; he might try again.

I received a letter from England that said my eldest sister had a car accident, so I considered an excuse to travel to escape Kenya. Babu summoned us to return and to live at the staff house for a couple of weeks, where we stayed before.

The final journey to Nairobi was set for early morning; to avoid any suspicion about our departure to the UK, we left our belongings behind. We decided to take only one bag each. Everything went to plan as we set off for Nairobi for the last time. I was very weak and unwell; I just prayed the journey would not be too bumpy and prolonged. We arrived in suitable time, and I explained to Amin's two sons and his brother that my sister was in hospital, and I must go back to England for two weeks to see her. They were very sympathetic having just lost Amin. They suggested I should go but Dylan would remain with them to help in the casino. I told them it was not possible I could not travel alone.

> *"I am not well enough to go alone I'd never make it without him,"* I appealed.

After a brief discussion they agreed that under these circumstances it would not be right for me to go alone. We stayed at Amin's house for almost two weeks whilst I regained strength, and the family inspected my report. Finally, Babu requested a meeting at the casino for a get together meal. They were incredibly pleased with my report, and I would work at the Four Aces, on my return. Because of the issues I outlined, the decision to sell the run-down Flamingo Casino became the better possibility. Rather than invest in refurbishment, and it was too far away to keep an eye on it. I believed the conclusion to sell the Flamingo Casino was the right one.

ESCAPING FROM NAIROBI

A DAY AT THE RACES

After almost two week's rest a surprise opportunity to visit our friend Judy, Duncan's girlfriend and go to the races for the day. Although I was still tired, I needed to get out. We met up with Judy and Duncan in Gypsies for a few drinks, they were very pleased to see us alive, after hearing some of the Nairobi gossip. They were aware of Amin's passing and the funeral.

Off to the races and back to reality, it was so reassuring to be out with friends. We bumped into several people we had met in Nairobi before the Namanga and Kisumu adventure and shared some stories about it. A wonderful day especially not having to worry about Reiner, and a few of us ended up having a meal at Gypsies Bar.

I noticed Major Paula Enselmo sitting with a young, attractive white man, another random coincidence I thought!

MEETING UP WITH JUDY TO ESCAPE NAIROBI

I called Judy to meet up at Gypsies Bar, then on to her house for a light lunch. We really needed her help to plan our escape from Kenya. Judy had connections with secret police and government officials through her husband, so she was the right person to advise us. Judy was fully aware of the entire story and told us to be mindful of Reiner and that his making peace or the truce, was a trap to catch us off guard.

The following day Babu invited us to the Four Aces, and we chatted about the journey home to the UK. We were in Amin's old office it felt very strange without him there. Amin's brother opened a wall safe and then handed over $1,000 US and told me it was our ticket money.

> *"You worked so hard for Amin, and I know that you have not received a salary. You have had so much to endure, and this is the very least we can do for you. When you return to Nairobi you will have your own apartment with a maid. A Mercedes car and security guard will look after you and drive you around. Your food and drink will be free, and your salary will be particularly good also. You will be an assistant to the manager as head of the catering. Dylan will help by doing something with security. Are you happy with this arrangement Janette?"*

"Yes, thank you it sounds wonderful."

We enjoyed a delicious meal with the family and later bought our flight tickets, in a small agency away from Reiner's spies. After two days we met up with Judy and her lover at Gypsies Bar and driven to our house to pick up the luggage bags. Then he took us to meet Judy, parked discreetly in a posh area near her home, where we transferred the bags to her jeep. Judy was very composed and began the journey chatting about the day at the races. We stopped at the traffic lights when two young men tried to distract us, a failed robbery we guessed. We became very vigilant and nervous after that. A long journey trying to weave our way through the chaotic city. At the airport we thought we recognised local police who were friends to Reiner. Judy kissed me on the cheek and hugged and said loudly.

"Have a nice break and see you in two weeks, take care both of you."

"I know I will never see you again," she whispered.

Turning away, she walked back to the jeep without a glance. We were so apprehensive and by now everyone looked suspicious to us. The waiting seemed endless. Our flight came up on screen and the announcement followed, that all passengers flying to London Heathrow would make their way to the departure lounge. We sat quietly and attentively watching for any sudden moves from anyone near us. Sitting on the edge of the seat waiting to board the plane was now only moments away. People were pushing and shoving in the queue, I became quite paranoid and anxious.

Gradually the queue began to move slowly towards the boarding area, then we handed over our flight tickets at the gate. Almost breathless and sweating profusely we gripped hands and boarded. The stewardess directed us to the middle of the plane, and as we looked for our seats, we heard a commotion and glanced to see activity going on by the entrance. I felt sick and thought Reiner was boarding. We sat down and prayed for the lift off. By now the tension was so great floods of tears rolled down my face as I tried desperately to remain composed. Finally, we had lift-off and a nine-hour flight ahead of us.

Dylan was constantly vigilant for any suspicious behaviour or anyone watching us. We drank small bottles of brandy and settled down having alternate snoozing. The journey was exceptionally smooth with only a short experience of turbulence.

Then we heard, prepare for landing it was music to my ears. We gathered our flight bags and headed to the entrance. The doors opened with a sudden rush of cold damp air sending chills up my spine. As my bloodshot eyes adjusted to the daylight, I could clearly see that it was grey and overcast. Typically, England, but I was home and safe. We sat for two hours expecting Dylan's sister to pick us up, however she was waiting at the wrong gate and had no idea where we were. When she appeared, she was aloof and strangely indifferent. It was a long and silent journey back to foggy Norfolk, as Dylan and I held each other and drifted off into a semi unconscious state with jet lag. Now we were homeless and forced to stay at Dylan's mother's house. On the plane we chatted about our homecoming and imagined a big Sunday roast dinner and a warm welcome. However, greeted with the harsh reality of an angry mother and a cold uninviting house.

A very stern looking mother at the door, no hug or kiss for either of us.

"Hello mate!" she quipped.

No aroma of a roast dinner that we envisaged on our arrival, there was no Sunday meal. A large, chipped mug of weak tea and a hot cross bun shoved under my nose, followed by hours of interrogation by the family. Dylan and I were so exhausted with jet lag and the past few weeks stress. I simply wanted to rest and did not need a bloody interrogation.

We needed to sleep and awaken to a new life without Reiner and all the horror we had endured. However, we had to sit on a hard sofa like two naughty kids and reprimanded for going off to Kenya.

We went from one nightmare scenario to another.

The love affair began over three years ago in Norfolk and here we were back where it all started. I sold a few things at auction that were stored at his mother's house. Within a month we moved to our own home in a small village. I bought an electric typewriter and typed up the notes and journals, and memories. I just wanted to get the Kenya encounter out of my mind and to never forget those salient experiences, albeit life changing moments.

SUMMARY

SIX YEARS IN NORFOLK

Over the next six years we were very content settling back into a different way of life in Norfolk. We worked tirelessly making small furniture, and a very successful spiritual, metaphysical teaching healing centre, and crystal shop.

We married.

After we married Dylan confessed to sleeping with several girls in Kenya. Including the mysterious girl on the boat trip to Walter's Island and our maid Alice, the sweet Christian girl.

Then one chilly afternoon a tall thin gypsy woman in her late thirties entered our lives. She joined our meditation classes, became a Reiki student and worked in our crystal shop part-time. Dylan had an affair with her and later they left town together, leaving me to pick up the pieces. Abandoned and heartbroken, alone, and desperate. I thought to kill myself. It was a bitter cold and freezing winter, with deep snow on the ground. I woke up crying feeling sorry for myself. I could not cope with the loss of Dylan especially after all I had been through with him. I took a bottle of vodka into the garage and a handful of sleeping pills; I was wrapped up in a thick blanket in my slippers as I shuffled to my car. My intent was to drink the bottle of vodka, take the pills and leave the car running with the exhaust fumes filling the garage, and it would end my misery.

It was freezing in the garage, I sighed and noticed my breath hanging in the still cold air, and thought is that my spirit? I stopped moving towards the car, for a moment I became motionless. Suddenly my hands were shaking, my feet were fixed to the ground. Then a mystical small bright white light emerged before me; I cried out I am not dying in this cold garage; I am not dying here today!

I returned to the living room and lit a big log fire, as the flames grew it reminded me of Kindani and the campfire experience. I made hot chocolate and put the vodka back in the cupboard. I snuggled down on the big sheepskin rug with my cosy blanket and wept.

Then I thought to myself.

I had survived malaria three times, betrayed by my Romany gypsy Dylan, conned and raped by Reiner the German mafia criminal, African black magic, the loss of Amin, losing my business and money, disgusting and appalling places I worked in, so surely, I could endure this nightmare too.

It was not my time to die.
It was not my ending, not this way.
Yet it was the end of my Romany gypsy love and me.
That's all.
We were together for almost nine years.

AFTER DYLAN LEFT ME

I had shelved my Kenya story in a green box file. There were piles of old notes, photos, the original typed one hundred pages, and parts of the journal. Then two years passed by when my dear friend Tim Kenning aka TFK, asked me what the box called Kenya was all about.

> *"Hey Jan, what is this file called Kenya?"*
>
> *"It's a journal, notes and photos of the three years in Kenya with Dylan."*
>
> *"You must write this story; I will help you,"* he smiled and took the file to his house.

Tim and I would occasionally revisit the file over the next twenty years we pieced it all together from the notes and memories. There was no rush as far as I was concerned. I wasn't really interested about it becoming a book, but he was. It was my journal and my story.

Sadly, Tim suddenly passed away June 1st, 2022, the Kenya story stayed in the file until February 2024, when I felt guided by Tim's spirit to complete it.

From the file of original jumbled notes, unfinished manuscripts stained with red wine, battered scruffy journals and the one hundred pages of typed memories.

Kenya, my story…

PHOTOS

&

INFORMATION

Tusks of Mombasa

Simba Village Diani Beach - My Apartment

At work in my office - African Oasis, Ukunda

African Oasis - off to Indian Ocean Hotel

Shimba Hills near Tanzania Timber Merchant

With James visiting his father, the Juju

Bootleggers' delivery

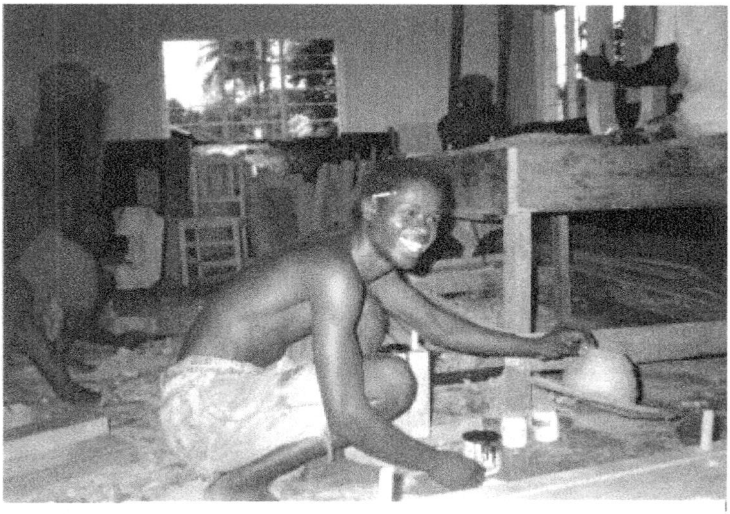

Patrick working inside

Collecting Makuti with Dylan for factory extension

Peter the pastor (first person), Francis (fourth person) and friends at the open church

Singing and dancing with the Ukunda children

Big house Christmas party with Tyson

Shakatak Club owned by Foxy Fuchs - Diani Beach

Ben and Jenny Pont - film producers of Michael Jackson's Earth Song *movie*

Namanga streets with Masai

Namanga Safari Lodge - Noah's Ark

Dylan and I back home in Norfolk

DAILY NATION, FRIDAY, NOVEMBER 26, 1993

Weekender *ENTERTAINMENT GUIDE*

Walji (Kanu-MP Westlands): "I am an organised politician."

Striving to make real his promises

IN HIGH PLACES

When he vied for the parliamentary seat on a Kanu ticket, he promised his voters that if elected he would give priority to the problems of insecurity, communication and unemployment in the area.

During the General Elections Amin Mohamed Sadrudin Walji won the Westlands seat by garnering 8,687 votes to 7,602 votes of his closest rival, Wang'uhu Ng'ang'a (FORD-Asili).

And now in parliament, Walji, who is an Assistant Minister for Local Government says: The problem of communication, too, is being tackled. "I have tried to repair most of the roads in Westlands and assisted in bringing water to the people. I have so far helped over 300 job-seekers to get employment."

And indeed Walji's offices either in Westlands or the ministry's headquarters at Jogoo House are full of people seeking help.

But he thinks something still has to be done about the insecurity situation which has adversely affected Asian community who have been killed without the culprits being found and brought to book.

Walji says since going to parliament he has presided over several harambee meetings where he has had to raise funds to pay school fees for students from the needy families who are either abroad or proceeding there.

Amin Walji was Kenyan Asian politician who was elected as the (KANU) representative for the Westlands Constituency in the Kenyan general election, 1992, the first multi-party elections since independence in 1963.

The Westlands Constituency was a marginal seat, and Walji challenged the incumbent Njoroge Mungai for the KANU by nomination. There were claims that Mungai had won the first ballots, but concern over irregularities in the nomination process led to the nomination process being carried out three times, with a third candidate dropping out complaining that non-resident voters were being imported to rig the nominations.

He died in 1996.

Wiki-

THURSDAY, NOVEMBER 2, 1995

NATION

ABC MEMBER OF THE AUDIT BUREAU OF CIRCULATION

on
ts

er developments, it still re- unclear on who, between Kenya Ports Authority, was le for the inability to rail umes of cargo from the ombasa.

g to the issue, the Caltex elations Manager, Mr said the payment prob- n old issue which started Government still con- oleum prices.

ernment, he said, used s for the transportation m products at 40cents Railways demanded the oil companies.

Mr Murt a said Caltex cipate a gas shortage he railway transport

y had enough stocks rt to road transpor-

d the liberalisation n industry gave the dom to set gas d claims of exces-

A German national, Mr Andreas Koeltz, poses outside the law court yesterday with a policeman after an extradition order was issued against him to face charges of stealing about Sh92 million in Germany. Mr Koeltz went back to the Nairobi Hospital, awaiting formal discharge by his doctor.

Kenya extradites wanted German

By ADIERI MULAA

A German wanted in his country for theft should be extradited today, a Nairobi court ruled yesterday.

The Nairobi Chief Magistrate, Mrs Uniter Kidullah, ordered Mr Andreas Koeltz to be sent back to Germany to be tried for an alleged theft of DM2.37 million (more than Sh92 million).

He allegedly stole the money from a company he worked for in Germany before he came to Kenya.

Mrs Kidullah said: "The subject, Andreas Koeltz is hereby extradited to Germany to stand trial for the said alleged offence(s)".

However, the magistrate allowed Mr Koeltz an overnight stay at the Nairobi Hospital, where he has been hospitalised, to be formally discharged by his doctor.

Mr Koeltz allegedly committed the before he came to Kenya.

Mrs Kidullah ordered that Mr Koeltz be delivered to the custody of the Commissioner of Police until he is handed over to the Interpol.

"Mr Koeltz is hereby delivered to the custody of the Attorney-General and more particularly to the Commissioner of Police awaiting to be conveyed to the German police".

The German was represented by lawyer Margaret Osolika.

Mrs Kidullah said the court had considered the fact that a warrant of arrest issued by a court Judge of the County Court of Bielefeld, Germany had been executed.

She said Mr Koeltz had no objection to being repatriated to stand trial in Germany.

The magistrate ruled that the alleged offence was one of those listed in schedule of the Mutual Extradition Treaty between Germany and Kenya.

In allowing Mr Koeltz an overnight stay at the hospital, Mrs Kidullah agreed with the defence counsel that it was only fair that he be taken back to be seen by the doctors treating him.

Responding to the defence counsel's application, Senior Principal State Counsel Horace Okumu said travel documents for Mr Koeltz were ready for him to be flown back to Germany today.

Andreas Koeltz deportation from Kenya - 1995

FOCUS Magazine | No. 41 (1995)

CRIME In Mafia Paradise

In the Mafia Paradise - FOCUS online

Millionaire thief Andreas Költz was gutted like a Christmas goose in Kenya. The people in Kilifi could not believe their eyes. Several dozen police officers rattled their cars through the streets of the poor Kenyan village near Mombasa. A few minutes later, they stormed into a whitewashed house and arrested a tanned German with dark hair and a high forehead.

Short luxury. When the handcuffs clicked, Andreas Költz's dream was over. On July 6, 1995, the 33-year-old had relieved his employer, the Bielefeld security company ADS (1,600 employees), of exactly 2,482,765.94 marks. The spectacular robbery of millions made headlines, but the new prosperity of the small security guard (monthly wage 4900 marks) lasted just under three months.

Költz had come to the West from Leipzig after the fall of the Berlin Wall. He did not feel comfortable in the former GDR. In 1982, he had been picked up during an attempted "flight from the Republic" on the Baltic Sea. At ADS, where he was hired, he marvelled at the millions that the money drivers stacked in seven vaults every day. He couldn't watch it for long. During the night shift, he cracked two safes by tampering with the computer system. In a three-page farewell letter, Költz poured ridicule and malice on his company: "Grant me the few marks."

"Embarrassing, extremely embarrassing," lamented ADS boss Peter Walpurgis after the robbery. A short time later, he is determined: "I'll grab it."

Safe cracker Költz returns to his hometown of Leipzig after the nightly robbery. Here, as a bartender in the international press club of the Karl Marx University, he already felt a touch of luxury in the early 80s. Now he throws the bills around. He lets school friend Michael K. in on his coup, and they both celebrate for three days in the "Interconti" hotel with champagne and paid girls.

On the side, Költz plans his escape. In Zurich, he deposits 1.5 million in an account of the Swiss Bank Company. Michael K. hides at least 250,000 marks behind the wardrobe in his apartment.

Andreas Költz makes his way out of Leipzig on July 10, completely unmolested. Via Prague, London, Cairo and Nairobi, he heads for his dream destination: Diani Beach, 30 kilometres south of Mombasa. A holiday paradise, where he already vacationed with his brother in February, enjoyed the easy life to the fullest and swore to himself: "I want to live here."

Költz dreamed of palm trees, white beaches, luxury villas, class hotels and, above all, willing black girls for less than 50 marks a night. What he didn't know was that the Mafia rules in Diani Beach. The deputy German ambassador to Kenya, Erich Kristof, warns against the pseudo-paradise: "The mafia operates prostitution, drug trafficking, girl trafficking and real estate transactions." The embassy says that Germans and Austrians rule in Diani Beach. Corruption is the order of the day.

Two sizes too big. Millionaire thief Andreas Költz is no match for the professional gangsters. He is gutted like a Christmas goose. After a short time, the Munich architect Joseph Brunlehner and his partner xxxxx xxxxx sold him a 300-square-metre dream villa in the "Palm Park Villas", thatched roof with a swimming pool in front of the door. After three days, the deal is settled. Költz pays in small bills. xxxxx: "Twenties, fifties and hundreds." Brunlehner's wife, a wealthy Kenyan Indian, counts for three hours: 300,000 marks.

She suspects that there is still more to be gained. Correct. The former Ferrari dealer xxxxx sells Költz his Harley-Davidson motorcycle for 50,000 marks. The profiteers milk their new cow and get him a new Mitsubishi Pajero SUV. Költz throws the money out of the window, buys jet skis, luxury furniture and a satellite system with a diameter of 3.80 metres. The millionaire robber is the only one on the coast to receive 27 European TV channels.

Hundreds of thousands squandered. On the hot nights, Költz chooses the "Shakatak" as his regular hangout. The brothel disco belongs to the former Hamburg neighbourhood star "Foxi" Fuchs. Within a few weeks, Andreas Költz squandered all the money he had dragged with him to Kenya in his suitcase: 700,000 marks.

Then he needs supplies. He orders from Michael K. in Leipzig via cell phone: "I need 200,000 marks, bring the money to Dieter J. in Langenfeld, he can bring it with him." Költz had met Dieter J. in Diani Beach. He is his neighbour. The man with the suitcase of money flies back to Kenya and hands Költz the coals. He gains confidence and shows his courier a FOCUS report on the million-dollar coup: "On page 54, that's me."

Költz is fearless. In the meantime, he knows: Many of his neighbours, architects, lawyers and doctors, bought the houses with black money. The millionaire thief generously grants the neighbour and building contractor Dieter A. a loan of 60,000 marks.

At the beginning of September, ADS detectives track down their ex-colleague. When they observe him, they can't believe their eyes. The little security guard Költz, whose professional glory moment came when he played the bodyguard for actor Roger Moore and tennis star Jimmy Connors, is now a star in his own right.

The detectives give the police a tip. In the early morning of September 13, Kenyan officials drag Költz out of bed. But he doesn't stay long in the 20-man cell of the prison in Mombasa. New friends such as hotel and nightclub owner Reiner Moser get him the best lawyer in Kenya. For a fee of 50,000 marks, Moses Kurgat brought his client back to freedom five days later.

Corruption. Judge Karanja Kanyi demands a bail of 30,000 marks. Költz pays easily. Kanyi, who is called "Mister 10 percent" in Mombasa, is also generously paid. Bielefeld's police chief Horst Kruse even knows: "Even an Interpol agent has been bribed."

Költz goes into hiding. Now the detectives are resorting to tougher bandages. First, they have the Költz property confiscated. Brunlehner and xxxxx even help and claim: "We don't want people like that here." They are currently trying to sell the house again.

The trap of the captors. Together with the Kenyan police, the detectives lie in wait for Költz in front of the "Reef Hotel" in Mombasa. But at the last second, the wanted man flees. His bodyguard, whom he now affords, has been recognised by the police in the dead end. The new Költz friend Moser hides the crook in the village of Kifili. Not for free, of course. He demands plenty of protection money.

The last resort: The ADS hunters advertise a wanted poster with a photo of Költz in the newspaper "East African Standard". For his arrest, they offer a reward of the equivalent of about 8,000 marks. An average Kenyan must work for ten years to achieve this. It only takes a few days before the fugitive is betrayed.

At the second arrest in Kifili, Költz is at his wit's end. xxxxx, who is present at the arrest, he shouts: "Volker, don't say anything about the checks." In vain. Because xxxxx has already led the authorities to the million-dollar hiding place in Switzerland. Millionaire man Költz had committed another fatal stupidity. He paid for the Harley-Davidson with traveller's checks from the Zurich bank, where his loot is stored. The money has been confiscated. Költz is waiting for his delivery.

THE TRAIL OF THE MILLIONAIRE THIEF

16 JULY: Andreas Költz disappears from the vaults of the ADS company with 2.5 million marks. He celebrates his coup for three days at the Leipzig "Interconti" with champagne and light girls.

10 JULY: Költz has deposited 1.5 million in a bank account in Zurich. Via Prague, London and Cairo, he flies to Nairobi and on to Diani Beach.

24 JULY: Költz buys a dream villa. He pays the 300,000 marks in small notes.

SEPTEMBER 1: ADS detectives track down Költz in Kenya and shadow him. Less than two weeks later, the police arrested him for the first time.

18 SEPTEMBER: Investigating judge Kanyi releases Költz on bail of just under 30,000 marks. The millionaire robber is hidden by "friends".

OCTOBER 1: Kenyans betray Költz, they collect a reward of 8,000 marks. The police arrest him. He is at the end of his rope and wants to turn himself in to the authorities in Germany.

Aussie Mike (Funzi Furniture Factory)

http://www.funzifurniture.com

Available worldwide from Amazon
and all good bookstores

Michael Terence
Publishing

www.mtp.agency

mtp.agency

@mtp_agency

Printed in Dunstable, United Kingdom

63807563R00238